GROWING UP IN AMERICA

Growing Up in America

THE POWER OF RACE IN THE LIVES OF TEENS

Brad Christerson, Korie L. Edwards,
and Richard Flory

STANFORD UNIVERSITY PRESS
Stanford, California 2010

Stanford University Press
Stanford, California

Library of Congress Cataloging-in-Publication Data

Christerson, Brad.
   Growing up in America : the power of race in the lives of teens / Brad Christerson,
Korie L. Edwards, and Richard Flory
      p. cm.
   Includes bibliographical references and index.
   ISBN 978-0-8047-6051-5 (cloth : alk. paper) —
   ISBN 978-0-8047-6052-2 (pbk. : alk. paper)

   1. Teenagers—United States—Social conditions.   2. Teenagers—United States—
Attitudes.   3. Race—Social aspects—United States. 4. Socialization—United States.
I. Edwards, Korie L.   II. Flory, Richard W.   III. Title.

   HQ796.C4596   2010
   305.235089'00973—dc22   2009044479

Typeset at Stanford University Press in 10/14 Minion

To Carin, Mark, and Malia
With love always

CONTENTS

Acknowledgments   xi

1 Introduction   1
2 Family: Learning Authority, Autonomy, and Responsibility   12
3 Peers: Influencing Attitudes, Social Acceptance, and
   Personal Relationships   41
4 School: Motivating Achievement, Aspirations, and
   Opportunity   71
5 Religion: Developing Beliefs, Experiences, and Practices   110
6 Conclusion   145

Appendixes
A. Methodology, 165. B. Frequencies of Racial/Ethnic Groups, 167.
C. Regression Analyses of NSYR Survey Data, 168

Notes   181
References   187
Index   197

TABLES

2.1	Household Structure of Teens by Race/Ethnicity	22
2.2	Teen-Family Contact and Supervision by Race/Ethnicity	25
2.3	Teen-Family Relationships and Communication by Race/Ethnicity	32
2.4	Summary of Family Types	35
3.1	Attributes of Friends by Race/Ethnicity	53
3.2	Body Image by Race/Ethnicity	55
3.3	Substance Use by Race/Ethnicity	56
3.4	Dating and Sexual Relationships by Race/Ethnicity	63
4.1	Academic Views and Future Aspirations by Race/Ethnicity	81
5.1	Teen Religious Beliefs by Race/Ethnicity	120
5.2	Teen Religious Practice and Experience by Race/Ethnicity	128
5.3	Teen Involvement in and Attitudes Toward Religious Institutions by Race/Ethnicity	134
C.1	Logistic Regression Model Predicting Likelihood of Teen Living in Female-Headed Single-Parent Household	168
C.2	Logistic Regression Model Predicting Likelihood of Teen Spending at Least One Evening per Week with No Adult Supervision	169
C.3	Logistic Regression Model Predicting Likelihood of Teen Spending Eight Hours per Week or More in One or More Weeknight Extracurricular Activity	170
C.4	Logistic Regression Model Predicting Likelihood of Teen Having Been Drunk at Least Once in the Past Year	171
C.5	Logistic Regression Model Predicting Likelihood of Teen Having Had Sex at Least Once	172
C.6	Ordered Logistic Regression Model Estimating Liklihood that Female Teen "Feels Happy About Her Physical Appearance"	173

C.7 Odds Ratios of Academic Views and Future Aspirations Predicted by Race/Ethnicity   174

C.8 Logistic Regression Model Predicting Likelihood of Teen Saying Religious Faith Is Very or Extremely Important in Shaping Daily Life   175

C.9 Logistic Regression Model Predicting Likelihood of Teen Praying Alone at Least Once a Day   176

C.10 Logistic Regression Model Predicting Likelihood of Teen Saying Their Church Is a Very or Fairly Good Place to Talk to Adults   177

ACKNOWLEDGMENTS

This book has been a long time coming to fruition, largely because of the logistics of juggling three sets of responsibilities, schedules, and locations. Our work together has been an equal partnership and collaboration, beginning with our first conversations about writing the book to generating and refining our ideas, to dividing the writing labor. We have found working together to be quite an enjoyable and profitable experience, although at times it was like herding fish to coordinate our responsibilities and schedules and, occasionally, to actually meet in person. We engaged in many conversations while thinking about and writing this book—over the telephone, through e-mail, and in person, and in such disparate locations as Chapel Hill, Kansas City, Portland, Columbus, Boston, San Francisco, and Newport Beach. Along the way, we have benefited tremendously from many colleagues and institutions that have supported our efforts, provided critical input, and generally kept us committed to completing the task.

Most importantly, we would like to thank the entire National Study of Youth and Religion (NSYR) crew for being great friends, colleagues, and conversation partners and for making our joint efforts at understanding the lives of American teens an enjoyable experience. We thank in particular Christian Smith, Lisa Pearce, and Melinda Denton for inviting us to be part of the NSYR project and allowing us to use this rich source of data. The National Study of Youth and Religion (http://www.youthandreligion.org), whose data were used here by permission, has been generously funded by Lilly Endowment, Inc., and is under the direction of Christian Smith, Department of Sociology at the University of Notre Dame, and Lisa Pearce, Department of Sociology at the University of North Carolina at Chapel Hill.

We are also grateful to Jim Lewis and the Louisville Institute for providing support for course releases, research assistants, and the like as we were working on this book. And we truly appreciate the efforts of our research assistants, Cheryl Ceralde-Elson, Alvina Kubeka, and Carolyn Zambrano, on this project. Many people have read all or part of this book or have heard presentations that were based on various portions of it. We are particularly indebted to two anonymous reviewers for comments at the proposal stage and when the manuscript was complete, as well as many others who have read portions or heard presentations, and have provided insights on our thinking about and understanding of teens. We also want to express our appreciation to Kate Wahl—along with her staff at Stanford University Press—for her enthusiastic and patient support of this book from our very first conversation. Finally, we are especially grateful for the love and support of our families in this and in all of our endeavors.

GROWING UP IN AMERICA

1 INTRODUCTION

"Children are our future." We have heard this saying many times, haven't we? Songs have even been written about it. Packed into this four-word cliché is the idea that society needs to invest in its children. Society ought to provide the support, knowledge, and skills members of the next generation will need one day when they are in control and responsible for strong, healthy, advancing communities.

Now when we actually look at a variety of social and economic "outcomes" for young people in the United States, what do we find? We learn that our society seems to consider some young people more vital to our future than others. In particular, *society invests in young white people more than young people of color*. This is evident in a variety of arenas. For example, white youth are more likely to have health coverage than racial and ethnic minority youth.[1] More money is spent on the education of white youth than on youth of color. Up-to-date computers and the Internet are more easily accessed by white youth than racial and ethnic minority youth, resulting in youth of color being left behind in the Digital Age.[2]

Of course, other factors, particularly *class*, influence society's investment in young people. But even before the United States was a country, people have been organized primarily around *race* and *ethnicity*. These characteristics have in many ways dictated people's upward socioeconomic mobility. Most of us are well aware of the United States' history of slavery, followed by Jim Crow in the South. But it is also true that neighborhoods and suburbs in the North orchestrated what amounted to segregation by adopting policies that prevented homeowners from selling to African-Americans. With few exceptions, labor unions limited African-Americans' opportunities to jobs with the least chance for advancement and the lowest pay.[3] Latinos and Asians were also systematically ghettoized, particularly across the West. Housing opportunities for Latinos and Asians were often limited to company-owned tenements.[4]

State and federal governments facilitated practices that subordinated African-Americans, Latinos, and Asians. For instance, until 1870 only free whites (for a time there were whites in the United States who were indentured servants and therefore not "free") could naturalize as citizens of the United States, at which time naturalization rights expanded to include people of African descent. (But it was not until 1952 that all racial or ethnic qualifiers were lifted to make people of *any* racial or ethnic background potentially eligible for citizenship.[5]) California passed a law in 1852 that taxed the work of foreign miners only, most of whom were Chinese and Mexican, who could not naturalize as citizens.[6] The federal government passed the National Origins Act in 1924, which fully excluded immigration by Asians to the United States, something no other racial or ethnic group has experienced in this country. The government also conducted mass deportations of Mexicans, both immigrants and United States citizens, during the first half of the twentieth century.[7] These laws and public practices marginalized people of color and validated, if not encouraged, private racism and discrimination.

Beginning in the 1950s, however, federal legislatures passed laws banning racial and ethnic discrimination in immigration, housing, and the workplace, removing many of the mechanisms that organized people's lives along racial and ethnic lines. Since then, formal racial prejudice has declined steadily.[8] People of color have occupied some of the most powerful positions in our institutions in recent decades, such as CEOs, mayors, and most recently the presidency. Still, race and ethnicity continue to be central forces in American life, influencing where people live, work, and attend school and how they spend their leisure time. And so, while racial disparities have narrowed over the past forty years, persistent gaps in education, wealth, power, and health and well-being still exist between groups of different racial and ethnic backgrounds in America. It is just that *the practices that perpetuate racial and ethnic inequality have become subtle and more covert.*[9]

Much of the contemporary research on racial inequality emphasizes the experiences of people after they have reached adulthood. Some studies point to culture as the primary reason for these continued disparities,[10] others focus on social networks.[11] Racist and prejudicial attitudes, as well as institutional discrimination, are common explanations.[12] Macrolevel changes, such as major shifts in the economy, are seen by some researchers as the main impetus for racial inequality among adults.[13]

In this book we take another approach. We look at the experiences of people *before* they become adults, in particular young people between the ages of thirteen and seventeen. Our intent is to understand the "precursors to racialized outcomes"; that is, we ask, *Does society differentially invest in youth of different racial and ethnic backgrounds, thereby predisposing them to follow certain paths and fulfill particular roles in society as adults?* Are white, Asian-American, African-American, and Latino teens socialized—that is, taught how to live in society—in different ways? If so, what effects do these different socialization experiences have on youth of various racial and ethnic backgrounds? And *how might these different experiences reproduce, or perpetuate, racial and ethnic inequalities?*

Focusing on four key social institutions, the *family, peers, school*, and *religion*, we argue in this book that youth of different racial and ethnic backgrounds are indeed socialized in different ways. This is in part because these institutions are themselves already racialized. They are often racially segregated. And more important, race really impacts how people experience life—their relationships, opportunities, and physical and social environment—in these institutions. The segregated institutions of families, peer groups, schools, and religious organizations produce distinct cultures and structures that reflect the social situations of the various racial and ethnic groups. In stating this, we are affirming the abundance of existing literature briefly sampled above (see Notes 10–13) that focuses on racial disparities among *adults*. Nevertheless, African-American, Asian-American, white, and Latino youth experience particular socialization processes that have been forged within disparate social conditions. The racialized experiences of youth produce advantages and disadvantages that arguably lead to unequal outcomes for youth and, later, for adults. We acknowledge that youth within a given racial or ethnic group are exposed to a diverse array of social structural experiences, and that there is no such thing as a typical experience for white, African-American, Latino, or Asian-American teenagers.[14] Still, our findings reveal that *teen socialization experiences follow distinct racial and ethnic patterns within families, schools, religious organizations, and peer groups, which persist across class and geographic lines.* These patterns have direct implications for the quality of teens' lives as well as their life chances as adults.

IMPLICATIONS FOR TEENS' LIVES

It may seem logical, or even obvious, that teens of one racial or ethnic group or another are at an advantage or disadvantage in relation to teens of other groups in their preparation for involvement in the American socioeconomic system. We believe the implications for teens, and their futures, is more complex than that statement may imply. We would not want to assert that teens of different racial or ethnic identities are simply "different" in how they are socialized and leave it at that. Nor would we conclude that the four areas that we investigate in this book—family, peers, schools, and religion—in acting as socializing agents, merely help to pass on the cultural values and social roles of American society to teenagers, although this is certainly partly true. Instead, we believe a better way to think about how teenagers are prepared for participation in American society is to rethink "socialization" in a much broader frame, one that includes not only the reproduction of cultural values and roles but also the idea that teens are building "stores of capital"—something we call *capital portfolios*—through the way they experience the world. Capital portfolios are packages of investments which include cultural, social, human, and religious capital (analogous, say, to stock investments). They contain resources teens can access in their current and future participation in American society; they are also related to the reproduction of inequalities inherent in the American socioeconomic system.

We return to the idea of capital portfolios in more depth in the concluding chapter. For now, we want to suggest that the concept of capital (and our use of it in arguing that teens tend to build capital portfolios containing different mixes of types of capital, stemming at least partly from race or ethnicity) is an important theoretical tool which can uncover hidden processes that serve to reproduce social inequality in society. In this we follow Amanda Lewis, who argues that understanding capital is important because it "challenges one of the dominant narratives for understanding educational success and failure—the ideology of meritocracy: people are understood to be successful solely because of their individual efforts and abilities."[15] Capital here is considered a resource to be used in advancing one's position in particular social contexts.[16] However, we move beyond Lewis in suggesting that the different forms of capital teens may develop may have both positive and negative effects in the larger scheme of teens' lives, and that some forms of capital may purchase more benefits in the larger socioeconomic system than others.

We will argue that teens, indeed children from the earliest ages, are building stores of capital—social, cultural, human, and religious—through experiences in their families, schools, religious organizations, and among peers. They will draw on these stores and put them to use as they come of age and enter the American socioeconomic system. Further, as teens differentially experience the world through family, peer relationships, school, and their involvement with religious institutions, their capital portfolio is being built with its particular mix of amounts and types of social, cultural, human, and religious capital. The particular mix yields different dividends in success, types of jobs, status, personal well-being, or other payoffs, and it varies by individual; yet that individual variation is bounded by the types of capital that tend to be developed within different racial and ethnic groups. Our position is not that there is one standardized capital portfolio for each racial or ethnic group—there is in fact considerable diversity in the investment by individuals within each group. We do suggest, however, that the capital portfolios which teens develop, and which they and others invest in, tend to follow distinct racial or ethnic patterns. *By uncovering the components of youths' capital portfolios and the socialization processes that produce them, we will better understand the sources of racial and ethnic disparities in American life.*

STUDIES ON RACE, ETHNICITY, AND YOUTH IN THE UNITED STATES

Several books have studied youth in the United States and how race and ethnicity matter in their lives. These studies have largely focused on racial and ethnic "identity formation" among youth of color; how youth of color participate in this process; and the role of race and ethnicity in youths' lives. Jennifer Lee and Min Zhou, for example, focus on the ways in which Asian-American youth construct and perform their own unique culture, and ethnic and racial identities.[17] In *Asian American Youth*, these authors discuss how Asian-American youth must perform this process in a society where they are simultaneously invisible and forced to combat racial stereotypes, such as the model minority, the gangbanger, and the perpetual foreigner. They also find that Asian-American youth construct their identities in response to those of their immigrant parents, whom they often view as constrictive, backward, and un-American. Since these youth are more acculturated than their parents, they become American by using tools from both Asian and American cultures.

Another example is Beverly Tatum's *Why Are All the Black Kids Sitting To-*

gether in the Cafeteria?[18] Tatum explores the role of self-segregation among youth of color, especially black adolescents, as she constructs what it means to be of a racial minority within a society that is as race conscious as the United States. She contends that self-segregation is a positive developmental action for African-American youth, even necessary, for developing a strong sense of belonging.

We do not address racial and ethnic identity formation among American youth. But what we take away from studies such as these is that Asian-American, African-American, and Latino youth construct distinct racial and ethnic identities in response to their unique social experiences and location. Being a youth of color who is being raised in, for instance, an immigrant family versus a native-born family, has different meanings and implies different tools for negotiating one's identity in society. Yet in other ways, all youth of color must deal with similar mechanisms imposed on them by the dominant society. Mechanisms such as racial and ethnic stereotypes, which mark youth as not normative, influence how they think of themselves.

Similarly with socialization, we find that African-American, Asian-American, and Latino youth experience unique processes that produce distinct advantages and disadvantages for their lives. Their individual capital portfolios are quite varied as a result. In other ways, there is a clearer white-nonwhite dichotomy in socialization processes. This division results in white youth possessing valuable forms of capital that are less available to African-American, Asian-American, and Latino youth; the reverse may pertain in forms of capital that are more common among youth of color and rarer among white youth.

We are interested in understanding the racialized socialization experiences among youth and their *potential* effect on eventual adult outcomes; in short, how race and ethnicity might affect socialization and its outcomes. Most studies on race, ethnicity, and youth have not emphasized these sorts of relationships. When there has been an attempt to explain these processes, the studies tend to focus exclusively on the family or draw conclusions about youth in general that are based largely on samples of white youth.[19] But there are notable exceptions.

Annette Lareau, for example, in her book *Unequal Childhoods,* draws on eighty-eight interviews with third- and fourth-grade children at two schools, one located in a working-class community and another in a middle-class community.[20] The children were African-American and white and came from poor, working-class, and middle-class families. Lareau's research team also conducted intensive ethnographic studies, which involved sustained observation of and interaction with twelve families of children in the interview sample. She argues that social class plays a much larger role than race in how families raise their children. Middle-class parents prepare their children for socioeconomic advancement in adulthood by engaging in what she calls *concerted cultivation*. Provided with a wealth of experiences in adult-organized nonfamily activities, such as sports, music lessons, and summer camps, middle-class children not only develop important skills but also learn to see adults as equals, share their thoughts with and make demands of those in authority, and expect to be served by institutions. In contrast, Lareau finds that working-class parents do not engage in concerted cultivation; instead, they emphasize obedience to parents and allow for long periods of unstructured time with family and extended family rather than in organized outside activities, a socialization pattern which she calls the *accomplishment of natural growth*. Both methods of child-rearing have advantages and disadvantages, according to Lareau: the overscheduled lifestyle of soccer games, band camps, and dance recitals may better prepare middle-class children for success at school than their lower-class counterparts, but they are also likely to be more stressed. The working-class and poor kids, in contrast, may have closer family ties but sometimes miss participating in extracurricular activities. From these findings Lareau argues that schools and other institutions need to be more realistic about the limited educational resources many parents enjoy and more sensitive to the second parenting style.

Although *Unequal Childhoods* focuses primarily on family socialization processes, the up-close-and-personal view into the worlds of poor, working-, and middle-class African-American and white families provides a valuable, detailed understanding of how families teach their children in the United States. We draw on Lareau's conceptual framework to begin to make sense of how families socialize their adolescent children. But we depart from Lareau in several ways. The family is a central agent of socialization for young people; however, other institutions also play key roles. By examining youth's experiences with school, religion, and peers, in addition to the family, we gain a more complete understanding of how society invests in youth and prepares them for future roles. Moreover, we are looking at adolescents. During this stage of life, institutions outside the family become increasingly important to young people's sense of self, their understanding of the world, and their place in it. As the final stage of childhood prior to becoming an adult, adolescence and its socialization experiences are more predictive of adult outcomes than those of third- and fourth-graders. We also depart from Lareau in our emphasis on race and ethnicity. As discussed above, race and ethnicity have been the main factors organizing human relations and social outcomes in the United States. Further, the meanings of class status differ by race and ethnicity. This is evident among the experiences of adolescents. In *Black Picket Fences*, for example, Mary Pattillo-McCoy reveals how being an African-American middle-class youth differs from being a white middle-class youth.[21] Black youths' opportunities for upward mobility are constrained compared to white youths', particularly since the macroeconomic conditions that spurred their parents into the middle class no longer exist. Thus, African-American middle-class youth are more inclined to live in socioeconomically diverse neighborhoods, exposing them to greater criminal deviance and greater negative consequences.

Still, class is an important factor in the socialization experiences of youth. Our analysis does not dispute the role of class. Nor do our data allow a test to determine which is more important, race or class, in the socialization experiences of youth. The data do show, however, that race and ethnicity have an effect independent of class. For example, as we will show, our statistical analyses reveal that when controlling for income (and other demographic factors), racial differences are still large and significant. Our analysis of different subgroups further reveals that while factors like parental authority and family responsibility are a common facet of families of color, they get played out in very different ways depending on the particular racial or ethnic group. So, while we recognize the importance of class for youth, there is considerable evidence that race and ethnicity influence the mobility trajectories of youth.

Legacies: The Story of the Immigrant Second Generation, by Alejandro Portes and Ruben Rumbaut, is an impressive study of second-generation youth in the United States from varied racial, ethnic, and socioeconomic backgrounds.[22] Drawing on ethnographies, as well as survey and school-level data, this book explores the world of second-generation youth, looking at patterns of parent-child conflict and cohesion within immigrant families, the role of peer groups and school subcultures, and factors affecting academic achievement, among other areas of adolescent life, to understand the process of socioeconomic mobility for recent immigrants. A central finding of *Legacies* is that the immigrant experience varies considerably. The acculturation process is much smoother for certain immigrant groups because society welcomes and privileges them over other immigrants. In addition to culture, socioeconomic status, and immigrant community networks and resources, race (or what the authors refer to as "color") is a primary factor affecting the extent to which immigrants are incorporated into American society. Immigrants who more closely look like the dominant group are, as Portes and Rumbaut put it, "chosen" to acculturate and ushered toward an easier trajectory of upward socioeconomic mobility.

Portes and Rumbaut highlight the complexity of mobility for second-generation youth in America. In our study we build on *Legacies* by focusing on the role of race and ethnicity in the socialization processes of American youth as we explore the views and experiences of immigrant and native-born adolescents. We also address immigrant "generation status," particularly for Latinos. We find, for example, that for Latino youth the greatest distinction in generation status is between the second and third generation. Additionally, we explore the role of religion in the lives of youth. Religion is central to the culture, identity, and social cohesion of communities of color because, in the United States, it has consistently been the main institution where minority groups can exercise full control. Our findings demonstrate how religious organizations and networks invest in youth and make valuable contributions to their capital portfolios.

One study on race and socialization experiences of students, which has been controversial but influential, is John Ogbu's qualitative study *Black American Students in an Affluent Suburb*.[23] The youth in his study attended high school in the affluent Shaker Heights suburb of Cleveland. While the academic performance of African-American youth in Shaker Heights was above the state and national averages for African-American teens, it was markedly lower than that of white peers in their school. Ogbu aims to make sense of why African-American students, who seemingly have the resources and life conditions conducive to academic success, still perform far below their white counterparts. He argues that the peer culture of African-American youth discourages academic excellence. African-American youth are ambivalent about achieving academic success because it is perceived as "acting white." Several scholars disagree with Ogbu's claims, finding that African-American youth, as well as Latino youth, care as much or more about doing well in school as their white peers.[24] We too find little evidence for Ogbu's position, which we discuss in Chapter 4. Still, Ogbu's work has pushed our thinking on the influence of peers on the academic views and experiences of minority youth.

OVERVIEW OF BOOK

This study uses a multimethod approach to understand the socialization experiences of youth in America. We draw primarily on the National Study of

Youth and Religion (NSYR). The NSYR, based at the University of North Carolina at Chapel Hill, includes survey data generated from a nationally representative telephone survey of 3,290 U.S. English- and Spanish-speaking teenagers between the ages of thirteen and seventeen and their parents in 2002 and 2003, and 267 in-depth interviews from a subsample of the adolescents who participated in the survey (some of whom turned eighteen by the time the interviews were conducted). The survey and in-depth interviews explore a wide range of topics, including religion, family life, dating and sex, school experiences, peer relations, drug use, entertainment, future aspirations, and other topics. In our analysis, the survey data serve as a first-cut determination of the largest differences and similarities among African-American, Asian-American, Latino, and white youth. The interviews provide engaging, visceral accounts and deep insights into how teens from these four largest racial and ethnic groups in America experience family, school, religious, and peer life. *By examining nationally representative survey data along with in-depth interviews, we provide an intimate yet comprehensive view of the racialized socialization experiences of youth in the United States today.* (See Appendix A for more on methodology.)

We now move on to the four chapters on family, peers, school, and religion. In Chapter 2, building on previous research, we propose four types of family socialization patterns. These patterns reflect the importance families place on autonomy, authority, community, and success, and the processes families engage in to instill these values in their children. Chapter 3 looks at how peers matter in youths' lives. Compared to youth of color, white youth are given greater autonomy to spend more time with their peers. This makes white youth more susceptible to deviant behaviors, which can pose threats to their well-being. Chapter 4 highlights the connection between teacher-student relationships and youths' academic views. White youths' experiences show that schools, through teachers, provide important resources that privilege them academically in the short and long run. In Chapter 5 we show how religious institutions, beliefs, and practices serve to reinforce what teens have learned in the other institutional spheres of their lives, in particular how teens of different racial or ethnic groups relate to authority and hierarchies, and how they are expected to participate within the religious organization.

Each of these chapters explores how youth in America experience and think about the institution examined. With the survey results as a backdrop, we focus on what young people have shared about their lives during the interviews. Near the beginning of each chapter, we tell the stories of four persons with different racial or ethnic backgrounds. Altogether then, the stories introduce you to sixteen of the adolescents interviewed in the study. We highlighted the stories of these teenagers not because they are typical or representative of their particular racial or ethnic group—there is no such thing. Instead, we chose these youths' accounts because their experiences underscore certain aspects of family, school, religious, or peer life that, according to the survey and interview data, follow distinct racial or ethnic patterns. Taken together, the stories also demonstrate similarities among youth across differing racial and ethnic backgrounds and, conversely, variation among youth of the same race or ethnicity.

In the concluding chapter we return to the discussion of how youths' capital portfolios are constructed. Citing examples from previous chapters, we look at the inputs institutions make into youths' capital portfolios and the social dividends that result. We suggest that African-American, Asian-American, Latino, and white youth are endowed with various kinds and amounts of capital. It is not the case that white youth are generally better off in all areas of life relative to youth of color. It is rather that the dominant society often makes available to white youth those forms of capital that it *values.* And society is structured such that white youth are better situated to receive returns on those valued forms of capital, returns that are perceived as being more important. This is where and why racial inequality, particularly socioeconomic racial inequality, persists, we propose. Yet youth of color are endowed with capital that is largely absent from the portfolios of white youth. These forms of capital protect and prepare youth of color in ways that are not accessible to white youth. This capital is constructed in part as a response to their racial and ethnic communities' subordinate position in the dominant social structure, but it also arises out of differing community worldviews and perspectives.

Unfolding in the following pages are rich firsthand accounts of the different social worlds inhabited by teens of different racial and ethnic groups in America. You will hear teens in their own voice describe their conflicts with parents, pressures from other teens, teachers who have influenced their self-esteem, and religious beliefs that drive their understanding of the world. It is our hope that these voices will reveal the challenges and triumphs of adolescents today, and bring to light the impact of race and ethnicity on the resources available to youth as they move toward adulthood.

2 FAMILY
Learning Authority, Autonomy, and Responsibility

I love my Mom very much. She does all kinds of things for me.
She's always there when I need her. Me and her are the best
of friends right now. We have our differences sometimes. Like
when I wanna go somewhere she doesn't approve of . . . I get
mad but I get over it.

—Donald Lewis, age 14, African-American

Social scientists universally agree that the family is a central agent of socialization in all societies—the family is a key place where, as children, we learn the scripts we are to follow in our future roles as adults. Families impose expectations on children that reflect social norms and seek to instill patterns of behavior that are adaptive within their social context.[1] Thus, parents of different cultural or ethnic backgrounds often vary in their socialization goals for their children. In particular, they differ in the extent to which certain values such as independence, self-expression, autonomy, obedience to authority, and collectivism are promoted.[2] In this chapter we explore these diverse patterns and their effects on the experiences of teenagers.

Before exploring racial and ethnic differences in teen family life, it is worth noting the substantial *similarities* we found in teen family experiences among the major racial and ethnic groups in America. Virtually all teens love their parents and want to be loved by them and to please them. Likewise, virtually all parents love their children and want the best for them. This may seem obvious, but it is still worth mentioning. Sixty percent or more of parents of all racial and ethnic groups see their teens as at least sometimes hard to understand and at least a little rebellious—there was no significant racial or ethnic difference in these opinions. Half of teens interviewed stated that they at least sometimes do things they hope their parents never find out about, and a great majority—95 percent—also stated that their parents would be "very" or "extremely" upset if they used drugs. These responses had no significant racial or ethnic variance. Nor was there any racial or ethnic difference in the 45 percent of parents who reported their teen to be "doing wonderfully" in life. Further, in the areas where significant racial and ethnic differences in teen family experiences exist, we find still quite a bit of overlap between groups (see Tables 2.1–2.3 in later sections of this chapter).

Despite these striking similarities, we found important variations in how teens experienced their family life, and in how families had socialized their teens. The broadest differences were in orientations toward *authority*, *autonomy*, and *responsibility* toward the family. White teens, compared with other groups, are given the most freedom to disengage from family and pursue outside interests, and they had the lowest levels of parental control. Compared with the other racial and ethnic groups, white teens displayed a greater sense of equality with adults, and an attitude that family life is meant to serve their needs and interests rather than a sense that they are meant to serve their families. In all of the nonwhite racial and ethnic groups we found much more emphasis on authority and parental control, and a much more reciprocal relationship in which teens had high levels of responsibility as well as privileges. We also found significant differences in orientations to socialization among African-American, Latino, and Asian-American families.

DEREK WILLIAMS

Derek Williams is a fifteen-year-old African-American teen living in a working-class neighborhood of a large southeastern city. Tall, soft-spoken, and well mannered, Derek approaches life carefully and thoughtfully. He gets good grades—mostly A's—and is hopeful and confident about his future. He shuns drugs and alcohol and says that he doesn't face much pressure from friends to use them. Derek lives with his mother and his soon-to-be-adopted three-year-old brother. He describes his relationship with his mother as very warm and close and says he wouldn't change anything about their relationship. "We're really close. I can talk to her about anything. She'll be always there for me. Any problems, I can just talk to her." Derek's mother also keeps a set of strict "house rules" that he has to follow or else face immediate consequences. He has daily and weekly chores, which include mopping the floor, cleaning the kitchen, and cutting the grass. He has a strict curfew and says that his mother knows where he is at all times. If he breaks one of the house rules, his mother will take away his television privileges, limit his access to the Internet or phone, or give him more chores to do. Derek's mother is very involved in his education as well. She made a point to transfer Derek to a better high school than the low-performing school in their neighborhood. She is a PTA member and knows all of Derek's friends at school.

Extended family also plays an important role in Derek's life, particularly his grandparents, aunt, and uncle. His grandparents live within walking distance from his house, and he stops by to visit them every day. He describes his relationship with his grandmother as "really close" and says that his grandfather is the person he most admires in the world. "He's a really hard worker and . . . he always has lots of integrity, and he's honest and he works for what he needs, and he's kind of like a family man. He always is very supportive for my grandmother and everything, and I'd like to be like that." Derek's maternal aunt, uncle, and cousin also live nearby in a place he calls his "second home." He visits them on most weekends, playing pool with his uncle and cousin or going with them to the local park to play sports. He and all of his extended-family members attend church together every Sunday.

The role modeling that his grandfather and uncle provide seems important to Derek because he has never met his father. He was born out of wedlock and doesn't know where his father lives. This is upsetting to Derek for a number of reasons. When asked what he would change, if anything, about his life, he mentioned only his father.

> INTERVIEWER: What are some good and bad things about your life as a teenager?
> RESPONDENT: [The] good thing is [that] my mom and my grandparents really support me, and the bad thing is that I don't have a father, a father figure in my life; that's what my mom says I need, so that's kind of like a bad thing about my life.
> I: Do you ever feel sad or depressed?
> R: Sometimes.
> I: Are there any particular things that make you feel that way?
> R: Knowing that my dad left me when I was just like really young, yeah, that's it.

Derek also feels upset that his mother has to work so hard to support the family without any help. He says, "I wish my father would be there for me. I feel kind of left out, and it doesn't feel too good to see that—how your mom works, works to support the family, so I'd probably wish that he was there, you know, to help us out and everything."

Derek's religious faith and church community provide support and a moral purpose for his life. His mother and grandmother have been central in passing down the Christian faith to him, and he attends church every week with his mother.

Derek has a lot of family support and a positive attitude toward life. He is well supervised, has learned to take care of himself, and contributes his labor to the household workload. The support from his extended family and church community give him a sense of confidence and the feeling of being loved. It seems that the facet of his life he is struggling most with emotionally is the absence of his father, which clearly affects the family's resources and places financial burdens on his mother. Support from his grandparents, aunt, and uncle, however, may compensate much for the emotional effects of his father's absence.

CARA SANDERS

Cara Sanders is a fourteen-year-old white teen who lives in a small city in the Western United States. She lives with her mother, stepfather, seven-year-old stepbrother, and eighteen-year-old biological brother. Her dark eyes, blond hair, and slightly chubby young face give her a look that is at the same time charming and intense. She is energetic and frank—someone who doesn't pull any punches and lets people know exactly where they stand with her.

Cara's parents divorced when she was four. Her father lives in a nearby city, but she says she sees him "only when I want something." Cara has moved numerous times with her mother and stepfather to different cities around the state. She says this has made her life difficult as it's hard to make friends, especially in small towns, where everyone knows everyone. She says she "used to be popular" until she began moving every two years or so. Her mother and stepfather have moved for financial reasons and job opportunities each time. Her stepfather is currently a cook for a local juvenile corrections facility, and her mother works for a cable television company.

Cara describes her relationship with her mother as pretty good, "with the occasional blowout." According to Cara, most of their fights can be attributed to her talking back and sassing her mother.

While Cara has father figures in her life, her relationships with them are strained. Cara describes her relationship with her father as "pretty much non-existent." Although he lives in a nearby town and Cara says he would like to spend more time with her, she would rather spend time with her friends. Her relationship with her father deteriorated when she turned eleven; at that point she "started having more of a life and having more friends to hang out with and stuff, and then he didn't like that" and as a result "got really controlling." Currently, she calls him only when she needs money, requests he is happy to oblige. Her relationship with her stepfather is also troubled. "I don't like him; he doesn't act like he likes me . . . he's rude."

Cara states that fights between her and her stepfather rarely get resolved. Like her relationship with her dad, things deteriorated when she turned eleven. "Just then I realized I wasn't a little kid anymore, and like my dad and [my stepdad] were treating me like one."

Cara appears to get little discipline from her parents. She says she gets grounded sometimes and has her phone taken away, but she sees the punishments as being inconsistent. She also describes kids in her neighborhood as having very little parental supervision. "A lot of parents let their kids just run around the streets; they don't care what they do, what they wear. As long as they're out of their hair." Cara often goes to parties at the homes of other kids where there is no parental supervision. She says they can get "pretty wild." Her mother knows that she attends these parties, but does not know that they are unsupervised and doesn't ask. Despite her attendance at these parties, Cara says she does not drink or smoke. Many of the kids around her, however, drink and smoke pot regularly.

Cara goes to church with her family every Sunday at a charismatic evangelical church. She says she considers herself a Christian but "could be stronger." She is not involved in the youth group and has no friends there. She claims not to have any significant adults in her life other than her parents and stepfather. Cara has no extended family nearby but says she is close to two of her aunts, both of whom live in other states. One of them travels for work and therefore can visit Cara's family around once a month.

Overall, it seems that Cara mostly wants to be left alone by her family. She has wide latitude to spend time away from them and to openly disagree with them. Because she "hates" the state where she lives, she wants to move far away to attend college. Her parents seem willing and able to support her financially, but they seem limited in their ability to support her emotionally. Because she has moved so often, she has little stability in her social networks, including friends and extended family. She has to this point avoided risky behavior such as sex and substance abuse, but given the habits of friends around her and the lack of parental supervision in her peer group, it seems that these activities could potentially be a part of her future.[3]

EVELYN CABRERA

Evelyn Cabrera is a seventeen-year-old second-generation Mexican-American living in a working-class neighborhood of a large urban area in the southwest with her parents, three brothers, and one sister. She is energetic and polite, with a kind smile. She is also very open to discussing her life. She describes herself as moody sometimes, but overall she has a positive view of life and her future. She spends most of her time at school, her job, a local theme park, family events, and with her boyfriend.

Evelyn describes her relationship with her mother as very close:

We're close, like really close; we communicate a lot. For example, when I have a problem, I tell her what's going on in my life, about my boyfriend, or about my friends, in school; yeah, we're pretty close.

She says there is nothing she wouldn't tell her mother. Evelyn describes her relationship with her father as equally close. She doesn't communicate as often with her father because he works long hours, but she feels she can talk to him about anything as well—that is, except for her relationship with her boyfriend. Evelyn and her boyfriend are serious, talking and thinking of marriage. He is older—in his twenties—and has a steady job as an office manager for a health care company. Evelyn is Daddy's little girl, and he has a hard time thinking about letting her go:

I'm Daddy's little girl, so I mean my mom tells him, you know, she's growing up, she's gonna go to college, but the thing is that my dad's afraid because he thinks that sooner or later, I'm gonna get married, but I guess he loves me so much, he's afraid of me leaving the house, you know. Now that I'm with my boyfriend, [my dad] calls me up on the cell phone every little time—you know, how are you doing or everything's fine, and I'm like, Dad, it's fine; he worries about me too much.

Evelyn's father thinks she is too young for this level of seriousness in a relationship, and he tries to limit their contact by keeping her involved in family activities and responsibilities. Still, she spends a lot of time with her boyfriend.

Evelyn goes to parties frequently and has a large group of friends, mostly other Mexican-American kids. Although drugs and alcohol are occasionally present at these gatherings, she stays away from both. She says that her parents would be extremely disappointed in her if she drank or did drugs, and that they trust her to do the right thing. Despite this trust, her parents carefully monitor whom she goes out with, and they require that she have her cell phone on at all times. She says that all of her friends' parents know one another, so that if one of them does something wrong, they all find out quickly:

Like, for example, if one of my friends does something wrong, you know, my parents gonna find out, and if I don't want them to find out, they're gonna find out by her parents. You know, so you can't really hide nothing between friends and family, 'cause they're always gonna find out.

In fact, most of the parties Evelyn and her friends attend are family parties, with parents, cousins, friends, and her friends' parents. Her parents and her friends' parents spend time together, and they all go to the same neighborhood Catholic church. On the rare occasions when Evelyn has broken the trust of her parents and done something wrong, she says that making their disappointment known to her is all the punishment she required:

I: So if you were to get in trouble, though, how would they discipline you?
R: Oh, they would be just disappointed.
I: So they wouldn't send you to your room or anything, or ground you?
R: They would go, you know, we have so much trust in you, and how could you do this to us, you know.
I: They'd make you feel guilty?
R: God, so much.
I: So that's worse than being punished, huh?
R: Yeah.

Evelyn's parents are strong Catholics and have gone to church regularly together ever since she can remember. Evelyn is now a kindergarten Sunday school teacher at church. Church seems to be a large factor in keeping family relationships close. Evelyn explains that her older brother (age 22) had been negative about church for a long time. As he got older, he stopped going with the family. However, she says that now "God is changing him," and he has started to go to church with them again. She seems very happy about this and says it has brought him closer to the family again. Evelyn has another older brother (age 21) and a younger brother and sister. She is closest to her oldest brother but gets along with the others as well. While there are family fights and arguments, overall they are very happy together.

Similar to Derek, Evelyn is close to a number of adults in her life, many of whom are extended-family members but also adults from her church. Her mother's sister and Evelyn are particularly close. "Yeah, aunties, you know, my mom's younger sister, she's like twenty-three; yeah, she's already married. She has a baby; we're so close, yeah, we talk about relationships, we talk about guys." Much of her extended family is in Mexico, but those in the United States live close by, and she sees them on a regular basis. "We're all close," she says. "We're all the same; we get along, you know. We never lose communication with each other." Evelyn also has a supportive network of adult women at church who help her when she has problems or needs advice:

They're always helping me in everything, you know: Evelyn, do this, you know this is good for you, and when I say, oh, I think I did [something] wrong . . . they're like, oh, you know what? You're right. It is wrong. But when I have problems like, for example, if I talk to my parents about my boyfriend or my friends, and I tell the ladies that I know from church, they help me out the same way as my parents. They're like another part of my family.

Overall, Evelyn appears to be a well loved, well supported, and confident young woman. Her free time is mostly filled with family responsibilities, parties with friends' families, and spending time with her boyfriend. She is immersed in a network of friends and family that always know where she is and what she is doing. She gets decent grades at school (A's and B's with an occasional C) and plans to work and go to college when she graduates next year. She seems, however, extremely focused on her boyfriend. She says her boyfriend wants her to go to college, as do her parents, but the seriousness of their relationship seems likely to complicate these plans, which is worrying her parents. She says that worries about older boyfriends are an issue with many Latina (*Latina* means a female) teens and their parents. Evelyn is adamant, however, that she is not having sex and will wait for marriage for that. She wants to go to college and become a detective, just like her uncle. After college, she plans to get married and have a child, but just one. Evelyn appears determined to achieve her goals.

ERIC LI

Eric Li is an eighteen-year-old Chinese-American living with his parents in a medium-sized city on the East Coast. He is the only child of his parents, who moved to the United States when he was twelve so that his father could pursue a Ph.D. at a large research university. Energetic, fun, and openhearted, Eric is popular among his racially diverse peer group at school and at the upscale Chinese restaurant where he works as a waiter. Although he has lived in America for only six years, he appears very American in his clothes and in the way he carries himself.

Eric describes his relationship with his parents as generally good, but conflicts have emerged over the way American culture has influenced him:

Sometimes we'll get along fine, just like best friends, and then the next moment, you know, one of us will just snap, and then, you know, the whole household will just be like yelling and stuff, so well it's, it's kind of strange. They want me to be the traditional, obedient Chinese son, you know, so that's sort of like a tradition in China, but then since I've spent almost a third of my life here, you know, I grew up with both the Chinese ideas and the American ideals and then just trying to combine those two. Sometimes what I think is not necessarily what they want me to think, so that leads to a lot of conflicts.

Eric describes his mother as being supportive, but he doesn't share too much with her about what's going on inside:

Sometimes we will have talks and stuff, like one of those long, two-hour, three-hour talks, but then I never really put in any feedback, you know; I just listen, and she's always doing most of the talking, and so I wouldn't say we're like that close.

> I: What things would you try and avoid talking to her about?
> R: Um, I don't know how, how I'm really feeling inside, you know? And how I really feel about her or the, or the whole situation with living with them and stuff. I don't really know why, it's just I don't; I'm not the type of person who likes to share a lot of feelings, especially with people I know, 'cause then, you know, I'm afraid like they might judge me or something.

Eric says that his mother is worried about him, because once he graduates from high school, his parents might move back to China and he would stay to attend college here in the United States, living on his own. It seems that her worries are justified—his transition into adolescence was not smooth. A few years ago he began hanging out with friends who used drugs, and he currently struggles with what seems to be an addiction to alcohol. His parents were unaware of his drug and alcohol use for years. They found out recently and have told him that if he doesn't stop using, they will send him back to China.

In general, Eric says he doesn't talk much to his father, and hasn't for as long as he can remember:

We don't really talk much on a normal basis. He does his thing, I do my thing, and he kind of has like this thing where he trusts me to make my own decisions and stuff, and then if he sees something that I'm not doing right, he would just say it once.... I would say we're, we're kind of distant. I mean not, not to the point where like the relationship is strained; we just don't talk much.

Eric says that his parents get along pretty well; they have fights every now and then, mostly about him. He says that as a rule, his family doesn't solve conflicts well.

Eric's parents have high aspirations for his career. They expect him to get a Ph.D. and enter a lucrative profession. This is another source of conflict between Eric and his parents:

Their idea is go to school, go to graduate school, get a doctorate, get a lot of college out and some office, you know, wear a tie to work every day and make money, have a family, all that stuff. My idea is, I don't really care about money; I want to do something fun that I like to do, even if it doesn't pay much, you know? And then I want to just enjoy life while I'm still young, and to them that's just like more of an American way of thinking rather than, you know, you should be thinking about your financial future and all that stuff; so they think that I'm thinking that way because I grew up here, but I've, I've pretty much had the same ideas even when I was little. I didn't like school; I didn't like being told what to do.

Eric gets good grades, mostly A's, and is on the math team at school; but he rarely studies and finds school boring and unchallenging. He says that he doesn't get along well with his teachers, because his father has always treated him as one of his students:

I never really studied, never; slept through class and stuff and so [my teachers] were annoyed with that, and I understand their reason why, because my Dad was a teacher too. Ever since I was little, he always treated me like one of his students, so, at a very young age, I grew up resenting teachers. So I never really got along well with teachers.

Eric has the benefit of being intellectually gifted, which will hopefully allow him to make a successful transition into adulthood. He also has parents who are able to support and encourage the pursuit of higher education. His struggle with alcohol seems likely to be an obstacle to this transition, and his parents appear to not know how to deal with this problem or support their son. The physical absence of his parents after he graduates will mean that they will not be there for support or guidance. He will be truly on his own.

These stories highlight distinct racial and ethnic patterns in three important areas of family life: household structure, family contact and supervision, and family support. Our analysis shows how race and ethnicity matter in the ways teens experience these aspects of family life differently.

HOUSEHOLD STRUCTURE

Our data show that Asian-American teens are the most likely group to live in a household with both biological parents ("bionuclear" structure) (67%), followed by white (58%), Latino (44%), and African-American (27%) teens (see Table 2.1[4]). These racial and ethnic differences were statistically significant when controlling for income and other demographic variables.[5] African-American

TABLE 2.1

Household Structure of Teens by Race/Ethnicity

	White	African-American	Asian-American	Latino (generation)			
				All	First	Second	Third+
Family Type (percent)							
Bio-nuclear	58	27	67	44	51	57	33
Single-mother-headed	19	41	15	33	24	32	37
Step family	14	16	10	15	19	7	18
Other	9	16	8	8	6	4	12
Household Members							
Average number of people under 18 in household	1.98	2.24	1.71	2.44	2.49	2.45	2.42
Average number of people 18 or older in household other than parents	1.26	1.40	1.20	1.38	1.36	1.49	1.32

Source: NSYR survey.

Note: All differences between racial/ethnic groups are significant at $p < .01$ (Pearson's chi-square test). $N = 3,290$.

teens are the most likely to live in a one-parent, single-mother-headed family (41%). The percentage of third-or-more-generation Latino teens living in one-parent single-mother-headed families is similar to those of African-American teens (37%), while the single-mother percentages for first- and second-genera-tion Latino families are similar to those of white families. Latino teens live in families with the highest average number of children in the household, and African-American teens live in families with the highest average number of nonfamily adults in the household.

The debate over the functionality of single-parent families has been the most explosive and central issue in the race and family literature. It is not the purpose of this study to enter the debate as to the causes for higher rates of single-par-ent families among African-Americans and third-or-more-generation Latinos, or for that matter the high rates of bionuclear-structured households of Asian-American families. Nor do we explore the data on outcomes in later life to argue whether teens from bionuclear families have a lasting advantage over those from single-parent families. Almost forty years of research have addressed these ques-tions. Our contribution here is simply to explore the lived experiences of teens from different family structures by listening to the voices of the children them-selves. As we listen to these voices, we find that in all racial and ethnic groups adolescents with distant or absent fathers pay both an emotional and an instrumental price. Like Derek Williams, whom we met above, many of the teens from single-parent families stated that having a closer relationship with their fathers would be the one thing in their life they would change:

I: Do you ever feel sad or depressed?

R [sixteen-year-old Latina]: Yeah, sometimes when I think about my father and that's it.

I: What are the things in your life that get you the most excited or enthusiastic?

R: Like excited in my life? Probably, thinking that something could happen, like me and my father having a relationship or something. Being close like me and my mother are.

R [fourteen-year-old African-American male]: Well, I mean, I'm a teen, and I think he went through things that I went through; he's a man, you know, and I just want the love and care that a father would give me.

Many other teens from all racial and ethnic groups talked extensively about the economic hardships that came to their families when their fathers left:

R [fifteen-year-old white female]: Not having a dad around kind of made it a lot harder on me, and I had to survive myself because my mom worked three jobs to support us.

I: Wow.

R: And by the time that she got three jobs, I was five, so I basically learned how to cook, get up, wash clothes, and, you know, like walk to school.

Since African-American and third-or-more-generation Latino families are more likely to be headed by a single mother, teens from these groups are more likely to be experiencing the costs of having a distant or absent father. Our survey data show that African-American teens are the least likely of all groups to say they have a close relationship with their fathers (see Table 2.3 in later section). However, African-American teens were the most likely to say that they had father-like relationships with other family members. As with Derek Williams, grandfathers, uncles, and older brothers and cousins often fulfill some of the emotional, if not economic, role of their missing fathers:

Since I didn't have a dad when I was young, my [significantly older] brother was my father figure; I mean, my mother told him, you know, when I was small, to take me wherever he goes. So I saw everything, I learned my surroundings and everything. Where he used to go. I mean, he taught me the basic things of what a father would teach, you know. It's like no other man could compare to what he did, because he taught me those things. [fifteen-year-old African-American male]

Glowing and emotional reports like this one of having an older male family member mentor was a commonly heard refrain among African-American males. It appears that African-American teens in single-parent families have greater access to extended-family father figures than teens of other racial and ethnic groups, which likely lessens some of the effects of father absence. We did not find as many third-or-more-generation Latino teens with surrogate father relationships. Overall, however, African-American and third-or-more-generation Latino teens are more likely to experience emotional and instrumental costs because of an absent father.

FAMILY CONTACT AND SUPERVISION

Interestingly, our data show that despite the lower likelihood of living in two-parent families, African-American teens had more regular contact with at least one parent and were more closely supervised by a parent than were white and Asian-American teens. They also reported more household duties, stricter discipline, and a more hierarchical relationship with parents than did white teens. Like Derek Williams, other interview subjects illustrated the high levels of responsibility and discipline given by African-American parents. Punishment is strict and sometimes physical. Mothers often use cell phones and other family members to monitor what their teens are doing at all times. A sixteen-year-old African-American female described a common pattern of discipline found in many of our interviews with African-American teens:

I: If your mom found out you did something wrong, do you know you'll get disciplined?

R: Yes.

I: Is there ever a time when she doesn't?

R: No.

I: How does she discipline you?

R: How does she? She might hit me or something, or punish me.

I: How does she punish you?

R: You know, no phone or TV, or you know, that's about it, sent to your room for like a month or something, come home from school, you go to your room.

I: For a month?

R: Yeah.

I: What happened the last time you were disciplined?

R: Um, let me think; oh, we got a whoopin', I got a whoopin'.

I: What happened? Why did you get a whoopin'?

R: Oh, it was July 4th, right? We were out and it was late; we were just walking around, looking at the fireworks, and we forgot what time it was, and we were walking around and nobody knew where we were. And she had a fit when we came back.

I: Do you feel like you're able to do what you want without much adult interference?

R: No.

I: Do you feel like you're watched too closely?

R: Sometimes. Sometimes she'll be a little too close.

I: What kind of things does she do to supervise you?

R: Like, okay, if I, let's see, if I ever, if I go somewhere, with my boyfriend, she'll want me, my sister's got to tag along and be third party, and I think, okay, ma. He wanted me to go to his family reunion, and my sister got to go, and I'm like, ma, there's gonna be a whole bunch of adults, and she just, she always wants me to be supervised, everywhere I go.

In our interviews as well as our survey data, we found the level of supervision and control of African-American teens on average significantly higher than that of white and Asian-American teens but similar to first- and second-generation Latino teens (see Table 2.2). This is not to say, however, that all Afri-

TABLE 2.2

Teen-Family Contact and Supervision by Race/Ethnicity

Percentage of teens . . .	White	African-American	Asian-American	Latino (generation)			
				All	First	Second	Third+
Having dinner with parents every night	41	46	43	51	65	45	49
Having two or more nonfamily weeknight organized activities per week	47	37	45	33	18	38	45
Spending at least one evening per week with no adult supervision	71	61	67	56	36	52	64
Saying their parents "always" discipline them when they do something wrong	35	41	42	34	33	36	32
Saying parents would be extremely upset if they found out they were skipping school	65	71	79	61	57	64	61

Source: NSYR survey.
Note: All differences between racial/ethnic groups are significant at $p < .01$ (Pearson's chi-square test). $N = 3,290$.

can-American teens are supervised heavily and always disciplined strictly. We found many others who were not. However, compared to other ethnic groups, African-American parents, mothers in particular, are highly involved in their teens' lives emotionally as well as through monitoring and discipline.

White teens, overall, had the least family contact of all the racial and ethnic groups we examined. They spend less time with family, have more outside activities, have less parental supervision and discipline, and are the least likely to be close to siblings and other extended-family members. They also have more freedom to express their opinions in their families, and feel the most comfortable interacting with adults outside of the family (Tables 2.2 and 2.3).

Like Cara Sanders, a large number of the white teens we interviewed seemed to see their parents as primarily a nuisance that kept them from pursuing what they wanted to pursue. Many wanted simply to be left alone. One seventeen-year-old white male was particularly annoyed that his stepfather, because of his work schedule, was often home during the day:

R: For six years, he's been around every day, and that's the only thing I don't really like about him, he's always there; it was better off before he got there, you know. Normally, he's home, I can't bring people over, you know, and do stuff with my friends 'cause he's gonna be there.

I: So the home is not like an open, free place to do stuff for a while—

R: Yeah, I guess; I mean, even if he's not around, I can do whatever.

This shows a common attitude we found among white teens who would rather be with friends and not have their parents around. This attitude was much less prevalent in our interviews with teens of other racial and ethnic groups.

The families of white teens seem to allow a much greater degree of autonomy to pursue outside interests and freedom to challenge parental authority. We heard white teens repeatedly express frustration at their parents' not treating them like adults, which reveals an expectation that they should be on a par with adults in some respects. White teens seem to have fewer household responsibilities and expectations from parents compared to the other racial and ethnic groups, and they feel the most freedom to express their own views to their parents. Their time is more likely to be consumed by activities apart from the family (Table 2.2).

It was also clear from our interviews that white teens received less supervision and discipline from parents than other groups did. Cara Sanders, for example, doesn't like spending time with her family and chooses to have fun with friends instead. Her parents have few restrictions on her coming and going. Other white teens expressed the same pattern. As one white male reported, "I can do whatever I want, as long as I get my homework done." A fifteen-year-old white teen from a small town in the West expressed a freedom from parental interference in most of her activities:

I: How consistently do your parents discipline you when they find out you've done something wrong?

R: Barely ever. It's do whatever you want; if you get caught, you get caught type thing.

I: How do you feel about that?

R: I think it's really good, 'cause I don't like being grounded, especially living out in the middle of nowhere. It's not that fun.

I: So, if you do get disciplined, then it's grounding?

R: No, I have to do a lot of chores. I won't get my cell phone taken away; I'll probably get grounded off the computer, which I'm never on the computer anyways. Or I can't have phone calls past nine. I can have phone calls basically anytime I want. Like last night [a boyfriend] called me at 3:45 in the morning when I was sleeping. My mom didn't get mad; she just didn't care.

I: Do your parents monitor or supervise your behaviors closely or not?

R: No.

I: Do you feel like you can pretty much do anything you want?

R: I can do anything I want and everything I want, but I just don't do it. My mom has a pretty high trust in me; she respects my decisions.

This was not true of all white teens, however. Many, particularly those with religiously conservative parents, received much more monitoring and discipline. Some (although a minority of) religiously conservative white teens are home-schooled so that parents can not only teach their values through the curriculum but also have a closer watch on the behavior of their teens. This homeschooled fourteen-year-old white teen reported being tightly monitored by her parents:

I: Do [your parents] check up on you to see where you are or what you are doing?

R: No, they usually know where I'm going, because they usually take me [laughs].

I: Do you feel like you can do pretty much what you want without adult interference?

R: Ah, not really. My mom has this thing where she doesn't want me to go see any movie that she thinks would be too mature for me. Um, so, like whenever I go to movies, she's like, I want to see what movie you saw.

I: Right, so she does try and keep a watchdog eye.

R: Yeah.

I: And do you think that that, that your homeschooling, affects your parents' discipline and supervision of you in any way?

R: Um, sort of; I'm by my mom all the time, so she sees a lot of the stuff that I do.

Despite these exceptions, white teens overall experienced higher levels of freedom from supervision and discipline than did teens in the other racial and ethnic groups. The lives of most white teens were focused on friends, school, church, and organized activities.

Our interviews generally portrayed first- and second-generation Latino teens as deeply embedded in tight family and community social networks. Of all the racial and ethnic groups, first-generation Latino teens were the most likely to say they had dinner with their parents every night and were the least likely to spend time unsupervised by an adult or spend evenings away from the family in organized activities.

Like Evelyn Cabrera, many of the first- and second-generation Latino teens we interviewed are embedded in a strong extended family, often residing in close proximity. Interaction is reinforced through family events such as birthday parties, holiday parties, and attendance at a local church. A fifteen-year-old Latino teen describes the extended family that lives in his apartment complex in a small East Coast city:

On the first floor, my grandparents live there, and my cousins just came from Colombia a couple of years ago. And then on another floor, my aunt lives with her son. And then, my cousin lived on the third floor with his sister and his parents, but then they just bought a new house just down the street.

This close proximity to family gives this teen a constant source of activity and support, as well as higher levels of responsibility. He is responsible for looking after younger children, helping with housework, and being there for family functions. Similar to African-American teens, Latino teens also had more adult supervision and strict discipline than their white counterparts. However, supervision seemed to be more in the form of community monitoring rather than individual parental control, as is the case with African-American teens:

I: Okay, and do your parents monitor or supervise your behaviors closely or not, usually?

R [thirteen-year-old Latina]: Well, now, they definitely want to know where I am. As long as they know who I'm with, they usually have my friends' number or their parents' cell phone number, so they are always able to contact, um, them or me.

I: What about parties: do you go to those much, or is that something that is common?

R: Um, the only parties that we have are birthday parties, and those are usually supervised.

This picture of the large Latino household embedded in close family and community ties certainly does not fit the experience of all Latino teens. Many third-plus-generation teens closely resembled the families of the more autonomous white teens. In addition, the likelihood of living in a single-parent family was much higher for third-plus-generation Latino teens—similar to African-American teens. On average, however, Latino teens were the most likely to be embedded in strong family and community networks, and the least likely to be involved in nonfamily activities and commitments.

Our data show that on average, Asian-American teens have the highest levels of discipline and expectations for behavior, but not necessarily the highest levels of supervision or contact with family. In addition, they have the least open communication with their parents. Asian-American parents were more likely than parents from other racial and ethnic groups to express that they had difficulty talking to and understanding their teens.[6] As with Eric Li, many Asian-American teens do not have emotionally close relationships with their parents, but parents do encourage their participation in school and extracurricular activities and have high expectations for them to succeed in these endeavors. These high expectations may often lead to conflict and guilt. One sixteen-year-old Asian-American male we interviewed had been expelled from an elite private high school for yelling at a teacher, as well as other disruptive behavior. This caused considerable shame and guilt for this teen in the ensuing conflict with his parents. Interestingly, the greatest disappointment he felt from his parents was how this turn of events would affect his prospects for college: "They want me to go to the best college possible, to be successful in life, to drive a good car, and I have been, um, something of a disappointment in that." This teen is still on track (mostly B's) for academic success in his current public high school; his aspirations for college have dropped from the Ivy League to the state university. He feels a tremendous burden of guilt over his perceived declining prospects, and he experiences constant conflict with his parents over grades. This level of career anxiety is surprising for a sixteen-year-old still two years away from graduation.

Despite these high parental expectations, Asian-American teens were monitored less than African-American and Latino teens, and like white teens their parents seemed unaware of what was going on in their lives. In addition, Asian-American teens were the most likely to report that they lied to their parents on occasion; however, they were the least likely to engage in risky behavior such as drinking alcohol, using drugs, and having sex. This interaction with a sixteen-year-old Asian-American male was similar to many others we had with Asian-American teens:

I: How consistently do your parents discipline you when they find out you've done something wrong?

R: Oh, quite consistently; I mean, not that it happens a lot.

I: Right, and how do they discipline you? In what ways?

R: You know, they have these very long, tedious discussions that are quite annoying, but um,

I: [laughs] So that's part of the discipline. Long tedious discussions.

R: Yeah.

I: Yeah, that's interesting. Okay, do your parents monitor or supervise your behaviors closely, or not so much?

R: Um, not so much, because in all honesty, they don't have a lot to monitor, and I think they realize that.

I: Uh-huh. So you're able to do what you want without much adult interference?

R: Yeah, but that's because I don't do much that adults would find to be very objectionable.

Overall, Asian-American teens are similar to white teens in the amount of contact with family. They are likely to live in smaller households, have less contact with extended family, and spend more time in nonfamily, outside activities. The difference with white teens, however, is that most Asian-American teens seem less free to pursue their own desires and interests, and feel more responsible to their families. Yet unlike Latino and African-American families, this responsibility is less likely to include household obligations and obeying house rules, and more likely to be focused on performing well in nonfamily activities, particularly in school. Many of the Asian-American teens we interviewed seem to have internalized this strong sense of responsibility to obey their parents' wishes, even if they disagreed with them. They feel the pressure from their parents to perform well in school and to stay out of trouble. Thus, it seems, even though Asian-American parents are often out of sight, they are not out of mind.

FAMILY CLOSENESS AND SUPPORT

Although the most likely to report being distant from their fathers, African-American teens were by far the most likely to report being "extremely close" to their mothers (see Table 2.3). They were also the most likely to report that they discussed personal subjects such as friendships, dating, and drinking with their mothers. In our interviews we repeatedly heard of very open and supportive relationships between African-American teens and their mothers:

There's nothing I wouldn't talk about with my mother, you know; I talk to her about everything—girlfriends I've had, you know, everything. Conflicts at school—I mean, it's great. [fifteen-year-old African-American male]

Compared to other racial and ethnic groups, African-American mothers are highly involved both in supervising their children and in emotionally supporting them by allowing them to openly share about their lives.

Asian-American teens, in contrast, seem to have the lowest levels of open communication with their parents. Asian-American teens were the least likely to report that they were "extremely close" to their mothers, and were the least likely to discuss personal issues like friends, dating, and drinking with their mothers (Table 2.3). As with Eric Li, many reported a lack of understanding between themselves and their parents, and this was distressing to many.

Asian-American teens who did report a good relationship with their parents spoke of their parents' supportiveness as encouragement to achieve rather than encouragement to openly share their problems, as was more common among African-American and white teens:

I: How supportive and understanding are your parents of you?

R [fifteen-year-old Asian-American female]: I think they're really supportive. Especially my mom.

I: Yeah? In what ways is she supportive of you?

R: She's always like pushing me to do the right thing.

I: Do you know what I mean when I say supportive? Okay, what about your dad?

R: Yeah, him too. Like if I get a good grade, you know, he'll be like, "Oh, good job," you know, "keep it up."

It is instructive that the interviewer (in this case an African-American woman) clearly had a different definition of "support and understanding" than the Asian-American respondent, who had a much more instrumental view of support: being pushed to do the right thing and to pursue high levels of achieve-

TABLE 2.3

Teen-Family Relationships and Communication by Race/Ethnicity

Percentage of teens . . .	White	African-American	Asian-American	Latino (generation)			
				All	First	Second	Third+
Describing relationship with mother as extremely close	33	45	29	33	32	33	33
Describing relationship with father as extremely or very close	49	31	44	41	48	41	38
Listing at least one immediate or extended-family member as one of five best friends	18	46	13	30	26	32	30
Getting along with siblings extremely or very well	23	39	27	41	55	45	34
Discussing personal subjects, such as friend-ships, dating, and drinking with mother very often	27	33	15	26	25	24	28
Saying they discuss personal subjects such as friendships, dating, and drinking with father fairly or very often	26	17	19	19	29	17	16
Saying they have too little freedom to openly express their own views	11	17	21	17	19	14	18
Saying they feel fairly or very comfortable talking to adults outside of their families	57	46	50	45	32	43	49

Source: NSYR survey.

Note: All differences between racial/ethnic groups are significant at $p < .01$ (Pearson's chi-square test). $N = 3,290$.

ment. In addition to supportive interactions, conflicts between Asian-American teens and their parents tended to revolve around levels of achievement.

Somewhat paradoxically, most white teens seem to have very open communication with parents even though they are less likely to spend time with them on a regular basis. They were second only to African-American teens in reporting that they talked openly with their parents about personal issues. As mentioned earlier, white teens also felt a higher degree of freedom to express their views to their parents than teens in the other racial and ethnic groups.

Their time was more likely to be consumed, however, by activities apart from the family. For many white teens, support seemed to be defined as allowing them the freedom to make their own decisions and pursue their own activities, and being upheld in those decisions. Conversely, conflicts between white teens and their parents were often surrounded by the issues of not being able to make their own decisions and "being treated like a child."

Many white teens described support from their parents as simply showing up at various activities outside the home:

I: So how supportive and understanding are your parents of you?

R [sixteen-year-old white female]: They're pretty supportive. They've been to all my school activities and what not.

This teen's time is so consumed with outside activities that she defines family support as their simply being present to watch her perform in school functions and sporting events.

In contrast to most of the white teens we interviewed, many Latino teens seemed to long for more time and attention from their parents. This is interesting given the fact that first- and second-generation Latino teens were the most likely to have dinner with their parents every night and the least likely to spend an evening without adult supervision. Much of this time, it seems, is large group, extended-family time with fewer opportunities to interact with parents one-on-one. In our phone survey, Latino teens were the most likely to say they didn't get enough attention from their parents.

The experience of this fourteen-year-old Latina was common in our interviews:

I: If you could change anything about your relationship with your parents, what would it be?

R: I don't know, I just want kind of like to spend more time with them because they're both working a lot now, and I'm usually the one with my brothers left home and taking care of them and . . . I like it when we're all together a lot.

I: Do you mind taking care of your brothers?

R: Um, no. I like taking care of them because they're really easy and we get along . . . and then by the time my mom comes back, she usually tries to go to the pool with us so she can spend time with us. Usually when my mom is trying to relax, she, like my mom and dad, they always try to find a time to spend time with us.

It is notable that this teen's responsibility to take care of her brothers did not seem to bother her. She did not complain that it limited her time with friends or for outside activities. Her main regret was that since both of her parents worked she could not spend more time with them. We rarely heard this sentiment from non-Latino teens.

CONCLUSION: RACE, CLASS, AND FAMILY LIFE

All parents seek to influence their children in ways that will make them more adaptive to their social environment.[7] Family researchers have created typologies (classifications based on types or categories) to conceptualize different parenting styles that reflect socialization strategies used by parents. These typologies are often configured on two axes of parenting: control/freedom and emotional closeness/distance. The best-known typology was created by Baumrind,[8] who distinguished between *permissive, authoritarian,* and *authoritative* parenting patterns.[9] The authoritarian style is characterized by high levels of control through punitive means and low levels of nurturance and support. Permissive parenting is the mirror image, with high levels of nurturance and support and low levels of parental control. Authoritative parenting combines high levels of nurturance, communication, and support with consistent rules-based control, where clear verbal explanations are given to children, and negotiation and disagreement with parents is possible. Punitive measures, particularly physical punishment are minimized in this type.

Many researchers have generally accepted that the authoritative parenting style is most likely to produce well-adapted children. In particular, this style is seen to produce independent, friendly, competent adults with high self-esteem.[10] Most of these studies, however, use only middle-class white families as their subjects, making generalizations beyond this subgroup problematic.[11]

Our results suggest that these typologies need to be expanded to account for the varying parenting patterns we found in our racially and ethnically diverse sample (see Table 2.4). Baumrind's typology fits most of the white families in our study, as we would categorize most white families into either the permissive or authoritative type. Most white teens we interviewed had open communication with parents and at least a moderate degree of emotional support from them. They also tended to feel very open expressing their feelings and disagreeing with parents, and felt they could negotiate with them. Many also felt very little control or monitoring from parents. Even in Baumrind's authoritative parenting style, by the time children reach adolescence parental control is expected to decrease, as by this age children have supposedly internalized the norms their parents desire.

TABLE 2.4

Summary of Family Types

Family type	Increased likelihood among	Emphasis on parental authority	Emotional closeness	Dominant method(s) of parental influence or control	Primary function of parenting
Nurturant authoritarian	African-American	High	High	Punishment	Developing respect for authority and personal responsibility
Instrumental authoritarian	Asian-American	High	Low	Verbal pressure/punishment	Training/skill development
Communal nurturant	First- and second-generation Latino	High	Moderate	Communal monitoring	Integration into extended family/community
Permissive	White and third-generation Latino	Low	Moderate/high	Rewards, verbal encouragement	Developing autonomy, self-esteem
Authoritative	White and third-generation Latino	Moderate	Moderate/high	Incentives, positive and negative reinforcement	Internalization of parental norms, developing autonomy

These various parenting models reflect key aspects of Anglo-American culture, such as therapeutic individualism and egalitarianism.[12] Children are expected to authentically express "how they feel" to their parents, and are given the opportunity to disagree with their superiors. As we will discuss below, these models also reflect middle-class values designed to groom children for autonomous decision making.

As predicted by Baumrind, our study suggests that authoritative parenting produces many confident, self-assured, and competent white teens, while permissive parenting styles seem to produce a number of maladaptive behaviors, including risky and delinquent behavior. When we examine other racial and ethnic groups, however, these typologies do not fit many of the families in our sample.

Many African-American families, for example, combine the high degrees of nurturance and emotional support of permissive or authoritative parenting with the high levels of control and punitive practices of authoritarian parenting styles. While Baumrind's and other models would predict less-than-adaptive outcomes from this combination, particularly the emphasis on control and punishment, it may be that in the context of their neighborhood, school, and economic strata, these families are socializing their teens in adaptive ways. In the public worlds of many African-Americans, there is little tolerance for disrespecting or negotiating with authority figures. In addition, African-Americans who break drug laws or commit other nonviolent offenses are approximately ten times more likely to be incarcerated than whites who break the same laws,[13] so the emphasis on obedience with the threat of punishment fits more completely with their external social world than does the more negotiated, incentive-based pattern of white authoritative parenting. We identify this parenting style found in many African-American families as "nurturant authoritarian," where obedience and respect for authority are demanded and punishment often used but where these are also coupled with close and open communication and high levels of emotional support. This style appears to produce teens who are very close to their parents, particularly mothers, and who respect authority and take responsibility very seriously.

Interestingly, many Asian-American families in our sample fit Baumrind's authoritarian type, with low levels of communication and emotional support and high levels of external control. Many family researchers who have studied white families see this as the most maladaptive parenting style, resulting in a lack of internalization of norms[14] and sometimes putting teens at risk for substance abuse and delinquent behavior.[15] We saw little evidence of these maladaptive outcomes among the Asian-American teens in our sample. In fact, they were the *least* likely teens to engage in risky behavior, and they tended toward high levels of achievement in school and extracurricular activities. Our data suggest that authoritarian parenting styles in a white context have different meanings in an Asian-American context. Many Asian-American teens interpreted the high levels of pressure and control from their parents as being supportive of them and wanting the best for them. They seemed to internalize their parents' desire to see them succeed and to view their parents' pressure as a means toward those internalized ends. These findings are similar to Chao's,[16] who demonstrated that Chinese-American parents were much more likely than white parents to see instrumental "training" as a goal of parenting rather than emotional support and adjustment. We call this type "instrumental/supportive authoritarian" and observed it commonly among Asian-American families.

Many first- and second-generation Latino teens seemed to experience a parenting style that does not seem to fit any of the categories generated by the family socialization literature. These teens reported high levels of nurturance and support, but support was spread out among extended-family members as well as parents. In fact, many first- and second-generation Latino teens wished they could spend more time with their busy parents yet felt supported by them and their extended families. They experienced high levels of supervision but in the form of communal monitoring rather than parental control per se. Teens did not feel entitled to negotiate and disagree with parents, at least to the extent that white teens did. These teens tend to avoid risky behavior simply to avoid being "found out" through the tight extended-family and community networks that monitor their behavior. They also had high expectations placed on them to take care of family responsibilities. These too, however, included extended-family obligations as well as those assigned by their parents.

First- and second-generation Latino families seem to function as a buffer between the individual and the formal organizations of society. First- and second-generation Latino teens spend the most amount of time in family activities and the least in outside organized activities of all the racial and ethnic groups in our sample. This seems to be preparing teens for a life in which the family is at the center and formal organizations are peripheral. Respect for family and fulfilling family obligations are paramount, while participation in outside activities are allowed only to the extent that they do not compromise the ability to meet family obligations. All of this suggests that first- and second-generation Latino teens are groomed for a world where family holds the greatest potential for support, satisfaction, and belonging while outside institutions hold less hope for enhancing the lives of the individual. Adaptation, therefore, needs to be defined differently for these teens. Adaptation would have to include the extent to which they are socialized into extended-family and community networks that will continue to play a central role in their adult lives. We propose a parenting type called "communal nurturance" to identify this combination of communal authority/control and nurturance. This is consistent with other studies that have demonstrated the high valuing of familism and collectivism among Latinos[17] and their effects on parenting practices.

In contrast, third-or-more-generation Latino families, in which the parents were born in the United States, mirrored white family types more closely, the majority being permissive or authoritative. These teens had much more freedom to openly disagree with their parents and to spend time in the absence of adult supervision and in extracurricular organized activities. However, as we will see in later chapters, third-plus-generation Latino youth tend to be less supported by their schools and external organizations than are white youth, making the consequences of a lack of family cohesion more dramatic and negative for these teens. The assimilation of Latino families to Anglo-American norms seems to produce a number of negative outcomes for Latino teens.

With regard to family structure, our results generally confirm the findings of a growing body of literature that documents the financial, emotional, and behavioral problems that come from having an absent father. While other studies have shown these costs much more comprehensively,[18] our data add to this literature through listening to the voices of the teens themselves. It was striking that many of the teens we interviewed who had absent fathers mentioned this disconnected relationship as the one thing they would change in their life. Many others mentioned it as the thing most likely to make them sad or depressed. Others spoke in detail of the financial hardships that occurred on the departure of their fathers and how that negatively affected their lives. African-American and third-or-more-generation Latino teens were more likely to experience these emotional and instrumental costs resulting from an absent father.

This is not to say that fathers and stepfathers who are living in the same home as teens are always emotionally supportive and present for their teens. Relationships with stepfathers in particular seem to be fraught with difficulty for many teens, especially white teens. Yet whatever their level of emotional support and ability to parent teens, fathers and stepfathers in the home do provide financial, logistical, and supervisory support that is beneficial in most cases. These functions fall completely on the mother in most single-parent homes, which is clearly a deficit for teens in these homes.

As mentioned above, most research on parent-child socialization has been done in the context of middle-class European-American families, which implicitly creates Eurocentric models of family socialization.[19] Other research, which has expanded the pool to families of color, has found some of the same effects our data show—for example, greater expectations of conformity to parental wishes and less emphasis on individual autonomy in Latino, Asian-American, and African-American families.[20] Others have found families of color to exert greater emphasis on collectivism, cooperation, obligation, and reciprocity than is the case within white families.[21] Our findings confirm these previous studies and specify ways these differences play themselves out in the lives of teens.

Other researchers, however, downplay racial and ethnic differences and see them as artifacts of *social class*.[22] It has long been established that parents whose jobs require them to be obedient to authority and to carry out tasks commissioned by others tend to instill the importance of obedience and respect for authority figures in their children. Conversely, parents whose jobs require creative thinking and decision making are likely to give their children more freedom to make their own decisions and to challenge authority figures, including themselves as parents.[23]

These studies show that parents, knowingly or unknowingly, socialize their children into the character traits and habits that will prepare them for their eventual socioeconomic role in society. Working-class children learn to work hard, respect authority, and to serve their families, anticipating the roles they will play in formal organizations. Middle-class children learn to have confidence in their own leadership, to see authority figures as equals, and to explore their own ideas and develop their own ways of completing tasks. These character traits are important for playing out the scripts they will eventually embody as middle-class adults.

These researchers tend to downplay race and ethnic differences, arguing that the lower socioeconomic strata of families of color explain the differences in socialization. Thus, the emphases within families of color on obedience, respecting authority, punishment, and family support rather than on independence are simply adaptations to their lower-class status rather than cultural differences.

Rather than arguing whether race or class is more important to the socialization process, we think it is more fruitful to consider how the two might be connected. The racial and ethnic differences we found were significant even when controlling for income levels, which suggests a racial and ethnic effect that is independent of class. This seemingly independent effect could be explained by the fact that the socioeconomic roles which particular racial and ethnic groups have played in American society have remained fairly static over time. Since the racial hierarchy in America has existed for many generations, the upward or downward mobility of an individual family is unlikely to completely alter their child-rearing practices, which have been developed by their racial and ethnic group for generations in response to their socioeconomic position in the American racial hierarchy.

White families, on average, socialize their children to develop a sense of autonomy and entitlement, which grooms them to function in a world where institutions are expected to serve them and where they are expected to be autonomous decision makers on an equal plane with those in authority. This gives them an important source of cultural capital in the white-dominated formal institutions of American society. Being willing to make demands of institutions and seeing oneself as equal to one's superiors are viewed as signs of "leadership potential" in American organizations.

It also appears that this dominant socialization pattern among white families has a downside. White teens had the lowest levels of family contact and supervision, giving them less relational closeness and parental guidance than in other groups. While a sense of independence from family likely allows them to feel free to pursue their dreams unhindered by family obligations, it also seems likely to result in risky behavior and relational isolation. At its extreme, freedom and independence can turn to anomie and isolation. A lack of teen supervision can also result in risky behavior that can hamper healthy growth and development into adulthood. A significant number of white teens we interviewed seemed involved in risky activities that are likely to lead to relational and emotional problems.

Families of color, to varying degrees, socialize their children into a world where their relationship to institutions is much more hierarchical and reciprocal. They are expected to serve the institutions of society as much as institutions are expected to serve them. While this prepares these teens well for subordinate roles in formal organizations, it may not provide the cultural capital necessary to advance to the higher ranks. However, teens of color, particularly African-American and first- and second-generation Latino teens receive a wealth of support from extended family, which they can use in ways that are not available to more autonomous white teens.

These patterns raise questions about the relationship between formal, public institutions and the institution of the family. Our data suggest that families are more protective and emotionally supportive among racial and ethnic groups in society that have the least to gain, and possibly the most to lose, from their involvement in public institutions. It makes sense that those who have less to gain from formal organizations would organize life around family and other mediating institutions while those who have the most to gain would seek meaning, belonging, and fulfillment in formal organizations. This also raises the question of whether people thrive more in a life oriented around family as opposed to advancement in the public realm. Surely a balance of the two is desirable, but it may be that those who seek fulfillment solely through advancement in formal organizations miss much of what makes life worth living.

3 PEERS

Influencing Attitudes, Social Acceptance, and Personal Relationships

I: What do you think are some of the biggest problems or pres-
sures facing teenagers today in general?
R: Probably I'd have to say, the way they look…the big pres-
sure on the way you look and succeeding, I guess, making good
grades, what you're going to become in your career.
—Sarah Travis, age 16, white

While the family continues to be the most researched aspect of child socialization, it is well recognized among researchers, parents, educators, and anyone else
that comes into frequent contact with teens that peers become important as a
socializing agent during adolescence.[1] Early work by family researchers tended
to pit parental and peer influence against each other, in attempts to discern
which reference group has a more powerful influence on teens.[2] The currently
wide consensus among family researchers, however, is that parents continue to
influence teens most powerfully even as the influence of peers increases.[3]

Sociologists, in contrast, have focused their attention on specific outcomes
related to peer relationships, such as delinquency, sexuality, or academic
achievement,[4] and conclude that peer networks exert a powerful influence in
these areas. As with research on families, most studies that look at the influence
of peers have focused on white middle-class youth.[5] Strikingly few studies on
the friendship patterns of adolescents of color have been conducted. This chapter explores racial and ethnic differences in peer relationships and their effect
on specific outcomes in the lives of teens.

As Youniss and Smollar note,[6] peer relationships are more accepting and
present-oriented than the more hierarchical and future-oriented parent-child
relationship. Importantly, this allows higher levels of trust and self-disclosure
among peers, making peer relationships an important source of social accep-

tance among teens.[7] Indeed, our interviews show that all teens highly value this "I can be myself" quality of their peer relationships. Somewhat paradoxically, for teens who are denied acceptance by their peers the horizontal nature of peer relationships heightens their discomfort, thereby providing peers with significant influence.

As we have seen in the area of family life, in many aspects of peer relationships teens of different racial and ethnic groups are more alike than different. For example, 95 percent of teens of all racial and ethnic groups were equally likely to have close friends; 55 percent think it is important to "act cool" in order to fit in with peers; 60 percent have at least one close friend of the opposite sex; 60 percent sometimes feel alone and misunderstood; and 53 percent say they are sometimes teased or made fun of by other kids. These seem to be common experiences of the majority of American teenagers regardless of race or ethnicity—there were no racial or ethnic differences on these questions. It is also worth noting that despite our emphasis in this chapter on risky behavior, most teens are not having sex or using drugs and alcohol. Contrary to public perceptions, for all of these activities and for all racial and ethnic groups there were far more abstainers than participants.

The tables in this chapter show statistically significant[8] racial and ethnic differences in the attributes of peer relationships as well as in peer-related behaviors and attitudes (see Tables 3.1–3.4 in later sections[9]). As was the case with family, these differences are relatively small, with significant overlap between groups and significant variation within groups. While relatively small, the racial and ethnic differences we found follow distinct patterns; when taken together, these differences point to important racial and ethnic differences in the ways teens experience their friends and peers. On further analysis of our data we found that the differences between racial and ethnic groups remained statistically significant when controlling for other factors, such as income, age, and area of residence.[10]

The broadest difference we found is that peers play a much larger role in the lives of white teens than of teens in other racial and ethnic groups. As we saw in Chapter 2, white teens move away from the influence of parents to a greater extent than do teens of other racial and ethnic groups. They spend less time with their parents and more time with friends, and they are less supervised by adults than are other racial and ethnic groups. It is not surprising therefore that peers play a larger role in the lives of white teens. The freedom to disengage from family allows white teens more freedom to engage with peers than other groups have.

However, in addition to offering more opportunities to enjoy friendships, this freedom exposes white teens to risky behaviors and negative peer influences.

Interestingly, Asian-American teens are similar to white teens in the amount of time they spend with peers, but they are on average less influenced by them. Asian-American teens have high levels of contact with peers and are highly embedded in non-Asian peer groups, yet do not seem to assimilate to the behavior patterns of their friends. They are constantly around teens of other ethnicities who engage in risky behavior yet tend not to participate themselves.

African-American teens have strong ties to family (as we saw in Chapter 2) and to religious communities (as we will see in Chapter 5), which moderate the influence of peers and may provide a strong source of self-esteem and moral purpose that is apart from peer group approval. Our data show African-American teens faring well in these areas as well as in low levels of risky activities, giving these teens a strong foundation for a healthy transition to adulthood. Against this mostly positive backdrop, African-American teens have relatively higher rates of sexual activity than the other groups.

As we observed with regard to family, Latino teens' experience with their peers differs greatly by immigrant generation. There appears to be a significant shift in the importance and influence of peers particularly when comparing first-, second-, and third-plus-generation Latino teens. As we saw in Chapter 2, contact with and importance of family is much lower for third-plus-generation teens than for first- and second-generation teens. As family contact and influence declines, peer contact and influence rises.

CHRIS CONNELY

Chris Connely is a seventeen-year-old white male from an upper-middle-class suburb of a large city on the East Coast. Tall, with short blond hair and blue eyes, Chris has the look of an All-American basketball player from another era. He lives with his mother and stepfather and stays with his biological father every other weekend. Chris is the only child in the house and has no biological siblings, only step-siblings, who do not live in the area.

Chris spends most of his time outside of school hanging out at friends' houses when there are no adults around, sometimes drinking and smoking pot. He also describes himself as a "hard-core skier" and often travels to the mountains in the winter with friends.

INTERVIEWER: So we talked some about what you and your peers do for fun. You say you go to a movie or hang out. What are the typical things you'll do?

RESPONDENT: It's like we can just chill and go to [my friend's] crib or do whatever, or maybe there's a party we're gonna go to, or maybe I'll call up the other kids at school and see who's having people.

I: Just go over to people's houses . . .

R: Yeah, I mean.

I: Are there parents home?

R: No.

I: Are these parties sort of low key and people are just hanging out and drinking, or are they completely wild, loud music?

R: No, the cops get called a lot, cops, well, [at] those ones; it's usually, you know, only crew parties now since big parties get broken up, so, you know, if you're not in the group of people where you know the ten heads who are gonna be there, [you don't go].

I: People smoke pot at these parties?

R: Ah, yeah, sometimes, you know, people go out on the back and, yeah, usually someone has weed at the parties.

I: Okay. Do you drink alcohol, or smoke pot, or do other drugs?

R: Yeah, sure, why not, yeah.

I: Let's focus on drinking first, the alcohol.

R: It depends. I really go through phases; I haven't drank much recently, but, you know, there are times where I drank like every other night during the week, you know, go to parties and stuff, other people's houses.

I: During the school year?

R: Yeah, at the beginning, . . . one of these guys I knew, and I always [drank] during the week, a couple times, three times a week, on weekends . . . and it's just like, hey, the last three weeks every, almost every night I've been out, but now I could say the last, like three weeks going back I haven't drank at all. So. It's a big difference.

Chris seems to come and go as he pleases, even on school nights, yet he sees his parents as strict compared to his friends' parents. Chris says that he has had sex several times with acquaintances at parties and with short-term girlfriends. He sees sex as fine for teens as long as they use condoms and "can handle it mentally."

While on the surface Chris seems to enjoy his life of parties, drinking, smoking, and having fun with friends, he also mentions that teen life can be depressing. He feels there is too much pressure for teens to conform and succeed. He seems to use his friends and parties as an escape from these pressures:

I: Some people say that many parents are really clueless about the realities of teenage life today, that they don't realize what it is really like, and what's really going on. Do you agree or disagree?

R: Ah, I don't know, it's, I think teenagers today are a lot more emotionally fragile, but I think that's about it.

I: Tell, tell me about that.

R: I really think that all the pressure put on, might be a little too much nowadays.

I: What kind of pressures?

R: Just to succeed and, you know, there are so many potential people to succeed, and there aren't enough successful roles for them all to play.

I: What do you mean by succeed?

R: I think the pressure to live up to expectations is high, and I think it's a little bit harder now 'cause you have to work to live up to them, you can't just automatically do well.

I: So when you say expectations, you mean school work or being a good person?

R: Everything.

Despite Chris's mediocre grades (mostly B's and C's) and police record, he is scheduled to attend a well-regarded private college in the fall semester. He sees his future as bright and full of successes. Given his admittance to this college and the resources of his family, this seems entirely likely. However, his substance abuse and preference for parties over homework may become an obstacle to this success.

TAMARA PHILLIPS

Tamara Phillips is a seventeen-year-old African-American living in a large urban area in the southeast. She is well dressed—her professional attire, stylish hair, and manicured nails give her the look of someone more mature than her age. She is also energetic and enjoyable to talk to.

Tamara has just graduated from a private Catholic high school and has a full-time clerical job for the summer before she leaves for college in another state in the fall. Tamara's mother transferred her to the private school because the local public school was too "wild" with "no discipline or authority." Tamara was doing poorly and having behavioral problems. The private school setting and teaching methods, according to Tamara, helped her get better grades—she graduated with a 2.75 GPA (grade point average).

Tamara seems to have many friends—some from school and some who are older. In fact she states that friendships are the best thing in her life:

I: Okay, what are the things in life that get you most excited?

R: My friends. Being around them. They'll be like, oh, you're coming over today, yes. Just being around the people that I really care about. And I'm saying my friends, a little bit more than my immediate family.

I: Yeah?

R: I say that because when I'm with my friends, I feel at peace, I'm feeling myself, so, that gets me most excited. More than my boyfriend, more than anybody, my friends, definitely. Uh-huh.

Tamara also says, however, that peer relationships, particularly competition to be intimidating, in her words, to "be the man," is the most difficult pressure teens face:

I: What do you think are some of the biggest problems or pressures facing teenagers these days?

R: Here in [the city], the biggest pressure is trying to be the man. When it comes down to trying to have the last word or trying to be the toughest. Or trying to be ahead or on top of everyone. Trying to intimidate others, I think that's a really big problem. I think that's why conflicts are so, you know, common. Um, no one in this city wants to be under anyone when it comes down to, um, being respected. They have to be on top of everybody. They have to be the dime; they have to be the godfather kind of thing. They don't want to be under anybody; they don't want people to see them as not being hard or being tough. So I think, um, that is a big problem.

I: Is this for guys and girls?

R: Oh, yeah. I think it's guys more than girls, but females, oh, umm-hum. Oh yeah, oh yes.

I: Okay, is there anything else that you feel like teenagers are facing today, big problems or pressures that you can think of?

R: That I can think of, I think, that comes quickly to mind because we deal with that all the time, all the time; we hear it on the news. Some guy, you know, how some people say, well, he stepped on my shoe kind of thing; it's bigger than that, you know—it's, um, retaliation, all the time.

Tamara speaks of several conflicts she has encountered with girls at school, some of which led to physical fighting. Overall, however, these incidents have been rare, and by and large she says she gets along with everyone fine.

Interestingly, the competition between girls at Tamara's high school seems to have more to do with toughness and intimidation (verbal and physical) than with clothes or attractiveness. Given the attention paid to eating disorders and the obsession with weight among white American high school girls, the fact that Tamara does not mention either of these as concerns seems noteworthy. She seems confident in her physical appearance and rarely worries about it:

I: In general, how happy or unhappy are you with your body and physical appearance?

R: I'm pretty happy, you know, um, no complaints. I'm very happy about myself. I'm happy that I'm not like anybody else. That's my happiness, right there. So I'm pretty confident in my life.

Tamara does not drink or use drugs, nor do any of her friends. She says she has been drunk once, and that was enough for her. She feels no pressure from anyone to use drugs or alcohol.

Tamara also has a boyfriend (age 19) and has been sexually active for some time, as are most of her friends. A tension prevails between her strict religious beliefs about sex and her sexual activity—a tension she has difficulty reconciling:

I: Okay. Um, does your religion have any particular teaching or morality when it comes to sex?

R: Wait till you're married.

I: Why is it that you do not agree with it?

R: Actually, I do agree with it. Uh, and there's really no buts about it, but, well, but [laughs] but, um, we as teens look at times [as] different. We're like, okay, this was written a bajillion years ago. Back in the Bible days, there was nothing to really, well, we think, there was nothing really to influence them.

I: Okay.

R: And there was nothing really around them that gave them a different idea or a different perspective. So it was basically just wait till you get married.

I: I see.

R: But now, we're surrounded with media, our friends, and, you know, we find it to be harder. Even though we try to use that as an excuse, but we really know it's not. So I do agree with it, yet we don't always follow.

I: Okay, why don't you always follow?

R: There's really no excuse. We feel like, we get the idea that it's a release, kind of. We hear people say, you know, this is what is supposed to happen when you care for somebody; this is what you're supposed to do.

I: Okay. How much is pregnancy or sexually transmitted disease a concern for teens thinking about sexual activity?

R: It's a concern because we're aware, but, uh, it doesn't change anything. I think that whether you're aware of something like that or not, it's not really gonna alter your—it could alter your decision very greatly, but for the most part, it doesn't. When it comes down to teenagers in my society. It doesn't. I mean, if you get pregnant, you have two choices. Have the kid or abort it. And that's it. I have friends my age that have children, so it's, it's really second nature to them; like I told you earlier, it's okay to have kids down here. So it's, people aren't gonna look at you different—well, they think that people don't look at you different; they think that life goes on, just normally.

Overall, Tamara appears to be a confident, capable young woman with a high likelihood of success. She is enrolled in college and seems motivated to succeed professionally, and she has a group of supportive friends and family. Her relationship with her boyfriend seems the only thing that might potentially interfere with her plans.

MIKE ORTIZ

Mike Ortiz is a seventeen-year-old, third-generation Latino living in a large city on the West Coast. Mike moved in with his grandparents, aunt, and uncle from his mother's house after he was expelled from his high school in another city for repeated drug use and possession. His mother thought that moving would give him a fresh start at a new school. His grandparents discipline him when he gets in trouble, but his transition to the new city has not been smooth. He and a friend were arrested for robbing a Wal-Mart store recently, and he was transferred to an alternative high school for troubled kids.

In Mike's world there is little "network closure"—a term sociologists use for describing the interconnections between kids, their families, and the families of their friends. His grandparents are unaware of whom he hangs out with, and they rarely if ever come into contact with his friends' families. He meets friends mostly through his passions—skateboarding and punk rock music:

I: What kind of people are your good friends?

R: Uh, they like to skate, go to shows, and uh . . . listen to music.

I: What kind of shows, what kind of music?

R: Like punk music; go down to [names of clubs] in [the city], places like that.

I: Those are clubs?

R: Yeah, where they have punk concerts and . . .

I: And so where did you meet your friends?

R: One day I was walking on [the street] up here, and I just met this one girl and this guy who just started talking to me, and they introduced me to these friends, and it just kind of broke the chain and just went down and down and down.

I: What do you do with them?

R: Uh, we go, we'll hang out a lot at school, and then we'll go skate, and after school we go down to [the city], the park down by [the high school] and just kick it, listen to music, skate, until I go home.

Interestingly, this circle of friendships based on skating and music is racially diverse:

I think I'm the only Mexican in the group of friends that I hang out with. I hang out with black kids, white kids, and I think I'm the only Mexican, and there are a couple Asians that I hang out with.

This group of friends seems to have little adult supervision and is involved in fairly risky activities. They stay out late during the week and weekends, sometimes returning the next day. According to Mike, he has many more restrictions than most of his friends.

Mike used to use drugs with his friends at his previous high school but says that his drug consumption is now limited to alcohol and cigarettes:

I: How much do you drink, and how often?
R: Uh . . . I drink about two forties [ouncers] maybe or take a couple shots of something, and I usually drink on weekends or maybe on a Friday, so, and that's like a couple times every week.
I: When did you start using drugs and drinking alcohol?
R: Uh, well, I started drinking when I was really little 'cause my dad used to give it to me; he used to give me a little in my cup or whatever. And then I started smoking weed when I turned ten and then started up smoking it again when I was fourteen, and then, you know, did acid when I was fifteen, and then did crystal meth sixteen, and that's it.

Mike is also sexually active with his girlfriend and has been for quite some time. He sees little reason to abstain from sex, other than the fear of pregnancy. He has a child with another girlfriend in his previous home city but has no contact with either of them.

Mike's life seems to revolve completely around his friends. He has little contact with family, school, or religious communities. His goals are primarily to have fun and eventually be in a punk band. Even if he graduates from his alternative high school, he will have little training or few skills he can use in the workforce. He seems headed for a lifetime of struggles.

JULIE KANESHIRO

Julie Kaneshiro is a fifteen-year-old second-generation Japanese-American living in a large city in the South. She is a fashionable but casual dresser, easygoing, sociable, and open. She lives with her Japanese-born mother and father along with her younger brother, older sister, and cousin.

Julie has a racially diverse group of friends that she describes as "loud, crazy, funny, and nice." Her best friend's parents were born in North Africa, and her best "guy friend" is "part Puerto Rican and part black." She is the only Asian-American in her group of friends. She says that friends and "guys" are the best part of her life:

> I: What are the things in life that get you most excited?
> R: Um, friends and guys.
> I: Okay, tell me about that.
> R: Uh, I love making new friends, and then it's always exciting when you meet a new guy you like.

Although Julie has had official "boyfriends" in the past, she says she doesn't want that in her life right now:

> I: Are you interested in going out with anyone now?
> R: Not right now.
> I: Not right now? Why?
> R: Um, I think it's always fun to—like right now it's just too complicated, and I don't want that in my life right now.
> I: Why is it too complicated?
> R: Uh, there's always your feelings and then the guy's feelings that you have to deal with.

Julie feels positive about her physical appearance; other than being a few inches taller, she would not change anything about it:

> I: In general, how happy or unhappy are you with your body and physical appearance?
> R: I think I'm pretty happy with it. I'm pretty confident about it.
> I: Okay. Okay. What is it about your body that you like?
> R: Uh, um, I don't know. I don't, I'm not like overweight, but I'm not like too skinny.
> I: Okay. Okay. Why do you think you feel this way about your body?
> R: Um, positive feedback from other people, I think.
> I: Okay, who are the other people?
> R: Friends and, like, adults, like my mom's friends.

Julie has not had sex but thinks it is fine for teenagers if it is with the "right person":

> I: What are your thoughts about teenagers and physical involvements and sex?
> R: Um [pause], I think that if you really like someone, I think it's fine. But I don't think you should be hopping around doing it just for fun.

I: Okay.

R: Um, sex, I think, again, like if you know that you know it's the right thing or the right person.

Although Julie has tried alcohol twice, she does not drink regularly and has never used drugs. She is worried about her friends who drink a lot and occasionally use drugs:

I: Do you have any concerns or worries about drinking?

R: I wouldn't do it to a point where I got wasted, 'cause I think I'm fine with what I do, but I worry about my friends.

I: Why do you worry about your friends?

R: 'Cause I think they drink too much. You know, I have friends that drink a lot, and, you know, they pass out, and I've never witnessed it, but I've heard stories.

I: Do you think that drinking, smoking pot, or doing other drugs is morally wrong?

R: Um [pause], no, I don't think so.

I: What is it that makes it okay?

R: It's like, to a certain point if that's all you do, then it is wrong, but if you just do it occasionally and it's not hurting anyone and it's not hurting you, then I think it's fine.

I: Do you feel there are any expectations for you or your friends to be involved in drinking, smoking, or drugs?

R: No, I don't think so.

Julie works hard in school but is not involved in extracurricular activities other than hanging out with her friends. She thinks about her future often and seems to have bright prospects. She gets good grades (3.98 GPA) and has decided she wants to get a Ph.D. and be a pediatrician, along with having a husband and family. She and her friend often talk about what they will name their kids. Given her upper-middle-class family background, achieving all of her high aspirations does not seem out of reach.

The teens described above are, once again, not "representative" of their respective race or ethnicity, but they do highlight certain distinct patterns we see in our data. In particular, we see significant racial and ethnic differences in three important areas: contact/closeness in friendships, peer influence, and romantic/sexual relationships. We will explore these three themes in the remainder of this chapter.

PEER COMPOSITION AND CLOSENESS WITH FRIENDS

Peers, as one would expect, are extremely important to teens. Indeed, the ability to connect with people of one's own age group and find friendship and acceptance there is particularly valuable to all teenagers. We heard repeatedly from teens of all racial and ethnic groups that having friends was one of the best things in their life:

> I: So, what are your friends like?
>
> R [thirteen-year-old Latina]: They're always able to put a smile on my face. Um, they're very caring; um, my best friend Justina is the best. She's nice and sweet, and she's not very—you know—she's a great listener. She's always easy to talk to, and my friend Jeff is great for a laugh.
>
> I: So, what are some good things about your life as a teenager?
>
> R [sixteen-year-old African-American male]: I got all my friends and stuff, and knowing that I'll always have somebody to go to.
>
> R [seventeen-year-old white male]: [My girlfriend], actually, is a huge excitement for me; I love spending time with her.

Emotional support, the ability to "be themselves" around friends, and the fun and laughter friends provide were the most commonly stated benefits of peer friendships across all racial and ethnic groups.

Despite the shared positive effects of friends across all groups, our findings suggest that peers are more important to white teens compared to other racial and ethnic groups. White teens spend more time with their friends, and our interviews suggest that spending time with friends is a higher priority than spending time with family. White and Asian-American teens are more likely to make friends through formal institutions (school and extracurricular activities) than teens of other racial and ethnic groups (see Table 3.1). This follows from what we found in Chapter 2—that white and Asian-American teens spend less time with family and more time in formal organizations and outside activities than African-American and Latino teens. Our data show that most white teens spend more than one night a week with extracurricular activities and at least one weekend night with friends. And most white teens spend more nonschool hours with friends than with their families. White and Asian-American teens were more likely to say they felt "especially close" to a best friend than were African-American and Latino teens. Asian-American teens were also by far the most likely to have friends who were racially or ethnically different from them, probably because they constitute a relatively small percentage of the population.

When we compare third-plus-generation Latino teens to second- and first-generation teens, they are much more likely to have friends of other races and religions and more friends in extracurricular activities at school (see Table 3.1).

TABLE 3.1

Attributes of Friends by Race/Ethnicity

Percentage of teens who say . . .	White	African-American	Asian-American	Latino (generation)				Total
				All	First	Second	Third+	
Family member is at least one of five best friends	18	46	13	29	26	31	30	24
All five best friends go to their school	46	32	34	40	35	48	36	42
At least one of five best friends is another race	34	42	95	60	49	65	62	40
All five best friends are the same religion	46	60	20	37	41	40	32	47
Three or more of five best friends are involved in extracurricular activities at school	49	38	65	27	16	26	32	45
They interact with three or more of five best friends many times a week	66	51	63	51	38	54	56	62
At least one of five best friends do drugs or drink a lot of alcohol	35	23	42	35	28	25	44	34

Source: NSYR survey.

Note: All differences between racial/ethnic groups are significant at $p < .01$ (Pearson's chi-square test).

$N = 3,290$.

They also have much more interaction with their friends: the percentage of teens who interact with three of their five best friends "many times per week" rises from 38 percent of first-generation teens to 56 percent of third-plus-generation teens.

African-American teens were the most likely to have a best friend that is a family member and the least likely to have met all five best friends through school. Although the differences from other racial and ethnic groups are small, they suggest that African-American teens' social networks are somewhat less tied to formal organizations and more tied to family than is the case for white and Asian-American teens. Latino teens were more likely than white and Asian-American teens to have an extended-family member as a best friend, but they were still significantly less likely than African-American teens to report this.

African-American teens also have fairly homogenous peer groups—they are the most likely to have friends that are the same religion and are second only to white teens in having the fewest friends of another race.

PEER INFLUENCE

While all teens are subject to peer pressure and the desire to "be cool," there are racial and ethnic differences in the influence of peer pressure on teens. Many of the white teens we interviewed, particularly females, felt enormous pressure from friends to look perfect, dress "cool," and to excel and achieve in school and extracurricular activities. This pressure seems to be a large source of stress and sometimes depression for many white teens. Recall Chris Connely's statement about the pressure to succeed, which makes his peers "emotionally fragile." Listen to a fourteen-year-old white female's views on body image:

I: Um, what do you think are some of the biggest problems or pressures facing teenagers today?

R: Body image.

I: Tell me more about that.

R: I mean, I've heard, "I'm so fat" so many times in my life from me and my sister and from other people.

I: You've heard people tell you that you're fat?

R: That they're fat.

I: That they say that about themselves?

R: Teenage girls are terrible about that. And, I know at my school academics is fairly pressuring, 'cause there's a lot of work at my school. But I think it's different depending on who you are and where you are.

We rarely heard statements such as these about weight and body image from teens of other racial and ethnic groups. Table 3.2 shows that white and Latino females as well as Asian-American males were less likely to feel good about their appearance than the other groups. In our interviews, white females were by far the most likely to talk at length about the pressure to look good and how unhappy they were about their appearance.

Along with pressure to look perfect and achieve in both school and extracurricular activities, white teens are also the most likely (with the exception of third-plus-generation Latino teens) to engage in substance abuse. Unsupervised parties with alcohol and drugs present were a common weekend activity for many white teens. We should not overstate this, as the majority of white teens do not smoke marijuana or drink excessively. However, the percentage of

TABLE 3.2

Body Image by Race/Ethnicity

Percentage of teens who are ...	White	African-American	Asian-American	Latino (generation)			
				All	First	Second	Third+
Very happy with their body and physical appearance (girls only)	32	54	50	34	29	29	41
Very happy with body and physical appearance (boys only)	44	71	12	46	53	44	44

Source: NSYR survey.
Note: All differences between racial/ethnic groups are significant at $p < .01$ (Pearson's chi-square test). $N = 3,290$.

white teens who at least occasionally get drunk is significantly higher than any of the other racial and ethnic groups (again with the exception of third-plus-generation Latino teens) (see Table 3.3). When speaking about drugs and alcohol, white teens generally did not say they felt pressured to use these substances, but many said that their easy availability made it more likely that they would:

I: Do you feel there are a lot of expectations from people your age that you're involved in drinking, smoking?

R [fifteen-year-old white female]: It's all pretty neutral. You just do it if you want it, and other people just let it slide. We don't brag about it, we don't talk about it, and if a friend happens to be spending the night on a Friday night and you have beer or a glass of wine, and if they want to try it, they can try it. You don't ask them if they want to try it; they ask you.

I: Is it pretty easy for you to find alcohol or, if you wanted, to smoke?

R: It's really easy for me.

I: If you wanted to smoke pot, would you know where to get it?

R: [My friend's] mom. And [other friend's] best friend. [Or his] legal guardian. But that's it.

One explanation for the higher drug use among white teens could simply be that white teens spend more time with their friends and therefore have fewer obstacles to using drugs and alcohol on a regular basis.

Despite their high degree of contact with peers, Asian-American teens are the least likely (along with African-Americans) to engage in substance abuse. This is particularly surprising since they were the *most* likely group to state that one of their five best friends "do drugs or drink a lot of alcohol." As with

TABLE 3.3

Substance Use by Race/Ethnicity

Percentage of teens who . . .	White	African-American	Asian-American	Latino (generation)				Total
				All	First	Second	Third+	
Have been drunk at least once in the last year	29	12	15	23	13	14	34	24
Smoke cigarettes at least once a day	10	4	2	6	11	2	7	8
Use marijuana occasionally or regularly	12	9	4	11	3	7	16	11

Source: NSYR survey.
Note: All differences between racial/ethnic groups are significant at $p < .01$ (Pearson's chi-square test).
$N = 3,290$.

Julie Kaneshiro, Asian-American teens seem to have no moral reasons against having sex or using drugs yet largely abstain from these risky behaviors, even though many of their friends do not abstain. This begs for an explanation.

Our data suggest two reasons. The first is parental pressure. Asian-American teens were the most likely to say that their parents would be "extremely upset" if they were found to be having sex. Even though Asian-American parents talk less to their teens about sensitive subjects such as sex, dating, and drinking (see Chapter 2), they somehow communicate the message that if their children are found to engage in these activities there will be serious consequences. Paradoxically, it appears that even though there is less open communication and less contact between Asian-American parents and their teens compared to other racial and ethnic groups, these parents seem to have more influence on their teens' behavior than do parents in other groups. It is difficult to discern from our data the mechanism behind their influence, but clearly it is strong. There may also be pragmatic reasons for the relative abstinence from sex and substance use. Asian-American teens seem highly motivated to succeed academically and professionally (in part because of pressure from parents), and they tend to see risky behavior as a possible obstacle to reaching these goals:

I: Do you think that drinking or doing drugs, pot, is that morally wrong or not?

R [sixteen-year-old Asian-American male]: I wouldn't say it's morally wrong, no; it's kind of stupid, but not unethical.

I: And what is it that makes it okay in some circumstances, or perhaps you're saying that it's not necessarily okay, but it's not morally wrong, I guess.

R: I wouldn't, I wouldn't say it's not okay; I mean, I don't think it should be something that you're doing, just in the effects that it might have on your health or the way you do things or your safety, but no, I don't think it's morally wrong.

It is interesting that this teen, like many of the Asian-American teens we interviewed, did not see drug use as a moral issue but rather as a pragmatic one. It's not that drugs are wrong; they just affect your ability to function well.

We see evidence of this pragmatic reasoning even with Asian-American teens who do participate in risky behavior. Consider Eric Li, whom we met in Chapter 2. Eric has smoked marijuana and abused alcohol for much of his teen life. Yet because he was getting all A's in school, he didn't see it as a problem:

I started smoking weed in, ah, after ninth grade, and it pretty much became a hobby; you can call it an addiction, you can call it a hobby, whatever. I like doing it, and, um, I did it every day. I'll just come home because, ah, school wasn't like a problem for me at all; I didn't have to do homework; I didn't really have to take notes in class, but I still got like straight A's, so I would come home and just get high every day.

This statement reveals a strong pragmatism—as long as an activity does not interfere with success in school, it is acceptable.

Because open communication, particularly about sensitive issues like drinking and sex, between Asian-American teens and their parents is limited, parents may be unaware of the risky behavior of their teens. When they do become aware, however, the consequences are swift and serious. The threat of serious consequences appears to keep many Asian-American teens from participating in self-destructive behavior. In the case of Eric Li, his parents threatened to send him to China if he did not stop his drug and alcohol use.

The Asian-American teens we interviewed felt high levels of pressure from parents to succeed academically. However, they did not feel pressure from *peers* to "look perfect" and excel academically or in sports or other extracurricular activities. This is interesting because most of their peers were non-Asian-American, mostly white. Why white teens (especially females) feel peer pressure to look perfect and excel at everything while Asian-American teens do not feel that pressure *from the same peers* is difficult to understand. Perhaps Asian-American females are not expected to meet the dominant beauty standard because they are not white, disqualifying them from the beauty sweepstakes. Or perhaps the pressure Asian-American teens feel from parents to succeed in school is so much stronger than the pressure they experience from their peers that peer pressure is experienced as negligible.

Compared to the first and second generations, third-plus-generation Latino teens were much more likely to say they had friends who were a "bad moral influence" on them and who used drugs or alcohol a lot. These teens were also much more likely to have had sex. Thus, third-plus-generation teens look much like white teens in peer contact, influence, and risky behavior. First-generation immigrant teens were radically different—spending more time with family and less with peers and engaging in risky behavior at much lower levels. These differences between the different immigrant cohorts are as large as the differences between Latinos overall and the other racial and ethnic groups. As we concluded in Chapter 2, it is difficult to generalize about Latino teens as a whole.

Mike Ortiz, whom we met at the beginning of the chapter, is an extreme example of this pattern among third-plus-generation Latino youth—his world is centered almost exclusively on his friends. He seems to have little contact with or supervision by family. His parents are divorced, and he lives with grandparents, who have little idea where he is or what he is doing most of the time. Contrast this with Evelyn Cabrera, whom we met in Chapter 2; she is a second-generation Latina whose contact with peers is tightly embedded in family and community networks. Recall that she attended parties often, but these were "family parties" where both teens and adults were present. She would never do anything risky, because someone her parents knew would surely report it to them immediately. Nothing could be further from the world of Mike Ortiz and many of the third-plus-generation Latino teens we interviewed. The difference between these two teens starkly illustrates the variation we found in the different immigrant-generation cohorts of Latino teens.

Second-generation teens were much more likely to be tied to their families, who exercised far more control over their choices than in third-plus-generation families. One eighteen-year-old second-generation Latina we interviewed still had a 10:30 P.M. curfew. She said she attended parties, but they were always at someone's house where she knew the family. She described these parties as "family oriented":

I: What about parties? Do you go to parties ever?
R: I go to parties with my sister and my friends sometime.
I: What kind of parties?
R: Um, the parties [at someone's house].
I: So, what kind of things happen? Is there a lot of alcohol and drugs?
R: There's alcohol, but there's not really many drugs, like much drugs, 'cause they usually have [people] there, you know, checking and stuff like that. The parties we go to,

they're more family oriented, you know, they're not really like, oh, bunch of teenagers all wild in the streets; they're not really bad like that.

This was common among the first- and second-generation teens we interviewed. The picture painted by many of the third-plus-generation Latinos we spoke to included a less regulated environment:

I: Uh-huh, so what kinds of things do you and your close friends do for fun?

R [seventeen-year-old third-generation Latina]: Some of us get high together; most of us sit there and talk, go out and party together, hang out, do whatever.

I: How often do you go to parties?

R: Every, every weekend.

I: Every weekend. Uh-huh, so tell me what a typical party's like.

R: Um, I really don't know 'cause I have really been to a bunch of different kind of parties; like I have gone to gay and lesbian parties before, I've gone to one of those gangster parties, one of those parties where there's been like where everybody's getting high and drinking party, I've been to like those dancing parties, been to all kinds of parties.

This is not to say that most third-plus-generation Latino kids get high regularly or that parents allow their kids to run wild. Rather, it is that we rarely heard a story like the one above from a first- or second-generation Latino teen, but we did hear a significant number of third-plus-generation teens say similar things. Thus, there appears to be a significant difference in parental supervision among Latino teens whose parents were born and grew up in America and those whose parents were born elsewhere.

The strong religiosity of many African-American teens, as we will discuss in Chapter 5, and the religious homogeneity of their peer networks may explain the low levels of risky behavior among African-American teens, at least when it comes to substance use. African-American teens (along with Asian-American teens) were the least likely to use drugs, alcohol, or cigarettes. While spending time with friends and having fun were clear priorities for African-American teens, by and large they did not see the fun in using drugs and alcohol. They were also the most likely to state that using drugs and alcohol is morally wrong. In our interviews most teens from other racial and ethnic groups stated that while they might not use drugs or alcohol, it's not necessarily morally wrong— "it's up to them." But over and over we heard African-American teens say that using is "just wrong," not just for them but for everyone:

I: Okay, um, do you, do you drink or smoke pot, or do other drugs?

R [fifteen-year-old African-American male]: Mm-mm [no].

I: Is there any particular reason that you don't do these things?

R: 'Cause they're wrong.

I: Do you feel that these things are morally wrong?

R: Yeah.

I: Okay, why?

R: 'Cause it's just wrong.

We heard similar statements from many African-American teens in our interviews.

African-American teens were also the most likely to report that they were happy with their physical appearance. The lack of pressure to "look perfect," especially among females, is particularly striking compared with their white counterparts. Other studies have found higher levels of self-esteem, fewer instances of dieting and unhealthy weight-control practices, and lower levels of depression among African-American adolescents compared to their white counterparts.[11] It may also be worth noting that contrary to popular media images, the vast majority of African-American teens we interviewed were not exposed to violence, gang activity, and drug consumption. A small minority of African-American teens (as well as Latino teens) reported strong pressure to join gangs as well as fear of kids who carry guns in their neighborhoods. These teens, however, were rare in our sample. This is not to say that violence among African-American teens is not a problem. African-American males from fifteen to twenty-four are roughly sixteen times more likely to be murdered than white males in the same age group.[12] But to put this in perspective, homicide victims compose less than one tenth of one percent of African-American males in this age group each year.

More common were reports of physical fighting and pressure to be tough and intimidating among peers. Recall Tamara Phillips stating that this is a pressure for African-American females as well as males. We heard this in our interviews numerous times. One study from the Centers for Disease Control and Prevention found that African-American teens were significantly more likely than white and Latino teens to have been in a physical fight in the previous thirty days (45% of African-American teens, compared to 40% of Latino teens and 32% of white teens).[13] In fact, a small but surprising number of African-American and Latino boys and girls we interviewed reported that they were currently being homeschooled because they were getting involved in too many fights at school.

Our interviews suggest that many of these fights arise out of peer pressure to retaliate after being slighted or disrespected by other teens. This sixteen-year-old African-American describes a fight, which resulted in his being suspended from school:

R: My friend got into a fight, and I was standing right there by him, and they all jumped on us.

I: So why did they jump on you?

R: [They] believed that my friend Eric disrespected one of them. Then all of them had to jump him 'cause they was all from the same hood, so it was like a whole gang against one.

I: And so you jumped in?

R: Yeah, I jumped in to help him.

I: Did he disrespect the guy, or was it not really?

R: Yeah, he went to get something to eat, and my friend Eric took his spot, and he came back and tried to ask for it back, and he's like, "I ain't getting up." You can't get punked a lot, like if you let somebody punk you, then everybody is going to try to do it.

This "you can't let people punk you" statement came up repeatedly in our interviews with African-American teens. Many of these teens spoke of feeling that their safety is more threatened by not responding to an act of disrespect than it is by getting involved in a physical fight, because other kids then see them as weak, thereby inviting more abuse in the future. Interestingly, this dynamic seems to apply to girls as well as boys. A number of African-American and Latino girls we interviewed spoke of frequent physical confrontations between girls that arise out of verbal disrespect:

I: You have mostly male friends?

R [fifteen-year-old African-American female]: Yeah, male friends.

I: Why is that?

R: Because girls, I don't like girls. Girls always have to have their arguments; always it's a argument, and I don't like to fight or nothing like that.

I: And how are your guy friends better or different or worse than your girlfriends?

R: Um, I have a boy that I used to go home from school with; I could, I could say something like, shut the hell up, and he would like take it as a joke, where with girls, you say that, you're gonna fight.

This teen was also currently being homeschooled, in part because of the frequent fights she was involved in at school.

Overall, students who attended predominantly African-American or Latino schools spoke often of the frequency of fights at school, and the necessity to respond when disrespected in order to keep from being harassed at school. It appears that the respect these teens seek from their peers is a zero-sum game, where respect usually comes at the expense of another through intimidation. This creates a volatile environment, where fights and verbal confrontations are common. While these confrontations are rarely physically dangerous (we rarely heard instances of the use of weapons or of serious physical injuries in these conflicts), they have important consequences, the most common being suspension from school or, in a surprising number of cases, being removed from the school altogether in order to avoid the charged environment.

SEXUAL RELATIONSHIPS

Another exception to the comparatively lower levels of risky behavior among African-American teens is in the area of sexuality. While there was no difference between white and African-American teens in the likelihood of having had intimate physical contact with a person of the opposite sex (such as oral sex or touching and petting), African-American teens are the most likely to have had sexual intercourse and, among those that are sexually active, tend to have had more partners compared to other racial and ethnic groups (see Table 3.4).

This is difficult to explain because of the strong influence of conservative religion and the absolutist morality among most of the African-American teens we interviewed. Like Tamara Phillips, many stated that they thought sex before marriage was morally wrong yet were sexually active themselves. When asked to explain this apparent contradiction, many had trouble doing so:

I: Does your religion have any particular teaching or morality when it comes to sex?

R [seventeen-year-old African-American male]: Yeah, they say no sex until marriage.

I: Do you agree with it?

R: Yeah. There are a lot of factors; number one, it's because the person they do it with first they say is a blood covering, and because blood is shed, you wanna be, you're yoked to that person, and they say only, only in the constraints of marriage it's, it's gonna be okay because, number one, the blood shed, you're with that person, regardless; you have to stay with that person 'cause you're married to them. And then they say sometimes, well, you want—you don't want to have a kid outside of wedlock and have them be a bastard, you know? And then again, they say that a lot of emotion and stuff is involved, and only when you're old enough to get married, that's when you'll be able to be mature enough to handle it. So that's why.

I: Well, that's what they say; do you agree?

R: That's what they say. I agree with it some, with that; it all depends on the type of

TABLE 3.4

Dating and Sexual Relationships by Race/Ethnicity

Percentage of teens who...	White	African-American	Asian-American	Latino (generation)				Total
				All	First	Second	Third+	
Are currently in a dating relationship	34	42	23	34	29	27	41	35
Have had sexual intercourse	20	28	8	21	14	15	28	22
Have had sexual intercourse (seventeen-year-olds only)	45	58	0	45	32	29	59	48
Have had sex with four or more partners (sexually active seventeen-year-olds only)	29	43	NA	30	44	39	28	33
Felt pressured to have sex by dates or friends	12	20	15	12	13	6	15	14
Say parents would be "extremely upset" if they had sex	78	67	89	76	81	82	70	76
Say it's morally okay for teens to have sex	30	33	38	29	25	24	29	30

Source: NSYR survey.
Note: All differences between racial/ethnic groups are significant at $p < .01$ (Pearson's chi-square test). NA = not available. $N = 3,290$.

person that actually engages in it. 'Cause a lot of people not, not ready for it; a lot of people are, conversely.

I: So it's okay for some?

R: Some, yeah, but like re-, religion, nah, it ... In regards to religion? It's not okay because it goes against religion.

I: Okay, so what do you think, though?

R: Me?

I: Yes.

R: Personally, I think, all right, well, if you want to, if you could, if you can handle it, just do it right now.

I: So how does, how do you think that's worked out in your own life?

R: Pretty good. I don't, I don't feel negative about anything; I don't feel guilty. [laughs] I sure as hell don't feel guilty!

We repeatedly heard statements like this from African-American teens in our interviews. It is clear that many are hearing a clear teaching from their religious congregations that sex outside of marriage is wrong, and most state that they agree with the teaching. At the same time, they state that it somehow doesn't apply to them or that if the person is "ready," then it's not wrong. The high incidence of these contradictory statements is quite striking and difficult to understand.

Another church-going fourteen-year-old male felt that waiting to have sex until marriage was problematic because marriage might not happen:

I: Do you think young people should wait to have sex until they are married or not?
R: Uh, no.
I: Why? Why not?
R: 'Cause what if you don't get married?

It could be that in poorer African-American communities, where marriage is less likely, this reasoning makes sense, that is, if lifelong sexual abstinence is not seen as an option. Yet this higher likelihood of African-American teens to be sexually active remained significant even after controlling for income differences.

African-American teens also reported the highest levels of pressure to have sex from friends and dates. This is true for both males and females, as roughly 20 percent of African-American males and females stated that they felt pressured to have sex by dates and friends. It is important to note, however, that despite their comparatively higher level of sexual activity on average, most African-American teens are not having sex, and many are not because of strong religious convictions. Only 28 percent of African-American teens in our total sample had engaged in sexual intercourse, and 58 percent of seventeen-year-old African-Americans in our sample had had sex. Many of the African-American teens in our interviews were waiting until marriage because of religious beliefs:

I: Are there things that you don't do because you are a Christian?
R [sixteen-year-old African-American male]: Um, yes.
I: Like what?
R: Like smoke and have sex and stuff, I don't. I don't do that because in the Bible it says wait 'til you're married to have sex, and that, um, that's it.

Still, early sexual activity is taking a toll on young African-American females. A recent Centers for Disease Control and Prevention study found that sexually transmitted disease (STD) rates among fourteen- to nineteen-year-old girls were significantly higher among African-American girls: nearly half had at least one STD, versus 20 percent among both whites and Mexican-Americans. Rates of teen pregnancies for African-American girls aged fifteen to nineteen are roughly double those of teen girls overall (134 per 1,000 versus 75 per 1,000).

Interestingly, while white teens had lower rates of sexual intercourse compared to African-American teens, they were the most likely group to have had oral sex and other forms of sexual contact beyond kissing (such as touching and petting). Thus if one includes oral sex and other forms of sexual contact short of intercourse in the definition of "sexually active," white teens are just as sexually active as African-American teens. This pattern of sexual activity for white teens, however, is less risky in being less likely to result in pregnancy or certain STDs (although a number of STDs are associated with unprotected oral sex[14]).

In his analysis of these same data Regnarus found that white middle- and upper-middle-class Jewish and mainline Protestant teens were more likely than other teens to engage in oral sex as a seemingly less risky substitute for vaginal intercourse.[15] These teens preferred oral sex, not out of any moral concern (such as remaining "technically a virgin") but rather as a strategic way to enjoy sexual contact without risking pregnancy or STDs. Many African-American teens, by contrast, thought premarital sex was morally wrong, yet they were sexually active, *and* they were against having oral sex because it seemed gross or unnatural. We heard many comments that were similar to this quote from an eighteen-year-old African-American female, who is religiously conservative and sexually active:

I: Does the type of sex make a difference in whether it's okay for young people, or not?

R: Well, for me, yeah. I'll never have oral or anal.

I: You'll never have oral or anal?

R: Uh-huh [yes] [laughs].

I: Okay, uh-huh. So do you think something's morally wrong with doing oral or anal?

R: I mean, to me it is because it's nasty. Hey, it just wasn't made to go there. So, that's how I see it: it wasn't made to go there.

This was also true of many religiously conservative evangelical and Mormon white teens—both groups were more likely to have had intercourse than oral sex, while the opposite was true for mainline Protestant and Jewish white teens. It could be that the religious conservatism of many African-American teens (and evangelical and Mormon white teens) actually drives them toward riskier sexual practices (among the sexually active) than the practices of more liberal, middle-class mainline Protestant and Jewish white teens, because the former groups are less strategic about their sexual practices and perhaps because they see intercourse as more "natural" and therefore morally preferable to other forms of sexual contact.

Asian-American teens are by far the least likely to be sexually active (Table 3.4) when considering rates of both oral sex and intercourse. This is particularly surprising since they were the *most* likely to state that they think it is morally okay for teenagers to have sex. Much like their middle-class Jewish and mainline Protestant white peers, they appear to define their sexual practices in terms of pragmatic outcomes rather than morality. However, this pragmatism among Asian-American teens seems more likely to result in sexual abstinence rather than simply substituting less risky sexual practices for more dangerous ones:

> I: What are your thoughts about teenagers and physical involvements and sex?
>
> R [sixteen-year-old Asian-American male]: Um, I think as a whole, sex with teenagers, um [pause] is not good, because emotionally I don't think people this age are ready for it, but I don't think that should discount all of it if they are emotionally ready for it.
>
> I: So then it would be appropriate or not appropriate to be physically involved, depending on being emotionally ready?
>
> R: Right.
>
> I: Okay, um, do you think that people should wait to have sex until they are married or not?
>
> R: Not necessarily, no.
>
> I: Okay, and why would it, why would they not need to?
>
> R: Uh, well, I think it all comes down to the issue of how responsible they are.
>
> I: Uh-huh.
>
> R: Um [pause] but I don't think marriage should be, um, the cutoff point.
>
> I: Right, and by responsible, you mean what exactly?
>
> R: Um, well, that they understand the possible consequences of it.

Interestingly, these pragmatic reasons for abstinence (risky behavior leads to harmful outcomes) seem more convincing to Asian-American teens than to teens of other groups, and strong enough to affect their behavior even when they are integrated into non-Asian-American peer groups who are highly involved in risky behavior.

CONCLUSION: RACE, CLASS, AND PEER SOCIALIZATION

Peer relationships take on a growing salience as children reach adolescence. As Youniss and Smollar note, peer relationships are more accepting than the more hierarchical and potentially judgmental parent-child relationship.[15] The higher levels of trust and self-disclosure make peers an important source of social acceptance among teens.[17]

Most studies of adolescent peer relationships have focused on middle-class white teens. Early studies in this area suggested that peer relationships take on a magnified importance among adolescents of color because of structural disadvantages that keep youth of color from succeeding in other areas of life.[18] Giordano calls this the "compensation hypothesis," as it predicts that youth of color will compensate for their disadvantages through higher levels of importance placed on peer relationships.[19] More recent studies, however, contradict this hypothesis,[20] as does our analysis.

Our data show that while all teens view their friends as important to them, white teens spend the most time with friends and are most heavily influenced by them. Not surprisingly, therefore, white teens were more worried about their appearance and their success in extracurricular activities, and were more likely to engage in risky behavior, particularly substance abuse.

The families of most adolescents of color appear to play a greater mediating role in peer relationships than those of most white teens, thus lessening the salience and influence of peers. The mechanisms of mediation vary, however, by racial and ethnic group. Many African-American extended families provide the emotional support and daily contact that form teens' most intimate relationships. Indeed, roughly half of African-American teens named a family member as one of their closest friends. Many first- and second-generation Latino teens form close friendships in the context of a close-knit community of groups of extended families, all residing in close proximity to one another and knowing each other's families. This community embeddedness not only provides opportunities to make friends but also serves as a structure of social control, in which the activities of teens are monitored through a network of adults.

The mediating mechanisms of many Asian-American families appear quite different. Asian-American teens, on average, spend as much unsupervised time with their (mostly white) peers as do white teens but are much less influenced by them. Parental influence, as mentioned in Chapter 2, seems to flow from parental authority rather than from actual contact and supervision. This authority appears to be used by many parents to instill a focused pragmatism that causes teens to avoid activities which might jeopardize instrumental goals.

The literature examining the effect of social class on adolescent peer relationships has similar currents to the race literature. On one hand, some studies propose a similar compensation hypothesis, theorizing that a lack of involvement in formal organizations and school activities propels lower-class youth to place greater importance on friendships.[21] Other studies suggest the opposite—that teens who lack a strong connection to school and other formal organizations have a less favorable space in which to form peer relationships, and that frequent moves among lower-class families make forming close peer relationships difficult for teens.[22] Still other studies have found that living in poor, unsafe neighborhoods is associated with a defensive posture toward peers; as a survival strategy, few are trusted, which limits the breadth and depth of peer relationships.[23]

Once again, our purpose is not to assess whether race or class is more important, in this case in structuring adolescent peer relationships, but rather how they might be related. Our regression analyses generally show that the racial and ethnic effects we found still exist when we hold income constant, suggesting an independent effect of race. It appears, however, that the two may be intertwined.

The "concerted cultivation" (which Lareau associates with middle-class families; see Chapter 1) that we see among many white families, in which teens spend numerous hours in nonfamily structured activities, provides a space for teens to form close ties with other peers. This, coupled with the individualistic, egalitarian ethos of many white families, leads to a lot of freedom for white teens to pursue unsupervised activities with peers as well. Thus, more than any other racial or ethnic group, for white teens peers become a powerful reference group. Many nonwhite middle-class teens (with the exception of third-plus-generation Latinos), while engaging in many of the same external activities, have more hierarchical and structured family lives, which mediate the role of peers as a reference group to a greater extent.

The freedom to pursue close relationships with peers is likely to benefit teens in many ways, such as in emotional support, self-expression, and freedom to explore new activities. However, it can also lead to more potential for self-destructive behavior. Numerous studies have demonstrated that white teens are significantly more likely to commit suicide and die in car accidents than are other racial and ethnic groups.[24] They are also at a higher risk for alcoholism and drug addiction,[25] as well as unhealthy dieting and eating disorders.[26] Thus some of the advantages of "concerted cultivation" may come at a price. To the extent that other racial and ethnic groups assimilate to the dominant white youth culture of freedom and independence from family, they too take on the risks of that independence.

Nowhere are the risks of assimilation more evident than among Latino teens. Third-plus-generation Latino teens appear highly assimilated to the individual freedoms enjoyed by white teens and actually exceed white teens in terms of risky behavior, while the first and second generations, still tied to family supervision and authority, behave in less risky ways. Most first- and many second-generation Latino teens are highly embedded in family and community networks that protect and nurture them, as well as demand sacrifices from them. This limits their freedom to pursue their own agendas but also limits the potential for risky behavior.

It appears that the traditional mechanisms that have insulated many Latino teens within the family structure and facilitated adult supervision have largely faded by the third generation. Yet those ties are not replaced by ties to formal institutions such as school, extracurricular activities, or tightly bound religious communities, as is the case with many white and African-American teens. This lack of institutional ties seems to leave third-plus-generation Latino teens floating; where there are few formal organizations to channel energy and focus, peers have the potential to lead teens into risky and potentially destructive activities. These teens also face the same risks as white teens do from the lack of ties to family and community. Our data show (as do other studies) that first- and second-generation Latino teens as a whole have fewer educational and financial resources than the third generation but are protected to a greater extent from the risks of the dominant youth culture.[27] Third-or-more-generation Latino teens appear to have the worst of both worlds and are the group of teens most at risk for potentially destructive activities.

Most African-American teens have strong ties to family (as we saw in Chapter 2) and to religious communities (as we will see in Chapter 5), which moderate the influence of peers and seem to give them a strong source of self-esteem and moral purpose that are apart from peer group approval. Our data show African-American teens faring well in these areas as well as in low levels of risky activities, giving these teens a strong foundation for a healthy transition to adulthood.

The high incidence of risky sexual activity among African-American teens is hard to explain against this mostly positive backdrop. If one includes oral sex and other forms of nonvaginal sexual activity in the definition of being sexually active, African-American teens are no more sexually active than white teens. But with regard to vaginal intercourse and a higher number of sexual partners, which increase the risks of pregnancy and the contraction of certain types of STDs, they stand out as the most risk-taking group in terms of sexual activity.

It appears that strong external peer pressure to have sex, and weak pressure to wait, are producing early entry into sexual activity. Somewhat paradoxically, religious and moral conservatism appears to lead African-American teens to prefer more-traditional yet riskier types of sexual activity (vaginal intercourse). This pattern holds obvious risks for these teens' futures, not only for their physical health but also for the possibility of an unwanted pregnancy, which affects socioeconomic opportunities.

The patterns we found among Asian-American teens are also difficult to understand. Asian-American teens have high levels of contact with peers and are highly embedded in non-Asian-American peer groups, yet they do not seem to assimilate to the behavioral patterns of their friends. They are consistently around other teens (mostly white) who engage in risky behavior yet tend not to participate themselves. They spend much of their time away from family yet are highly influenced by their parents. A likely explanation seems to be that parental pressure, even in the absence of direct supervision, drives this abstinence. Parental pressure, coupled with a pragmatic desire for educational and eventually economic success, rather than any absolutist morality give Asian-American teens a foundation for resisting the riskier aspects of youth culture. Yet these teens still have the freedom to engage and enjoy their peers as much as any other group. Asian-American teens seem to have both the freedom to pursue extracurricular involvements and a high level of family expectation to succeed and behave. This combination may be likely to produce socioeconomic success, if not individual self-fulfillment, as they move into adulthood.

In sum, the scripts by which teens are socialized by their families, which as we argued in Chapter 2 are structured by race and class, have clear effects on peer relationships. The "concerted cultivation" used by many white families to prepare youth for success in formal organizations actually poses dangers to the well-being of these teens by allowing peer groups to take on exaggerated importance as reference groups. The greater mediating role of family in the non-white groups, while variable according to group, serves to protect these teens to a greater extent from these dangers.

4 SCHOOL

Motivating Achievement, Aspirations, and Opportunity

School is the number one priority for me right now . . . It's do or die. You have to do good or you end up flipping burgers.

—Ricardo, age 17, Latino

A typical middle or high school student spends an estimated 1,300 hours per year at school. Many youth, as discussed in our chapter on family, spend even more time participating in school-related activities outside of normal school hours. For a large majority of youth, school is the first main public institution with which they interact. Schools symbolize what public institutions have to offer youth, what they will expect of them, and the extent to which public institutions are their allies. The main function of schools is academic instruction. However, schools fulfill many latent (or unstated) functions as well. Researchers have noted the role that schools play in teaching young people the dominant ideology,[1] integrating youth into the broader society,[2] or sifting youth deemed more talented into channels that lead to high-status positions.[3] When schools fulfill different functions for white youth and youth of color, they inevitably socialize adolescents of different racial and ethnic backgrounds in distinct ways. Beyond the family, then, schools are very important agents of socialization for youth. They are central to their lives.

Much of the research addressing educational and racial disparities among youth examines racial differences in academic achievement; these studies often emphasize the extent to which students value education or teacher-student relationships as explanations for the persistent disparities. In this chapter, we listen to youths' views on education and stories about their school experiences to better understand the meanings and functions of schooling for American teens—and if and why these meanings and functions differ for white youth and youth of color.

We find that *while youth across racial and ethnic backgrounds give similar reasons for caring about doing well in school, they differ in their propensity to select certain reasons over others.* A substantial majority of white youth interviewed explicitly say they care about achieving good grades so that they can increase their college opportunities. Youth of color also list college as a reason for doing well in school. But they also stress other reasons, something that white youth were not inclined to do. We also find that youth of color tend to be specific about their educational and career aspirations, far more so than white youth. Latino, Asian-American, and African-American youth, as early as fourteen years of age, have begun to contemplate careers they might want to pursue, fields to major in, or colleges to attend. Some have considered all three. Conversely, most white youth intend to go to college but have given little thought to what to do after they have been admitted. Our data further reveal that schools, through teachers' relationships with students, fulfill distinct functions for white youth and youth of color. We propose that these functions are consequential for youths' educational views and career aspirations and, subsequently, the perpetuation of racial inequality. White youth and youth of color have very different perceptions of their teachers and the kind of relationships students should expect with their teachers. White youth see teachers as positive influences in their lives. Teachers are supportive, helpful adults. White youth have friendly and often intimate relationships with their teachers. Teachers are mentors and play the role of second parents for some white youth. African-American, Latino, and Asian-American students do not generally share this view of their teachers. Several say they have "good teachers," but "good" does not have the same meaning for youth of color as it does for white youth. Indeed, most Asian-American, Latino, and African-American youth in our sample perceive their teachers as neutral or negative influences in their lives. This is irrespective of individual students' academic achievement. We discuss the implications of these findings for racial inequality as we conclude the chapter. We now introduce you to some of our respondents, focusing on their experiences with school; we begin with Dorian Hughes.

DORIAN HUGHES

Dorian Hughes is a sixteen-year-old African-American teen from a city in the northeast. He is the youngest of four children. It is just he and his mother and father at home now full time; his older siblings are off at college or work. He and his family have strong support from and friendships with their neighbors. During the interview at his home, several people from the community dropped by to say hello.

Dorian attends a majority white school in the city, "'cause it's like the best school for music and that's what I'm basically taking up [in high school]." His grades have been inconsistent. As a result, he has not been able to participate in school sports at times. As he explains, "If you fail more than one major subject or something, you can't be on the [track] team. So, I was like off and on for a couple years." But he believes he should be active in school: "I know in the long run it will help me out, especially for colleges, like . . . doing the clubs and doing volunteer work and everything." Although he has a C average, doing well in school is "important." He explains, "I know without it I won't be able to succeed and I won't be able to accomplish what I want. Achieve what I want to." No doubt he understands this from significant adults in his life. When asked "How do you think adults in your life view you in particular?" he says, "Well, I guess some . . . say . . . I can do better, but others feel like I'm doing like the best. . . . They look at me as just like the kid that goes to school around here, you know, trying to come up." When Dorian is asked to elaborate on what some adults mean by "do better," he explains that they would like for him to be "pulling 80s and 90s all the time."

Being known as "the kid that goes to school around here" shows that Dorian stands out from other youth in his neighborhood. Adults around him encourage him to do better. They believe that he has greater potential than what he has demonstrated. Later in the interview, he elaborates on this:

INTERVIEWER: One of the things you mentioned . . . that you think is different from your friends is that you have goals. . . . What are some of your goals?

RESPONDENT: Trying to become a computer engineer. And I'm looking to get my, definitely looking to get my Master's, and I don't know what else, yet.

I: Okay. What do you think makes the difference between . . . why you have goals and your friends seem not to have goals?

R: 'Cause of like throughout my lifetime, people always explaining to me how important school was, and that it wasn't—that you can't really do much without it, and I just decided to make sure that I, I did what I had to do in school.

Dorian wants to get a graduate degree in computer engineering. Unlike his friends he has had the privilege of having adults in his life who have consistently taught him about the importance of doing well in school. He attributes his educational and career goals to having these people in his life.

While Dorian is receiving considerable support from his family and other adults, his teachers can be another story. Teachers have not always been particularly helpful or encouraging to Dorian. When asked "How do you view your teachers?" he responds, "Some of them are all right, like, they're helpful, I mean, I feel like they're good teachers, and others, it just seem like, they're like, almost like a negative effect on me, like they're not too helpful and like they're only there to just put notes on the board, you know, just, just so that they get their paycheck." He goes on to say that he would like for his teachers to be "willing to help us out and . . . maybe if they can, stay after school . . . for tutoring or something if we needed it. . . . Just [a] willingness to speak with the students, understand their problems or whatever." Dorian would like more help with his classes from his teachers. As his grades suggest, he could use additional attention. However, many of his teachers are not, in his opinion, willing to provide him with the tools he needs to learn the material. They are not interested in making sure that students understand the coursework. Dorian would welcome the attention.

Dorian's parents have clearly instilled the importance of education in him, as they have with their other children; however, they would like to see him have a better school work ethic. When he and his parents have conflicts, school is one of the main reasons:

Me and my mother, we get along pretty well. You know. Of course everybody has their little ups and downs, conflicts. . . . Like sometimes I might be late for school or something, and like she gets, she gets real upset with me about it. . . . Then she start giving me speeches . . . like I'm about to drop out or something.

Despite his seeming irritation with his parents, Dorian admits that he has not done as well in school as he would like. Achieving his goals requires more than he previously thought. He will have to attend summer or night school to make up for "messing up in school." He says:

I see now that I have to work a lot harder to achieve my goals. Since I have been messing up in school . . . I really haven't been in any programs, you know, to look good on my résumé. I know I gotta join more programs. I'm gonna have to go to . . . P.M. school, summer school, you know, all that. You know, I'm gonna have a full day as a senior in my senior year, have a full school day instead of going home at 12:00.

Dorian's experience reveals the challenges that African-American youth may have in achieving their scholastic goals. He has been strongly encouraged to do well in school by significant adults in his life who clearly care about him and his future. Additionally, he and his family have a strong network of support in their community. Unlike many African-American youth, he comes from a two-parent household. In these ways Dorian is privileged compared to other African-American youth. And he realizes this. Dorian has to deal with competing influences in his life. Parents and friends of the family desire for him to achieve more than the average youth in his community. However, these youths are his friends. As Dorian sees it, his friends do not have the same kinds of social resources that he does. As a result, they are not aspiring to attend college and have professional careers. Friendship groups that are not academically oriented expose youth within these friendship networks to poor academic achievement.[4] Dorian has limited peer reinforcement to do as well in school as he would like and pursue his goal of becoming a computer engineer. Moreover, Dorian is not following a high school curriculum that best prepares him to major in computer engineering in college. Concentrating on music in high school means he will likely begin college at a disadvantage relative to other students intending to major in engineering.

JENNA MARTIN

Jenna Martin is an Asian-American youth, who was adopted by white American parents. She is fourteen years old and finishing up middle school. Jenna attends a private school, where being the only Asian-American was at first challenging. She explains that "on the first day of school, it was like horrible, 'cause I didn't know anybody at all, not one person. And so it was a little hard to try and fit in. And then I'm also like the only Asian in my entire school." But her friends are "pretty accepting" of her now; most of them are from school. One of their favorite things to do for fun is go shopping.

Unlike other Asian-American teens in the NSYR survey, who on average participate in nearly three school-related activities, Jenna is not yet especially active in school. She participated in the school play in the previous year, but that was it. The student body is small at her school, and she is still in middle school. Although she did not say it, she may become more active once she is in high school. Jenna is, however, a very good student. At the time of the interview she hadn't yet received her final report card but figured she would be "getting straight A's." Jenna takes grades quite seriously. Anything less than an A is not acceptable to her. This expectation does not come from her white, adoptive parents. She tells the interviewer, "If I don't get an A in a class, my parents won't care. They'll say, 'It's a good thing you still got a B,' or, 'I know you tried your hardest.' But I'll be the one upset at myself, so it's usually from me." Jenna's academic expectations may come from her teachers. She explains, "[Teachers] like me a lot; I mean, I'm nice to them. And . . . I respect them, which a lot of kids don't, so they like me." She also sees teachers as a good influence in her life because "they teach [me] stuff, for the most part. Not all of them do, but most of them try to." Her teachers also treat her differently from other students. She has a reputation of being the "smart" kid among them:

'Cause . . . I'm in more advanced classes than a lot of people and so . . . I get kind of a lot of attention from that, and like teachers, well, I kind of have a reputation among teachers as like being smart and everything, so I kind of get treated differently for that.

Jenna is pretty clear about why she "really cares" about doing well in school. She wants to get into Stanford. She further explains that "It's more of like a personal thing. Nobody else is telling me that I have to do well. It's just more like I wanna succeed, I wanna do well, and I wanna go to Stanford." When asked why she wants to go to Stanford, she is unsure: "I've wanted to go there since before kindergarten; I have no idea why. . . . And my mom can't even figure it out." Again, the messages she is receiving regarding school and academic aspirations are not coming from her parents. Jenna, like other Asian-American youth in our study, excels in her classes. But her academic excellence and emphasis on education are being reinforced by her teachers rather than her parents. Teachers may view her as the stereotypical "model minority" and treat her as such. She respects them, and they like her "a lot" in return. Jenna also has very particular goals for her life after graduating from high school, something we heard from other racial and ethnic minority youth.

LIZA JACOBS

Liza Jacobs is a white eighteen-year-old from the Midwest. She has grown up in a very small town. She recently graduated from high school and will be going to a state university in the fall, where she plans to major in occupational therapy. Only Liza and her father remain in the household. Her three older siblings have moved out, and her parents are divorced. Her mother moved out of the home about a year ago. Her father "works all the time," so over this last year she has experienced limited parental interaction.

Liza has a very active life. During high school she worked at a local restaurant as a waitress. She recently quit because she did not like the hours, and she is now looking for a new job, because she needs the income. Liza will be contributing to at least part of her college expenses—plus, she says she needs money to fix her car. In addition to working, she was very active in extracurricular activities in high school. Teachers pushed her "really hard in high school. [I] was given like a lot of stuff to do, too." Liza was editor of the school yearbook and president of the student council. She helped organize the homecoming dances and blood drives as well as activities for the Family Career Community Leaders of America, Future Business Leaders of America, and Future Farmers of America. She was also on the dance team for two years. And according to her, "now that [I'm] leaving, they quit, they've shut down [the dance team]." Liza's high level of participation in school activities is likely tied to the size of her school. There were probably a lot more opportunities to get involved in activities relative to youth who attend schools in larger towns or urban areas. Still, Liza does admit, "I got pretty stressed out a few times because I got myself too involved . . . with like too many things at once."

Liza also has done well in school, earning a 3.55 GPA on a 4.0 scale in her last year of school. Although she "kind of goofed off a couple times [in school]," she cares about doing well:

I worried about scholarships a lot this year. I mean, I goofed around a couple of times when I—I mean, my main priority this year was to try to get my grades as high as possible to get scholarships.

Liza recognizes that getting good grades increases her opportunities to receive college scholarships. This may be especially important to her since she is contributing to her college expenses.

Liza may not have much face-to-face interaction with her parents since their recent separation. But she has good relationships with her teachers. As she puts it, "teachers have always been positive influences" in her life:

Like . . . when you live in a small town . . . your teachers are more personal than you think. . . . My friend's mom was one of my high school teachers, and I'd go down to her house regularly; and my [other] friend's mom was my science teacher, and I'd go over there all the time. And my math teacher who works at the lake . . . I go out to his house and talk to him sometimes.

Liza's teachers also encourage her to excel in school:

They push me to go do stuff. Like they pushed me to get better grades and stuff; like if my grades are dropping to B's, they push me and make me do better in class, so I'd get my grades back up to A's.

Liza was a high-achieving student in high school, participating in many school activities and getting good grades. In many respects, this is due to the positive influence that teachers "have always" had on her life. She knows them well, and they are personally involved in her life. She feels comfortable going over to their homes and visiting with them. These teachers invest in Liza by encouraging her to do better in school, pushing her when her grades are slipping. When she is getting B's, they encourage her to strive for A's. As a result, Liza's teachers have not only provided emotional support but also put her on a more secure path to college. While she attributes her relationships with teachers to living in a small town, Liza's situation is not unique. As we discuss later, white youth overwhelmingly view their teachers positively and have good relationships with them. Youth of color from small towns did not speak of their teachers in this manner, as Cecilia, whom we will now meet, demonstrates.

CECILIA LOPEZ

Cecilia is an eighteen-year-old Latina. She lives with her parents in a small rural town in the West. She has a much older sister who is married with children and who lives in a nearby town. Cecilia recently finished high school, where she got "A's and B's." For some of her classes she has had to "work hard" to do well. She was "pretty involved" in high school activities, participating in the Spanish club and varsity softball. She also worked for two and a half years at a local restaurant while attending high school. She saved half her pay from this job for college. After high school, she began working at a center for disabled youth.

Cecilia says she was invested in doing well in high school because "I just wanted to do good . . . [and] that way I could get in college easier and get scholarships, stuff like that." She is planning to attend a local state college in the upcoming fall, living at home while commuting to school. Cecilia plans to study nursing, something she decided during her last year of school. When asked "What about [nursing] appeals to you?" she explains, "I think it's a real rewarding job, and I volunteered at [a medical center] in [the city] for like a year, so I liked it." Practical experience as a volunteer has helped to solidify Cecilia's career plans. Even now she is working in a closely related field.

Unlike Liza, Cecilia did not have particularly good relationships with her teachers. When asked about having significant relationships with other adults besides her parents, she mentions only family members, "grandma, and . . . like a few cousins" in another town in her state. The interviewer then asks her specifically about significant relationships with teachers or coaches:

I: What about like teachers, coaches?
R: No.

I: Instructors? Anything like that?

R: No.

I: Do you wish you did?

R: No.

I: You don't, you don't want to.

R: [laughs] Yeah.

Cecilia did not have relationships with any teachers or coaches in high school and says she does not care that she did not.

Cecilia has a clear sense of what she wants to do with her life. She was active in high school and did well in her classes. Her involvement in school was motivated by her desire to go to college. She recognizes the relevance of school for increasing her college opportunities. Cecilia's interest in excelling in school is not the result of any of her teachers' influence. In her view, teachers have had no significant impact on her life.

Dorian's, Jenna's, Liza's, and Cecilia's thoughts about education and their school experiences highlight themes as to why school is important to youth, how youth think about their futures, and the role teacher-student relationships play in the lives of youth. We now expand on these themes and illustrate how teens' views and experiences are structured by race and ethnicity.

YOUTHS' VIEWS ABOUT EDUCATION

There is considerable research on the role that attitudes play in the racial gap in academic achievement.[5] Some propose that Latinos and African-Americans place less importance on education than do whites and Asian-Americans.[6] Others propose no racial difference when it comes to attitudes regarding the importance of education, or that Latino and African-American youth place more importance on education than whites.[7] We support the latter position. Our analyses reveal that youth across race and ethnicity (and generation) care very much about doing well in school. Consistent with what others have found, we found that Latino and African-American youth cared more than white and Asian-American youth about doing well in school. We add to this debate around academic achievement by revealing *why*, according to them, youth care about doing well in school, something that is relatively absent in the literature. We also include Latino youth in our survey and interview analyses, which most studies have not done.

Academic Achievement

Youth were asked in the NSYR survey how important it is to do well in school. While a large majority of youth agree that doing well in school is important (87%), African-American youth were by far the most likely to say that it is *extremely* important to do well in school (70%). Latino students followed with 53 percent reporting that doing well in school is extremely important. However, looking at only first-generation Latino youth, we found the proportion to be 70 percent. Less than half of white (47%) and Asian-American (46%) youth have this view about school. Further, after controlling for family socioeconomic status, grades, and participation in school activities, among other factors, this pattern remains: African-Americans continue to be the most likely to say that doing well in school is extremely important. Among Latino youth, only those who are first generation are more likely than white youth to place an extreme importance on doing well in school. There is no difference between white and Asian-American students' views (see Table 4.1[8]; for statistical analyses see Appendix C).

While youth from all racial and ethnic groups care about doing well in high school, the interviews reveal that white youth are the most likely by far to value good grades explicitly because they see them as necessary for admittance to college. For example, Laura is a white teen who cares very much about her grades. She is sixteen years old and lives in a small town in the southeast. School is very stressful for her, so much so that it makes her "depressed." She spends several hours an evening on her schoolwork, often working from the time she gets home until midnight or 1:00 A.M. For Laura, A's and B's are the only acceptable grades. Later in the interview, she explains why:

I care that I do very well. It used to be at one point [that] I didn't care. I think that was during middle school. I don't know why, but now, when I [got] to high school, I want A's and B's. . . . I don't want it to be lower than an A or a B . . . because . . . you being accepted in college is maybe more likely better than if you have lower grades, and I want to be more than available.

Laura takes school seriously. She wants nothing lower than B's in her classes. Her primary motivation is the importance of good grades for getting into college. Other white youth are similarly motivated. As one sixteen-year-old white male put it, he cared about doing well in school to "get into a good college and get scholarships." A fourteen-year-old white boy says that doing well in high school prepares you for college "because if you don't do good in school here you're not going to really do well in college."

TABLE 4.1

Academic Views and Future Aspirations by Race/Ethnicity

Percentage of teens who...	White	African-American	Asian-American	Latino (generation)				Total
				All	First	Second	Third+	
Think it is extremely important to do well in school[a]	47	70	46	53	70	53	48	52
Say they would like to go to college[b]	89	88	95	86	78	88	87	88
Think they will actually go to college[c]	82	78	93	72	56	77	74	80

Source: NSYR survey.

Note: N = 2,785.

[a] All differences between racial/ethnic groups are significant at $p < .01$ (Pearson's chi-square test).

[b] There are no significant differences between racial/ethnic groups.

[c] All differences between racial/ethnic groups are significant at $p < .01$ (Pearson's chi-square test).

Although a less common response, several white youth mentioned parental pressure in stating the importance of doing well in school. These youth get the message from parents that they should do well in school, and they begin to care themselves about getting into college and behave accordingly. Mary is a white fifteen-year-old from a devout Christian family, which is actively involved in their church. She explains that her father has very high expectations for her academically. As a result, she is fearful to tell her father when she is having difficulty in school.

My dad is very school- and success-oriented. It's not like . . . you have to study ten hours a day or you're getting kicked out of the house or something. . . . But last year I had a problem with my history class. And I couldn't turn a report in on time, and I was like terrified to like tell my dad, because I thought he would like kill me.

Another example of white youth who experience pressure from parents is Henry. He is a seventeen-year-old boy from the southeast. Henry says, "Definitely, [doing well in school] is one of my priorities, because, ah, you need [good grades] to go to college, and I don't know, I just, I'd be kicked out of my school if I didn't get grades, good grades, this year, actually." Henry is especially motivated to do well in school to avoid expulsion. When asked about what influenced his view about grades, he explains, "that's mostly my parents yelling at me about doing good and do your homework."

Racial and ethnic minority youth give a variety of reasons for caring about doing well in school. They talk about college opportunities and parental pressures but also about getting good jobs, making money, finishing high school, and generally succeeding in life. While several of these other reasons were also heard in the conversations with white youth, they were rarely mentioned.

About a third of African-American youth interviewed and half of Asian-American and Latino youth interviewed say they care about doing well in school because of the role of grades in college admittance. Leanne is a fourteen-year-old African-American girl who comes from an upper-middle-class family. She lives in a small town on the East Coast. She is active in school, participating on the drill team. Although Leanne has only a C average in her classes, she cares a lot about doing well in school because she wants to go to college and knows that the better her grades are, the more options she will have. When asked if she cares about doing well in school, she responds:

I care a lot about school . . . because I really want to get into college; I want to get into a good college, and I know that without the grades it's not gonna happen; they're not just gonna let you in, you know, so, um, it, it, I, it's a big part; it determines—your grades determine—whether or not you get into the college of your choice, and I want to go to a college of my choice; I want to be able to choose where I go. And I want to be able to have a big selection. You know, you gotta work hard to get there.

Similarly, Ricardo, a seventeen-year-old Latino whose grades are, as he puts it, "pretty good, A's and B's," cares a lot about doing well in school because good grades are needed to get into college. Indeed, if he does not do well in school and go to college, he believes he could end up "flipping burgers":

I care, I mean, I care a lot . . . if you don't do well in school, then you don't get into a certain college, and I think that's the most important thing; so school is the number one priority for me right now, besides my religion. So . . . it's do or die; you have to do good or you end up flipping burgers at Burger King or something like that.

Leanne and Ricardo show that racial and ethnic minority youth have internalized the importance of doing well in school. This appears to be the case even when their grades do not necessarily reflect this attitude. But, nevertheless, it is clear that they at least understand that their academic performance will ultimately have an impact on their college opportunities.

As with several parents of white youth, strong parental influence is the reason some youth of color care about doing well in school. Javier is a seventeen-year-old Latino. His grades are "pretty good. Probably B average." Javier's parents, his father particularly, strongly encourage him to do well in school. His dad has clear expectations that Javier go to college. He has even directed Javier toward a specific profession:

I: How much do you care or not about doing well at school?

R: It's important. My dad, my dad pushes me, you know, because he wants me to go to college and everything and become an architect, so he pushes me to do well in school.

I: And why is it important, because your dad's influence or other things?

R: Um, because I know I need it in life to get a better job, you know, to be able to make sense of what I'm doing. I just need it.

Several Asian-American teens in our study were invested in their education because of parental pressure. Their parents had high academic expectations for them and strongly encouraged them to participate in extracurricular activities at school. This often led to conflict and guilt. Josh, who is sixteen years old, shared how parental pressures to do well in school affect him. He explained:

School is the main area of conflict [with my mother] and how well she wants me to do. She wants me to do really well, and sometimes she thinks I have to do certain things that I don't think I have to do to achieve that level of excellence.

He goes on to share about "when I didn't do as well as I could do. That makes me feel like I'm letting my parents down sometimes. And I feel guilty because of that 'cause I could've done something differently." We see, then, that Josh cares about doing well in school, but his aspirations are strongly influenced by his desire to not disappoint his parents. And when he feels that his parents are disappointed in his academic performance, it affects how he feels about himself.

Despite their greater success in school, our research suggests that Asian-American youth do not always exhibit an emotional investment in their academic achievement. For example, Vivian, an Asian-American teen who is a very good student—making practically all A's in the past school year—says she is only "doing pretty good." And she is not particularly invested in school. When asked "How much do you care or not about doing well at school?" she replies, "I care, but I don't study as much as I should be studying, or I don't listen as much in class as I should be." When asked about her seeming ambivalence towards school, she responds, "I don't know; I get really lazy, and, you know, I do homework at the last minute, and the projects are always at the last minute." School is easy for Vivian. Without paying much attention or putting forth much effort she can get nearly all A's. She cares about doing well in school but is not committed to school and perceives that she has a "lazy" approach to schoolwork.

In addition to college aspirations and parental expectations, youth of color care about doing well in school because they want to become wealthy or successful. College, if mentioned in these cases, is merely a means to achieving these goals. Consequently, these youth are not fully committed to higher education. If these teens find that they can achieve their ultimate goal without going to college, they may choose to do so. A fifteen-year-old African-American male with a B+ average put it this way: "I care a lot about doing well in school 'cause, you know, it's, uh, if I'm going to be rich, I'm going to have to get my education." Aaron, an eighteen-year-old African-American male from a city in the northeast, has similar aspirations. He is actively involved in football and basketball at his school. For his grades he gets "one of everything and then probably like two C's." Aaron also cares "a lot" about doing well in school, because he wants to "succeed," which to him means, "I want to make money, pretty much," and getting good grades helps to facilitate this.

A common narrative given by about half the Latino youth interviewed, particularly first-generation Latino youth, is that they care about doing well in school because they want to have a good future or succeed. Many believe that college or postsecondary education is an important step in achieving their ultimate goal of a better life. Mona is a seventeen-year-old, first-generation Latina who cares about doing well in school because she wants a better future. Her high school is majority white and Latino. She gets "straight A's, B's, C's" and feels that she is "doing good" in school. When asked how much she cares about doing well in school she responds, "I just care about my future, what am I doing in life . . . I want to be somebody." She further explains:

I care 'cause . . . my parents are not always gonna be there. I mean, they're gonna be there . . . when I [have] problems or [to] help me out on this, but . . . when I'm gonna go to college . . . they're not gonna be there [to] help me out. [With] certain little things . . . I have to stand up for myself. . . . When I get a problem at school or college, or I need money, well, I have to do it on my own, 'cause I'm working.

Mona is motivated to do well because she believes that academic success is important if she wants to do well in life, "to be somebody." Becoming somebody includes going to college, although she does not make this explicit until the interviewer has probed a couple of times about why she cares about doing well. Mona also recognizes that she will need to take care of herself once she is done with high school, and she has already begun taking on responsibility by working. Getting good grades is ultimately a step in the direction of becoming self-sufficient.

Still, other African-American and Latino youths' reasons for caring about doing well in school have nothing to do with going to college. These youth desire to do well because they want to graduate from high school or get a good job. Manuel is fourteen years old and Latino. He has gone between being home-schooled and attending public school since fifth grade because of "some troubles and . . . the pressure and all that of, of, you know, you don't learn at your own pace; you learn, you learn at what you're supposed to." When asked how much he cares about doing well in school, Manuel simply replies, "I want to get a good job." He may not be interested in going to college, at least at this point, because of the challenges he has experienced in school thus far. But youth of color who did not experience trouble in traditional school settings also did not primarily view good grades as important for college. Tanya, for example, an eighteen-year-old African-American teen from a small Southern town, who was quite well mannered, often responding with "yes ma'am" or "no ma'am" during the interview, says she cares "a lot" about doing well in school because good grades are needed to graduate from high school:

Because . . . if you pay attention in class, you gonna know what you need to know to get out of school, and if you have C's, well, I'm gonna say D's and F's, what's your purpose of sitting in class; it's like you wasting your time and the teacher time. . . . And I think it's very important.

Tanya has strong feelings about actively participating in one's education. This is because she wants to "get out of school." Just sitting in class and failing or barely passing is a waste of time for students and teachers. Tanya is like many of the African-American youth interviewed. In fact, completing high school was a more common reason provided by African-American youth for caring about doing well in school than going to college. Latino youth do not show much concern about graduating from high school despite having lower high school graduation rates than African-American youth.[9] This difference in African-American and Latino youths' educational aspirations may be, in part, because of a difference in life orientation. Whereas some African-American youth are focused on overcoming immediate hurdles in life, which for these youth is graduating from high school, the "success" narrative that we commonly heard among Latino youth emphasizes future outcomes. Thus Latino youth are more focused on mid- or long-term goals. Additionally, poverty- and minority-concentrated schools are associated with lower graduation rates.[10] Latino youth are less likely than African-American youth to attend poverty- or minority-concentrated schools. Therefore, African-American youth are likely exposed to greater proportions of youth who drop out of school than are Latino youth. They do not assume that they and their peers will graduate from high school.

In summary, white youth are primarily motivated to do well in school because of aspirations to go to college. They understand the connection between good grades and getting into college. Although mentioned far less, parental pressure also motivates white youth to do well in school. Many parents of white youth expect their children to get good grades, and if necessary, these parents will provide incentives to encourage their children to do so. Racial and ethnic minority youths' reasons for doing well in school are far more varied than white youths'. College and parental pressure are primary motivators, too. This is particularly true for Asian-American youth. But youth of color also believe that good grades are important for getting a good job (which may or may not require a college degree), graduating from high school, and being wealthy or successful.

Future Aspirations

White youth are most likely to care about doing well in school because of the role that academic achievement plays in broadening college opportunities. However, when youth are asked directly about their educational aspirations, all youth generally see college as a desirable goal. In our survey youth are asked, "Ideally, how far in school would you like to go?" A large majority of white (89%), Asian-American (95%), African-American (88%), and Latino (86%) youth say they want to go to college. Youth are also asked, "Given realistic limitations, how far in school do you think you actually will go?" The percentages who think they will, realistically, go to college decline for every group. The decline is the greatest for Latino youth (–14%), followed by African-American youth (–10%). Eighty-two percent of white youth expect to go to college, a difference of 7 percent, and 93 percent of Asian-American youth expect to go to college, a difference of only 2 percent. Nevertheless, a large majority of youth from each racial and ethnic group believe that realistically, they will go to college. Further analyses reveal that youths' college expectations do not vary by racial and ethnic background once other factors are taken into account. The most notable factors affecting youths' views on college are class-related (Table 4.1). Youth from various racial and ethnic backgrounds are getting the message that they should attend college. Youth also recognize realistic obstacles that may limit their ability to achieve this goal.

In the interviews, youth were asked to elaborate on their future aspirations. Consistent with the survey results, a large majority of youth interviewed aspire to go to college, regardless of racial or ethnic background. However, consistent with white youths' views on academic achievement, white youth are the least varied in their aspirations. Most white youth interviewed know they should go to college and are doing what they know to do in order to make this possible. But getting into college is as far as most white youth have considered their futures. One might expect white youth to have clearer long-term goals, given their greater exposure to adults in skilled or professional jobs. But this is not the case.

While close to 20 percent of white youth interviewed specify a career or field they are interested in, commonly citing science, medicine, or professional sports as fields they would like to work in, nearly 75 percent do not have any specific aspirations beyond getting into college. These youth have no idea what career path they would like to pursue. Nor do they know what they want to major in while in college. Having no specific academic goals or long-term career aspirations is not problematic for them, either. Here are a few examples of how these youth respond to a question regarding their future:

I: How far in school do you want to go?

R [sixteen-year-old white male]: I want to get a Ph.D.

I: But you don't know in what.

R: No, yeah, I just want to get a Ph.D. in something.

I: How far in school do you want to go?

R [seventeen-year-old white male]: Ah, college and eventually get a masters, at least.

I: Where would you like to go to college?

R: Um, no idea. [laughs]

I: What would you like to do?

R: Um, no idea. [laughs again]

I: What do you think about when you do think about the future?

R [sixteen-year-old white female]: I wanna like go to college first and get a really good education.

I: How far in school do you want to go?

R: I don't know; I haven't, I mean, I know I wanna go to college and get a degree, but I don't know.

Racial and ethnic minority youth have more varied ideas about their futures and are more specific about their future aspirations than white youth. Some are mainly focused on going to college. Other Latino, Asian-American, and African-

American youth as early as fourteen years old have begun to contemplate careers they want to pursue, fields they want to major in, or colleges they want to attend. In some cases, they have both a career *and* a college in mind. Still, there are Latino and African-American youth, in particular, who do not always have the knowledge and life experiences to achieve their educational and career goals.

About three-fourths of African-American youth interviewed want to go to college. While most African-American youth are specific about their educational and career aspirations, a substantial minority of them have not planned much beyond getting into college. When asked about his future plans, one eighteen-year-old African-American male, an A student who would be attending college in the fall, responded, "Right now I'm thinking about college, but, um, just mainly college right now." Another eighteen-year-old African-American male, who is a near straight-A student, had this to say when asked how far in school he would like to go:

R: Oh, I'd probably like want to go for a professional degree or something.
I: Like what?
R: Oh, what type of field or something? Oh—
I: Yeah, what kind of field or . . . ?
R: Psychology, I guess.
I: Okay, and do you think you'd just go to, um, undergrad? Or would you keep going?
R: Keep going.
I: Okay, why?
R: Um, because I've always heard and now I think that in order to get what you want, you just have to, you know, get it, like work hard. It may be difficult, but like in the end, it'll pay off.

This teen also knows that college is important. He intends to go as far as possible in school because this is what he understands is needed "in order to get what you want." Although he is going to college, he is somewhat ambivalent about a major or career. It is only when the interviewer probes a couple of times that he offers psychology. Still, he has given at least some thought to what he would like to do once he begins college.

About half of the African-American youth interviewed have a particular profession in mind that they want to pursue. Some fields mentioned were law, business, journalism, and sportscaster. Most of these professions require at least a four-year degree and sometimes a graduate or professional degree as well. Here is what one fourteen-year-old girl who has a B average in her classes has to say when asked about her future: "I want to be a hair designer . . . I want to do hair. . . . And be a lawyer." This adolescent has not firmly decided which career she would like to pursue, but she is at least oriented toward some kind of career path. A sixteen-year-old interviewee, an A student, is also interested in becoming a lawyer because it is a career that should provide him with financial stability. He jokes that with an English teacher for a mother he should make a good lawyer. "I want to go . . . to college, and I want to be financially stable; I think that's it. When I graduate from college, I want to have a good job, you know, maybe a lawyer." He goes on to explain that he has some lawyers in his family, although he does not know them well. He is thinking of law because "I love the fuss . . . I love to prove somebody wrong or prove myself right, you know. . . . And my mom's an English teacher, so English is in my blood, you know, reading . . . all that language arts . . . that's all in my blood. So, I think I'll make a good lawyer." Interestingly, as with this girl and boy, several other African-American and Latino youth mentioned law as a future career aspiration. We are not sure why this is the case, but it may be a result of close exposure to the legal system or the popularity of law-oriented television shows, in combination with law being a financially lucrative field.

Almost all Asian-American youth planned to go to at least a four-year college, and several had a college in mind. The schools Asian-American youth were most interested in were often private, prestigious universities. There was also a large minority of Asian-American youth interviewed who said they intended to go to graduate school; however, they were not sure what they wanted to study in graduate school. A fifteen-year-old says she has given "a lot" of thought to her future education and career. She wants to become a pediatrician and get a Ph.D.:

> I: What do you imagine you will do with your life when you are an adult?
> R: I think I'll have a husband, kids, and like hopefully be a pediatrician.
> I: So, what are your future education plans? I know you said go to college. How far in school do you want to go?
> R: I want to get a Ph.D.
> I: A Ph.D.? In what? Do you know yet?
> R: No.

This Asian-American adolescent is ambitious. She plans to become a pediatrician. She wants to get a graduate education of some kind. When pressed about her specific educational plans, she says she wants to get a Ph.D., although her career aspirations mean she would need to go to medical school. She may be unsure of which doctoral field to pursue, or she possibly thinks that a doctorate is a medical degree. As she is only a high school freshman, her confusion is quite understandable. Still, she aspires to follow a particular career path—a very prestigious, professional one at that.

Similar to this female teen, who is quite specific about her career goals despite some ambiguity about graduate school, about half of Asian-American youth interviewed specified a career in which they were interested in pursuing. For example, Bryan, who is fourteen, is quite specific about the career he would like to pursue. He wants to go to the Air Force Academy and become a pilot. Bryan wants to achieve this goal so much that he is stressed about getting a B in school for fear that he could jeopardize his chances of being accepted:

R: I think about [my future] a lot, like.

I: What do you think about?

R: I don't know, I guess I get stressed about school; like if I'm getting a B in a class, I'll be like, oh no, they're not gonna send me to college or something.

I: Where do you want to go to college?

R: I want to go to the Air Force Academy. And so I'm just like, 'cause I know it's a really hard college to get into, so.

I: So that's part of wanting to be a pilot.

Bryan, too, has high educational and career aspirations. He is quite clear about these at a young age.

A large majority of Latino youth interviewed (about three-fourths) have a career or field they are thinking about pursuing. In a few cases they even have an idea about what school they would like to attend. For example, when asked how much she thinks about her future, this thirteen-year-old Latina responds, "I don't really think of it that much, um, but I, I know what I want." She continues:

R: Um, I want to go to UM.

I: University of Miami?

R: Yeah, or FIU.

I: Okay.

R: Um, and like I want to study art, like singing or acting, or if not, I want to, um, [be a] lawyer.

Another Latino adolescent, a fifteen-year-old, is similarly specific about his future educational and career aspirations:

I: What are your future education plans?

R: UT.

I: Degree in?

R: I wanna get a [degree in] meteorology.

I: How far in school do you want to go?

R: All the way through four years of college.

Latino and African-American youth at times lack the tools needed to achieve their educational and career goals. These youth do not have sufficient knowledge about the college process and expectations for the careers they are interested in pursuing. This is implicit in some of the youths' responses above, such as the African-American adolescent thinking about becoming either a hairdresser or a lawyer, or the Asian-American teen aspiring to be a pediatrician but wanting to get a Ph.D. However, the ambiguity about college and career aspirations and the limited tools for socioeconomic mobility were far more apparent in other youth. Angela, for example, is a fourteen-year-old Latina. She is on the "honor roll" and is interested in becoming a probation officer. When asked what things she definitely wants to accomplish in life, she responds:

R: I wanna, um, maybe go into the military and become a probation officer, and I want to learn how to ride bikes, like dirt bikes or motorcycles, and stuff like that.

I: What makes you want to be a probation officer?

R: 'Cause my sister was on probation; my stepsister was on probation, my Mom was on parole, and, um, this lady came to our school, and she talked to us about it, and it seemed like a really cool thing to do, so.

Angela's mother's and sister's experiences give her up-close exposure to the penal system. She also heard more about being a probation officer during a presentation at her school (which provides some insight into the kinds of careers that schools believe Latino youth can pursue). These experiences led to Angela's interest in becoming a probation officer. However, Angela is less sure about what she needs to do to become a probation officer. Later in the interview she is asked, "How far do you want to go in school?" She says:

R: All the way.

I: All the way to what? College?

R: College. I have to, I have to go to police academy to be a probation officer.

Angela recognizes that she should go "all the way" to college. She has internalized this dominant ideology. Yet she thinks of the police academy as college, and she further connects attending the police academy to being a probation officer.

Of course, Angela is only fourteen; part of her lack of understanding can be attributed to her age. However, older teens similarly lacked specific direction on how to achieve their career goals, or they have life circumstances that make achieving their goals a challenge. Sylvia is a sixteen-year-old Latina, with a C average in school. She has been arrested for fighting in school, a fight in which she also hit a teacher who was attempting to break it up. According to Sylvia, she lives in a "messed up" community in a large northeastern city. She is determined to get out of her neighborhood though. She "want[s] to be a lawyer and just get out of [this city]." Why does she want to be a lawyer?

R: I don't know. I think there's a lawyer that I—that's what I'm going to school for. I want to be a lawyer, so, that's what like, lawyers—I admire them 'cause that's what I'd really like to be when I get older.

I: What about being a lawyer attracts you?

R: I don't know, I guess it's just the position you got; it's like fighting for somebody like, I would like to be, like, what am I saying, like somebody side that's right, like not somebody that did something and you're fighting for them; it's just, I would like to stand up for somebody if I know they're right and just be on their side.

I: Do you know any lawyers?

R: No, not really.

Sylvia is unsure about the specific steps she needs to take to achieve her career goal, and she has life circumstances that hinder her prospects for success. She wants to become a lawyer because she is drawn to the idea of "standing up for somebody." However, she has no practical exposure to the field. She has also been arrested, and she has a C average. All of these obstacles can be overcome, but they will make it difficult for Sylvia to leave her childhood lifestyle and achieve her career goal.

In summary, white youth overall aspire to go to college, although they think very little about their adult lives beyond college, rarely discussing a career or major they would like to pursue. Many African-American youth similarly intend to go to college, and some have also not given much thought to a major or career. However, they have often considered a university they would like to attend. Other African-American youth are far more focused on a particular career they would want to have as an adult. Asian-American youth also focus on going to college, and they are much more specific about their academic goals than white youth, often explaining which college they want to attend or field they would like to major in. Similarly, several college-aspiring Latino youth have very particular ideas about the college they want to attend and career they would like to have as an adult. But as with some African-American youth, many other Latino youth focus solely on a career they are interested in and have limited knowledge or network connections that could facilitate achieving their professional aspirations.

TEACHER-STUDENT RELATIONS

Youths' views about education and their futures are considerably similar across race and ethnicity. Nearly all youth care about doing well in school and consider college to be an important goal. Youth of all racial and ethnic backgrounds have thus received the dominant ideology that education and college are to be valued. There were differences in the reasons *why* they cared about academic excellence and in their thoughts on their futures. White youth stood apart from racial and ethnic minority youth in caring almost exclusively about college, although there was some overlap. We also saw distinct patterns across the various groups of teens of color. However, a very clear distinction between white youth and youth of color is revealed when it comes to teacher-student relations.

In our interviews youth were asked open-ended questions about whether they had other significant adults in their lives besides their parents. If they did not mention their teachers, respondents were prompted to talk about their relationships with and views of their teachers. Unlike most other research on students' views of teachers, the youth in this study were not restricted to a particular scale and could elaborate on their feelings. This allowed us to gain a more nuanced and clearer insight into how students' relationships with their teachers influence their academic achievement and educational views and cultivate teens' understanding about their place in society.

Teachers Care

About three-fourths of white youth we interviewed expressed *solely* positive views of their teachers. They had no negative views of their teachers, nor did they see any teacher as having a negative influence on their lives. As with Liza, at the beginning of the chapter, teachers who have positive influences on white youth are those that invest in them, not only academically but personally. For example, Valerie, a sixteen-year-old white youth from a small town in the South, when asked if there were any other adults besides her parents whom she considered to be a positive role model or influence in her life, shares this:

R: My volleyball teacher, Miss Beach, she was helping me figure out how I should do my SATs; she's like, she's a very positive person; I really like her, I enjoy being with her, really enjoy talking to her.

I: So, she mostly helps you with school things or personal things, or?

R: School things, like SATs or when I should take them, or the best time to take them [so] colleges can get [the] scores; she's telling me the best times it would be to take them. She's real supportive.

Miss Beach provides Valerie with very practical advice on how to navigate the college application process. Additionally, Miss Beach is someone Valerie enjoys being around and feels comfortable talking to. Interestingly, Valerie is asked an open-ended question about positive, significant adults generally, and next to her parents it is a teacher who is the most supportive, influential role model in her life. Jonathan, a fifteen-year-old boy from a town in the Midwest, when asked about his relationship with teachers, talked about how his football coach, who is also his science teacher, has been very influential and supportive of him. This teacher and coach went out of his way to tutor Jonathan and encourage him to maintain good grades:

I: Teachers, how well do you get along with them?

R: Well, one of my teachers is my football coach, and he's always on my back about getting good grades and all this stuff, so, it's kind of pretty good, but I get good grades anyway. I really try hard in school, trying to make it somewhere in life, so, he's always there for me, too. Like when I'm slipping in something, he helps me get through it and all that stuff. . . . Whenever I'm like missing an assignment or something like that, he comes and tells me I'm missing it, and I do it, and he gets it to the teacher, and we just kind of go through that; he does that with everybody, though.

I: Okay, so he's really involved with all you guys?

R: Oh yeah, he's like almost my, like I would say tutor or something like that; like whenever I'm not too sure about a test or something, he'll take me like during study hall or something and go through it with me and just break it down so I understand it a little more.

It is unclear whether this coach-teacher is partly motivated to help Jonathan out of a desire to keep him eligible for the football team. Still, this is less important than how Jonathan views their relationship and the benefits he is receiving from his coach-teacher's attention. For white youth, teachers not only fill the role of teacher but are often a confidant and mentor as well. As a fifteen-year-old girl from a Midwest city simply explained about her English teacher, "I could go to her with anything."

Nearly all white youth, girls and boys, have positive views of teachers. They perceive their teachers as advocates and people who care about them. A negative relationship with a teacher is uncommon for white youth. Yet, not all white teens viewed teachers as having only positive influences on their lives. About a quarter viewed teachers as having potentially good or bad influences on their lives or viewed them as being mainly negative influences. A small number of teens with these less positive views of teachers also did not do well in school or were involved in some kind of delinquent behavior. However, most were at least B students; thus, having negative views of teachers is not necessarily related to their performance in school. These students viewed some teachers positively, others negatively, and also felt comfortable making judgments about their teachers' performance. Additionally, a large majority of white teens with less than fully positive views of teachers were boys, which suggests that teacher-student relationships are also influenced by gender as well as race and ethnicity. Still, even white youth who have not had completely positive relationships with teachers have an understanding that teachers are supposed to be personally as well as academically invested in their development, and usually have some teachers who they feel care about them.

Matt, an eighteen-year-old from a wealthier suburb of Los Angeles, explains that most of his teachers have a good influence on him, and that many of his teachers are also friends. But other teachers are "just there to teach," suggesting that for a teacher to only teach students is somehow inadequate. Good teachers are friends to students as well:

I: How do you view your teachers in school?

R: They're, there's, there's some that are there to interact with you and to be your friend and also to teach you, and then there's some that's just there to teach and I don't know. I don't really view them as like, as an authority or something like that; they're there, and I've got to pass the class.

Jaime, a white seventeen-year-old from a town in the southwest who does not view all of his teachers favorably, also says that good teachers are those who care about youth. When asked how he views his teachers, he shares:

R: Most of them are pretty cool.

I: Okay, how, how do you get along with them?

R: Most of them are pretty good; there's a few of them that don't seem to really care for you, which makes it difficult.

The negative views some white teens have of some of their teachers have more to do with the extent to which they believe their teachers care about them, not their teachers' teaching abilities. Jaime even suggests that school is more challenging when teachers do not "really care" for students.

Teachers Teach

We very rarely heard racial and ethnic minority youth talk about their teachers providing them with practical advice about college or other future endeavors, as we heard from white youth. It was also rare that they discussed developing especially close relationships with their teachers. As we saw with Cecilia, at the beginning of the chapter, what also distinguished youth of color from white youth is that they placed little emphasis on whether teachers cared for them. For example, Lucy, a fifteen-year-old Asian-American youth, does not have a particularly positive view of or relationship with teachers, despite getting nearly straight A's in her classes. She says:

Since they have so many students, they can't really interact with you one on one, so it's kind of like, like he's just my teacher, you know? . . . It used to be like, they used to know you, and you could talk to them and they could talk to you, but now, no.

Lucy sees the limited interaction between teachers and students as a result of the greater student-to-teacher ratio in high school. This suggests that in grammar school she received more attention from her teachers. Now she has little connection to her teachers. They are impersonal adults who have very little direct impact on her life and who she is. She further explained that to her a teacher is "just a person standing up there talking."

Only about a third of Asian-American and Latino youth interviewed, and about half of African-American youth interviewed, had only positive views of their teachers. But, these youth considered teachers with positive influences as those that effectively taught students, not as people who cared about them. Additionally, a good relationship with a teacher was defined by mutual respect. Youth of color with positive views of their teachers emphasized their ability to respectfully interact with teachers.

Recall Jenna, the fourteen-year-old Asian-American girl from the West Coast who you met at the beginning of the chapter. When asked, "Do you think of [teachers] as a good influence in your life or a bad influence in your life?" she responded, "They're a good influence. I mean, they teach me stuff, for the most part. Not all of them do, but most of them try to." An eighteen-year-old African-American female, Brenda, from a small town in the South, who recently graduated from high school, had a similar view when asked about her teachers:

I didn't give them problems or anything. I guess 'cause I was quiet; I'm very quiet, and they [were] good teachers. I learned everything.

Brenda not only explains that her teachers were "good" influences because they taught her what she needed to learn, but by beginning her response explaining that she didn't give them any problems she also seems to believe that her teachers' ability to teach was dependent upon her obedience.

Joe, who is also eighteen and African-American, would agree that what makes a good teacher is one who teaches effectively. He lives in a small city in the South. He says that he "[gets] along with all [his] teachers." During the interview, he talked about his favorite teacher from high school, whom he had in his senior year. Why was this teacher his favorite? He explained:

I guess his classroom. . . . It was a history class, and history is not my favorite subject, and I guess he made it interesting; and one of the things I really admired about him was . . . that I could tell that he knew what he was talking about, so that, not that I've ever had a teacher where I thought they didn't know what they was talking about, but it's just like he knew a lot more than, you know, what was required for him to be a teacher, so I liked it, it was good. But I mean he was very understanding, um, helpful; uh, it was an advanced class, so he tried to run the class like a college, while it was in high school, so maybe that was, maybe that had an impact also; so, I don't know, it was a good class.

Similar to the girls quoted above, there is no discussion of his favorite teacher caring for students or for him personally. What makes a teacher especially good is if she or he is proficient at teaching students. For Joe, this also means being able to create an interesting, challenging learning environment and being willing to provide additional help when students are in need of extra guidance.

For youth of color, good teachers also teach youth responsibility and appropriate behavior. The following teens, who say they get along with their teachers, have this to say about the role of good teachers:

R [sixteen-year-old African-American male]:They're good. They'll make you, ah, be responsible for your actions and stuff like that. So if you do something wrong, you can't blame nobody else but yourself.

R [seventeen-year-old Latina, first generation]:My teachers [are] . . . obviously good because they are the ones that tell me what I have to do, right?

I: Do you think your teachers are a good influence in your life, or bad?

R [fourteen-year-old Latino male]: Good.

I: Like how?

R: Well 'cause they discipline me; they show me how to act in class; they just, yeah, they just teach me a lot.

I: Okay. You said they, they discipline you; like how, what kind of discipline is?

R: Like if they discipline us, say, if we have an assignment and we miss out, we have to like write another assignment or something; they discipline us to do our work.

These themes of what makes a teacher a good or bad influence were also echoed by racial and ethnic minority youth who had less positive views of their teachers. Teachers' ability or willingness to teach students also continues to be an important criterion that distinguishes good from bad teachers. But respect from teachers is more important for these teens. Justin, a sixteen-year-old Asian-American student who attends a private school where, he says, the teens are "all a lot richer than [me]," is active in school sports and has a B average. This is what he has to say when asked his views on his school:

Negative. . . . There's a lot of people at my school, two teachers . . . that I don't respect because of things they do or the way they treat students. I think students should be taught, I think . . . if I give a teacher respect, they should give me respect back. . . . I don't believe in the system where it's like, a teacher has a whole control over the class. . . . Like some teachers at our school just don't give students . . . respect, I think . . . [and] that has a negative effect on kids. I think compassion goes a longer way.

Leslie is a fourteen-year-old African-American student who comes from a lower-class family living in an East Coast inner-ring suburb. She is a confident girl who seems older than her years. She says she gets "B's and D's and bad grades." Similar to Justin above, Leslie thinks that in addition to explaining the class material to her, teachers ought to treat students with respect. This is an especially important quality of a good teacher. And as the following discussion demonstrates, she is comfortable confronting her teachers when she does not perceive that she is being treated respectfully:

I: How about teachers? How do you view your teachers?

R: Teachers. Um, I admire them for what they do, but I don't like a lot of them. A lot of teachers are just in it for the money—

I: Yeah—

R: A lot of them are in it 'cause they love it; a lot of them are in it 'cause they have nothing else to do; it's just, um, teachers, um, very disrespectful; I'm not gonna lie, if I like you and you respect me, I'll respect you. You disrespect me, I'll disrespect you; I don't care, that's the way I am; not to be smart or anything, but if a teacher can talk to me and explain stuff to me and not catch an attitude, I won't catch an attitude with them; I have no reason to, you know what I mean. . . . If they, they understand what I'm saying, and they respect what I'm saying and respect my opinion, then that's fine. But when they catch an attitude with me and expect me to sit there and say yes ma'am, yes, that's not gonna happen, not while I'm alive; that's not gonna happen.

To summarize, race and ethnicity clearly have impacts on students' views of teachers. White students have rather intimate relationships with teachers. They are comfortable talking to them about personal matters and enjoy spending time with their teachers. While some white male youth have negative relationships with some teachers, they also tend to have very good relationships with other teachers. They perceive that these teachers care about their well-being and are genuinely interested in them. The intimate relationships that white youth have with their teachers often facilitate the transference of valuable social resources to these youth—social resources that are not accessible to racial and ethnic minority youth.

It was rare to hear a racial or ethnic minority youth in our interviews talk about having a personally close connection to a teacher in the way that white youth did. Many liked their teachers and had good relationships with them, but these relationships were narrow, directly tied to classroom interactions. These were well-behaved students who did not "talk back" to teachers. Teachers apparently responded well to their obedience, which was an indication to these youth that they got along well with their teachers. However, unlike white youth, most racial and ethnic minority youth did not view their teachers positively. This view was not reflective of their academic performance: high and low academic achievers possessed these views. These teens highlighted a lack of mutual respect with their teachers, which characterized poorer teacher-student relationships. Or, they merely saw their teachers as having very limited influence on their lives beyond the classroom.

Moreover, white youth and racial and ethnic minority youth also prioritize different criteria when delineating between teachers who have a positive influence on them from those with a negative influence. For white youth, having teachers who could effectively teach students was largely taken for granted. Teachers teach. But it was expected that teachers should care about them as well. It was notable when teachers did not appear to care for them personally. Poorer teachers were thus not described as those who were unable to teach them but mainly as teachers who seemed not to care about students. In contrast, racial and ethnic minority youth did not expect teachers to care about them. Good teachers were described as teachers who could teach well. They were willing to provide additional help outside of class or introduce more engaging methods during class to ensure that students understood the material. Racial and ethnic minority youth did not take it for granted that teachers were capable of teaching them, or willing to.

CONCLUSION: ACHIEVEMENT, ASPIRATIONS, AND SCHOOLS

Education influences socioeconomic mobility.[11] Young people's experiences in school and their views about education are therefore important for understanding inequality. Central debates about how (and how much) education matters revolve around student attitudes and teacher-student relationships and their connection to academic achievement. The bulk of this research has focused on the racial gap in academic achievement. Over recent decades this gap has decreased,[12] but it continues to persist despite larger structural changes, such as the end of Jim Crow segregation and increases in educational opportunities.[13]

Several factors affect students' attitudes about education; socioeconomic class and parental characteristics, such as parental expectations and child-parent interactions, are chief among them. After we account for these factors, any racial differences in teens' views on the importance of education that may have existed often disappear; or, as several studies show, African-American, Latino, and Asian-American youth actually have higher educational aspirations than white youth.[14] For instance, African-American students are significantly more likely than white students to report that education is important for getting a job later in life. They are more optimistic about occupational aspirations than white students.[15] There is also evidence that youth of color are more likely than white youth to expect to achieve a professional or doctoral degree.[16]

Still, educational aspirations of youth are high across racial groups.[17] So, educational aspirations, it is suggested by some, are not reasonable indicators of academic achievement. Many have then focused on explaining what appears on the face to be a disconnect between the actual academic achievement of racial and ethnic minorities, particularly African-American and Latino youth, and their strong endorsement of education—what is commonly referred to as the *attitude-achievement paradox*. For decades it has been purported that racial and ethnic minority youth are just not as motivated as white youth to do well in school.[18] While they may have positive views about education in the abstract, youth of color are not willing to do what it takes to do better in school. Certain researchers have proposed that African-American and third-plus-generation Latino youth have lower academic achievement than other students because they place less importance on doing well in school than on other goals.[19] African-American and third-plus-generation Latino students value their reputation among their peers more than getting good grades—the latter being perceived as part of the dominant (that is, white) culture and not reflective of their peer culture. Another view is that although racial and ethnic minority youth do believe education is important at an abstract level[20]—that is to say they accept the "American Dream" ideology that education is important for socioeconomic upward mobility—these youth also have concrete attitudes about their everyday life and opportunities. These attitudes reflect the reality of their structural conditions, which may hinder their capacity to reap actual returns on an investment in their education. In other words, youth of color believe that education has the *potential* to improve people's socioeconomic conditions, but their own observations of adults in their racial group, within their families or neighborhoods for instance, tell them that education will not necessarily improve *their* chances for upward socioeconomic mobility. Some researchers argue, however, that we cannot conclude from these findings that youth of color are being disingenuous in their responses to survey questions about school and education. It has been found that the attitudes of African-American, Asian-American, and Latino youth are relatively predictive of educational outcomes; that is, overall a positive association exists between these students' attitudes about education and their academic achievement.[21]

Youth of color possess strong beliefs in the power of education. In some instances they are more inclined to believe in the importance of education for their future success than are white youth. But while there is a positive association between youths' attitudes and achievement for all youth, among African-American and Latino youth in particular a belief in the value of education does not appear to have the effect on their educational outcomes that it does for other youth. It has been suggested by others[22] that inconsistent results regarding the relationship between attitudes and academic achievement might be due to differences in methodology (ethnographic studies versus survey-based studies; or localized survey data versus national survey data). By drawing on both survey data and the stories of youth through in-depth interviews, our findings provide important insights into what youth believe about education and why the disparities in academic achievement persist.

We found that while youth across racial and ethnic backgrounds give a similar array of reasons for caring about doing well in school, they differ in their propensity to select certain reasons over others. College is by far the most common reason white youth give for caring about doing well in school. Besides college (and secondly parental pressure), other reasons were rarely provided. Of course, some white youth interviewed did not care much about academic achievement. As one white student explained, "If I like the class, then I'm going to want to learn, but otherwise I don't really care." Another simply said, "I don't really care . . . 'cause it just isn't very important to me." Usually these youths' grades reflect this view; they have a C average in their classes, or worse. Therefore, variation among white youths' views about academic achievement is more about the extent to which they care, not their reasons for caring. When white youth do care, and a very large majority of them do, it is because they are preparing to get into college. White youth possess an almost singular focus on getting into college. Interestingly, a large majority have not considered a career they would like to pursue or even a major they would take up in college. Their only goal seemingly is to get into college. They are not seriously thinking about what they want to be "when they grow up." Still, even if white youth have limited ideas about their futures beyond getting into college, achieving this very crucial step in the education process places them in a position to excel in the future. College is highly correlated with better incomes and more prestigious careers, particularly among whites.[23]

Many Asian-American youth have a career in mind. In nearly every case these careers require a college education. While they care then about doing well in school so that they can get into college, college is not the endgame. The ultimate goal is a specific career. It was also quite common for Asian-American youth interviewed to aspire to go to graduate school. Yet a substantial minority of Asian-American youth interviewed were ambivalent or did not care about doing well in school. As one Asian-American student who planned to go to graduate school explained, "I don't think school is any measure of how smart someone is . . . I think school is a measure of how much somebody can memorize a certain amount of material." There was much more variation then among Asian-American youth than white youth in views about doing well in school. This is surprising given that most Asian-American teens excel academically. These youths had not necessarily internalized their parents' views about school but did behave in ways their parents expected. Such behavior will likely ensure these students a more secure future, at least economically.

Both in our survey and interviews, Latino and African-American youth are more likely to care a lot about doing well in school. It was very rare for these youth to be the least bit ambivalent about the importance of doing well in school. However, unlike white and Asian-American youth who also said they cared about academic achievement, these Latino and African-American teens gave a variety of reasons for why they cared. Many cared about doing well in school because they wanted to go to college, but for other Latino and African-American youth the connection between the importance of doing well in high school and going to college was tenuous. They knew they should want to go to college and that college was important for social and economic mobility, but they were vague about the ways in which high school achievement might affect their chances of going to college. And for still other Latino and African-American youth, the reasons for caring about doing well in school were not at all related to college. Rather, they believed in doing well so that they could finish high school or get a good job. Most of these students had about a B average in school. Later in their interviews, when specifically asked about their futures, they often said that they aspire to go to college or have careers in mind which would require a college education. But their immediate reasons for doing well in high school—graduating from high school or getting a good job—demonstrate that they do not have a clear orientation toward college or an understanding of the expectations for college admittance.

Our results highlight the high level of importance all youth, but especially African-American and Latino youth, place on education. The results also highlight that youth have different reasons for valuing education. However, it is also clear that teens are receiving very different messages about academic achievement, college, and their future aspirations. These differences have profound implications.

Youth have different ideas about the standard for "doing well" in school. White youth are explicitly told by their parents and teachers that the minimum acceptable grade in their classes is a B. White youth often suffer negative consequences from their parents for getting lower grades. For example, one white youth explains, "My parents take my license away if I get anything less than a B." Another says he cares about doing well in school "because I'm not allowed to do sports unless I have A's and B's." For many Asian-American youth, anything less than an A is unacceptable. Latino and African-American youth are not receiving these messages about the dominant standard of doing well in school. They believe they are doing well with a B average that includes C's. For example, Mona said she was "doing good" while getting "A's and B's and C's," something that is unacceptable for white and Asian-American youth. And recall Leanne, who is getting mostly C's. She understands the importance of grades for college but expresses little concern about how her grades may affect her ability to attend the college of her choice. African-American and Latino youth do experience negative repercussions for poor academic performance from parents. However, the messages they are receiving about the standard for doing well are different from those for white and Asian-American youth. Because the standard of doing well for African-American and Latino youth is lower than that of white and Asian-American youth, Latino and African-American teens are, unbeknownst to them, at a severe disadvantage when competing in the college admittance and funding processes. Whereas white and Asian-American youth are likely applying with A's and B's, and in some cases all A's, African-American and Latino students' records probably include several C's. Many African-American and Latino youth are as a consequence less likely to get admitted to the better colleges and universities, and further, they are less likely to receive certain forms of financial aid. If the understanding about what it means to be doing well in classes extends throughout their college career, these students could graduate from college with lower GPAs than many white and Asian-American youth, ultimately making them less competitive in the job market.[24]

Another message a large proportion of Latino and African-American youth in our interviews are receiving that distinguishes them from most white and Asian-American youth is that they should get good grades so that they can graduate from high school or get a good job. Grace Kao, drawing on focus-group data, proposes that the aspirations of racial and ethnic minority youth stem from an internalization of stereotypes about their racial or ethnic group.[25] They either try to live up to these images projected onto them, or they try to be the exception. Asian-American youth believe that people have high expectations of them, and they aim to meet these expectations. We see some of this in our interviews. For example, teachers of Asian-American students considered Asian teens the "smart" kids. Asian-American youth internalized this characterization and lived up to it. Kao further proposes that African-American youth primarily aim to avoid failing. They are focused less on doing well than on not doing poorly. Latino youth believe society sees Latinos as manual laborers. The goal of Latino youth is to not follow this path.

Similar to Kao, we suggest that to better understand the role of attitudes in academic achievement, it is important to talk to youth in more depth. However, our interview findings suggest slightly different reasons for why African-American and Latino youth aspire to achieve academically. We did not hear African-American and Latino youth talk in terms of racial or ethnic stereotypes. They were not motivated to avoid a particular path or identity but rather to assume one—as a high school graduate or employed person. These reasons—which nearly half of the African-American and Latino interviewees together give for getting good grades—demonstrate that a substantial proportion of youth of color are not being explicitly socialized into the college process. Despite understanding that college is important and talking about going to college someday, they do not directly connect high school achievement to college, and they lack the kinds of concrete information needed to make college a reality for them. Further, since the academic standard that underlies the reasons these youth care a lot about doing well in school is *relatively* low, they are not likely to be sufficiently concerned about maintaining grade levels that are necessary for college admittance. This could severely limit or even eliminate the opportunities for many African-American and Latino youth to go to college, let alone get a good-paying job after high school. If these youth were socialized differently, that is, given knowledge about the *specific* role that high school achievement has in college admittance and funding, and then trained in the steps needed to get into college, they would gain a better understanding of the implications of good grades for postsecondary education, and some might be motivated to maintain or strive for better grades.

Why are youth receiving different messages about academic achievement, college, and future aspirations? Our results show that these differences stem, in part, from youths' differing relationships with teachers. Youths' relationships with teachers are important for several reasons. Next to parents, teachers are among the most influential adults in the lives of youth. Youth interact with their teachers on a near daily basis. Teachers' interactions with students are powerful determinants of school performance.[26] Teacher-student bonds can have a positive effect on students' academic achievement. Positive teacher-student bonds are also protective against adolescent deviance; students who report having relationships with their teachers are less likely to participate in school delinquency.[27] Moreover, teachers influence youths' sense of self, act as mentors in many cases, and can provide important advice and direction on matters that parents may be less knowledgeable about or unaware of, such as applying to colleges or taking college entrance exams.

Several factors have been shown to affect teacher-student relations. Race and ethnicity and class are foremost among them. Teachers have been to shown to

possess less positive views of minority youth than white youth.[28] More specifically, white teachers, particularly those from middle-class backgrounds, have
less favorable views of racial and ethnic minority and working- or lower-class
students than their white and middle-class students. African-American teachers
tend to have more favorable views and greater achievement expectations of African-American students than do white teachers.[29] Actually, African-American
teachers expect more of their students, regardless of racial and ethnic status,
than do white teachers.[30] Still, teachers generally do tend to negatively evaluate
their African-American students. They perceive them as not making enough effort on their schoolwork and being more frequently disruptive than other students.[31] While race and socioeconomic status affect teachers' views of students,
this does not appear to be the case for students' views of teachers. At least from
evidence based on survey measures, there is little variation in students' views
of their teachers, regardless of their racial and socioeconomic background.[32]
Survey results show that students generally view their teachers rather positively.
For example, on a scale from 1 to 5, where 5 is most positive, students give their
teachers an average score of between 3.7 and 3.8, depending on the race of the
student.[33] Taken together, existing studies suggest that students' views of teachers
and teachers' views of students are incongruent, at least for minority students.

What we found in our interviews, however, is that when given the opportunity to expand their views about teachers, teens' attitudes about teachers are
more consistent with what might be expected from the survey-based studies of
teachers' attitudes about students. Teachers and white students have mutual,
trusting relationships. Teachers invest in the lives of white youth, and these
investments affect white youths' views on education and their future aspirations, and subsequently their academic achievement. White youth have access
to valuable information and support through the social capital that exists in
their relationships with teachers. Their teachers encourage them to do better
in school and give them information about college. If need be, teachers tutor
them outside of class. White youth respond to the support and encouragement
from their teachers in kind by working to improve their grades and doing what
they should to prepare for college. This is not to say that other influences, like
parents, are not equally or more important for white youth; but teachers of
white youth are key partners with parents in ways they are not with the families
of youth of color. These partnerships facilitate favorable outcomes for white
youth, such as good grades and a focus on college. White youth are socialized
by both parents and teachers to go to college. They are on a path toward college

without knowing or caring where the path may ultimately lead them. But they understand and trust that they should be on it.

Asian-American, African-American, and Latino youth are quite familiar with the dominant narrative about education—that college is an important goal. However, unlike white youth, Asian-American, Latino, and African-American youths' socialization about the role school should have in their lives and future aspirations comes almost exclusively from their parents, as well as other significant sources (extended family, peers, and so on). From these relationships they learn why they should do well in school and what their academic standards should be. Schools, through teachers, do not invest in the academic progress and future of African-American, Latino, and Asian-American youth as they do for white students. In fact, there is some evidence that the structure of high schools works to diminish the aspirations of African-American and Latino adolescents. Youth across racial and ethnic backgrounds begin high school with plans to attend college, but tracking systems and poor counseling discourage students of color from pursuing higher education.[34] Still, racial and ethnic minority youths' specific understanding about school and their future varies depending on their structural circumstances, such as neighborhood conditions, socioeconomic status, and family structure. Since these structural circumstances are racialized, some racial and ethnic minorities are more equipped to actualize their aspirations than are other minorities. For example, Asian-American youth, who disproportionately come from two-parent, upper-middle-class families, have access to greater human capital than many African-American and Latino youth, specifically to the kind of social capital that facilitates socioeconomic upward mobility. These resources protect Asian-American youth from poor academic achievement. They aid in the transmission of valuable information about the role of school for college and the more financially lucrative and prestigious career paths.[35] Moreover, the families of Asian-American youth are more likely to have the financial capital to support their children's aspirations for a college education.[36] Conversely, the financial strain and deteriorating neighborhoods that Latino and African-American families disproportionately experience hinder youth like Sylvia, who said she lives in a "messed up" neighborhood, from engaging in the educational process and realizing upward mobility.[37]

Schools, through teachers, then play an essential role in the success of white youth, both in school and after graduating, by performing critical manifest and latent functions in their lives. While in school, white youth are taught academic material, a manifest function that is largely taken for granted. Latent functions, like hands-on help in their courses, encouragement to participate in school activities and get good grades, and information about the college admittance process, are also provided to white youth. Lower socioeconomic status is one of the main factors that precipitate lower academic achievement among all youth regardless of their racial and ethnic backgrounds.[38] Therefore, under circumstances in which a white youth does not have the benefits of middle-class status or for whatever reasons is not getting appropriate direction from other resources, these latent functions of schools are filling critical gaps. For white youth schools are bridging the class divide. Schools place white youth, regardless of their socioeconomic status, on a trajectory toward success, one that facilitates collegiate, career, and financial advancement.

Minority youth see schools as institutions that exist to fulfill the manifest function of teaching them academic material. They rarely speak of the latent functions that are offered to white students. Personal support, academic direction, scholastic encouragement—these resources are not readily available to African-American, Latino, or Asian-American youth. Youth of color, no matter their academic achievement, involvement in school activities, or socioeconomic status, are rarely helped by their schools to, for example, improve their grades or understand the college admittance process. Therefore, other institutions, particularly the family, become paramount for the success of these youth. Whereas schools share the burden with parents for nurturing white youth, the families of minority youth must undertake this task on their own or enlist other family members or organizations, like churches, to help. Survey-based studies support this. Parental involvement in the lives of African-American, Latino, and Asian-American youth has a particularly important impact on these youths' educational attitudes and aspirations.[39] While extended family or churches are likely better than schools for emotional nurturance, schools are arguably better at academic nurturance. When families and their support networks do not have access to the kinds of social capital necessary for understanding the role of high school in attending college or grasping the college admittance process, minority youths' academic and career success are severely minimized. Processes such as this highlight the salience of race and ethnicity and explain why white lower- and working-class youth can often outperform African-American and Latino youth academically.

Moreover, white youth learn through school—the main institution in which youth interact—that public institutions are generally places which advocate for them, care about their well-being, and provide them with tools to navigate society. Relationships that white youth have with teachers are also quite friendly in many cases, suggesting a kind of mutuality. In addition to receiving academic guidance and tutoring, white youth can talk to their teachers about personal matters. They may even visit their teachers' homes. Having these sorts of ties with teachers tells white youth that they can expect to engage public institutions. Schools, through teachers, are incorporating white youth into the core of society. As these youth move into adulthood, they will be more comfortable participating and leading in the business world as well as civic life. They will understand that society is meant to work for them.

Meanwhile, for youth of color, although schools do not fulfill the latent functions of emotional support, encouragement, and providing important information, they are fulfilling another latent function for these students, one that also has implications for the perpetuation of racial inequality. Our interviews reveal that the main latent function schools fulfill for African-American, Asian-American, and Latino youth is teaching them discipline and appropriate behavior. Recall from interviews these youth sharing that good teachers make them "responsible for their actions," "tell [them] what [they] have to do," and "discipline [them] and show [them] how to act." White youth did not talk about teachers fulfilling this role in their lives. While teachers are engaging in mutual, supportive, helpful relationships with white youth—ones that make these youth feel valued and cared for, foster upward social and economic mobility, and ultimately prepare them for roles as private and civic leaders—African-American, Asian-American, and Latino teens are learning that institutions exist to teach them how to behave and to keep them in line. Research shows that adolescents and young adults of color are less likely than majority youth to be civically engaged through community service, extracurricular school activities, or other voluntary organizations.[40] The latent function of teaching discipline reinforces, or may even help to generate, the limited civic participation of minority youth. African-American, Latino, and Asian-American youth are taught by their school experience that public institutions are places that disseminate information and establish boundaries for people. These youth are to submit to the authority of public institutions; they do not have nor should they expect the privilege of engaging public institutions or changing them for their personal benefit. In the end, minority youth are taught that they occupy a subordinate place in society. They come to understand that public institutions do not exist for *them*. As adults, they may be less likely to participate in civic life and challenge public social structures. And they will likely be less equipped to assume positions of authority in the political and business communities.

5 RELIGION
Developing Beliefs, Experiences, and Practices

Well some stuff, I just think couldn't happen, so I would not really care about that, but I take what I can from religion.
—Tim Hirano, 17, Asian-American

Although a growing body of literature within the sociology of religion shows generally positive outcomes of religious belief and practice among youth,[1] these rarely place the role of religion in comparison with other areas of youths' lives or compare differences across racial and ethnic groups, as we do in this book. This is unfortunate, as religion—including beliefs, practices, and institutional involvement—provides a rich and important area to investigate, particularly as it relates to how teens of different racial and ethnic groups are socialized and thus understand the world, and their place in it. Further, when we investigate minority youths' involvement in religion, and the effects of such involvement, it is with the understanding that this institution is central to the culture, identity, and social cohesion of their communities. More so than other social institutions, religion provides minority groups the chance to fully lead and govern their own organizations. In this chapter we investigate three areas of the religious lives of teens: *religious beliefs, religious experiences and practices,* and *experience in religious institutions.* These aspects of religious life serve as arenas where teens' experiences with, beliefs about, and behavior in other social institutions, such as family, peers, and schools, are reinforced. In what they believe, how they practice their beliefs, and how they are involved in their religious institutions youths can "try out" or exercise their agency in different ways.

As with each of the institutions we have explored thus far in this book—family, peers, and school—American teenagers exhibit broad similarities in how they think about, understand, and practice religion, regardless of their race or ethnicity. For example, most teens believe in a personal God, who is involved in people's lives. About half of all teens attend religious services at least two or three times a month. A majority of teens, regardless of their race or ethnicity, "maybe or definitely" believe in life after death and in miracles from God. A majority also believe that many religions may be true, yet they are interested in learning more about their own religion. However, despite such similarities, interesting and important differences between the four racial and ethnic groups suggest that the role religion plays in the lives of teens varies at least in part with their race or ethnicity (see Table 5.1 later in chapter). On further analysis of our data, we found that the differences between racial and ethnic groups were still statistically significant when controlling for other factors, such as income, age, and gender (see Appendix C).

A consistent pattern across racial and ethnic groups is expressed in a variety of ways in each of the three areas we investigated. African-American teens are consistently the most religious as defined by personal beliefs, attendance at services, and participation in congregational activities. Asian-American teens are consistently the least religious, and more than teens in other racial and ethnic groups they tend to defer to their parents' wishes in such things as participating in religious services or performing certain religious rituals—regardless of whether they actually believe the same things as their parents or whether they want to attend services. White and Latino teens are consistently between the poles represented by African-American and Asian-American teens, yet there are important differences between these two groups as well. Latino teens' beliefs and participation in religious institutions tend to revolve around their families; they often conceive of their church as an extension of their family or cite concrete examples of religion bringing about family solidarity. White teens are the most individualistic about their religious participation in that they consistently express their beliefs, experiences, practices, and involvement with religious institutions in words that emphasize the personal benefits that result.

KEESHA WILLIAMS

Keesha Williams is a sixteen-year-old African-American girl living in a suburb of a large city on the West Coast. She is dressed casually but neatly and has long curly hair and an engaging smile. By her own admission she is talkative, and several times during the interview she asked questions about the information we were collecting, and what our plans for it were. Keesha lives with her dad and younger brother, and sometimes her older sister lives with them as well. Her mother and father divorced when she was very young; when Keesha was thirteen, her mother died. She says "it's really crummy" that she doesn't have a mom, and she misses having her around at this time in her life. She remains close to her father, who she says is moody. Her way of dealing with the problems in her life has been to reach out to others and help them with their problems. She says this is just her reaction to "a lot of problems in my life and the whole broken home thing; I just reacted to it differently than they did. Instead of needing someone else to take care of me, I decided to act out by taking care of other people."

In many ways this perspective seems like a natural outgrowth of Keesha's religious commitments and moral code. Keesha's father is a Jehovah's Witness, but she says he put no pressure on her or her siblings to follow that faith:

Me and my family, we're Jehovah's Witnesses. My Dad has never forced religion on us; he's exposed us to the religion, but he made it clear that he wasn't gonna make us do anything and that we had to make a stand for ourselves and decide what we wanted to do. So I decided to be Jehovah's Witness.

Keesha's commitment to her religious beliefs and her determination to have them as a central organizing feature of her life is apparent as she describes different aspects of her faith. She says she "believes in organized religion. I believe that you can serve God in your own way, but you need other people as a sort of support group, because it is hard to do, and if you don't have those other people around to help you out, you falter and you fall short of what you're supposed to be doing." She says too that their shared faith helps to bring her family closer together: "I think it keeps us closer together. Like when things are bothering us, we'll, you know, we'll think about it; we'll think about the religion and like we're all supposed to be serving God together, and we can't do that if we're all apart and bickering, so, yeah, it brings us closer together."

Keesha attends services three times each week and often spends her weekends with other Jehovah's Witnesses knocking on doors and telling people about her faith. For Keesha, her faith forms the basis of her life, both religiously and morally:

INTERVIEWER: Do you think of yourself as a religious or spiritual person?
RESPONDENT: Yes.
I: In what ways?
R: My moral standards and values are based on the Bible; I read the Bible every week;

I go to church three times a week; my religion is a major part of my life, and it really affects the decisions I make and how I live my life.

I: When you think about God, what do you think of? Who or what is God to you?

R: Creator of earth, loving, powerful, wise, just, fair.

I: Do you think of God as personal or impersonal?

R: Personal.

I: Do you think of God as more loving and forgiving or demanding and judging or something else?

R: Loving and forgiving.

I: How did you get these ideas about God?

R: By reading the Bible and looking at examples of times that he has loved and forgiven, and, think about it, like, all the bad stuff that humans do, we wouldn't stand a chance if he was really that judgmental; there would really be no point to our existence, 'cause we mess up so much and so often, there'd be no point.

Keesha maintains her beliefs despite the fact that she feels "very different" from students her age because of these beliefs: "Jehovah's Witnesses always stick out in school like a sore thumb 'cause they are different from everyone else because they don't do the smoking and the drinking and drugs or the partying or the dating or the, the, any of it, so we really stick out, and so people don't like us goody-two-shoe Witnesses." In the end, Keesha's approach to religion is very much her outlook on life. When asked what she thought was valuable or important in religion, she replied:

A very firm belief in what you're doing. I mean, if you're in a religion just because your family did, or just because whatever, then you're gonna be very unhappy with it; you have to do something that you really believe in. Everyone needs to believe in something, 'cause if you don't believe in anything, I think that's really when you're worse off. When you don't believe anything, then you don't really have hope, and when you don't have hope, then everything's gone; you're not gonna try for anything, which means you're not gonna achieve anything. Because it's like, why bother? I mean your life really has no meaning and has no point, and you can look back and say, see, look my life has no meaning, it has no point. Well, no duh, it has no meaning, it has no point because you never gave it any direction, you never believed anything, you never tried for anything, so how can you be disappointed when you failed; you never tried!

Keesha is a very determined young woman who has overcome obstacles that other teens might allow to deter them from their goals. She has direction, which she attributes to her religious faith, and as such she seems on track to be a successful young woman as she continues through high school and on to college.

TIM HIRANO

Tim Hirano is a seventeen-year-old Asian-American boy who lives in a quiet suburb of a major city in the southwest. He arrived at the afternoon interview directly from taking his SAT exam, wearing shorts, a sweatshirt, and a knit cap with the name of his high school wrestling team on it. He is a short but strong guy, and had his right arm in a sling from recent surgery for a wrestling injury. Tim lives with his parents, his younger sister, and one of his older twin brothers. Tim is quiet but funny, and many of his answers to questions were short and to the point. He feels "pretty close, I guess" to his parents. Although he doesn't talk much to them about his life, he says he could share pretty much anything with them if he really needed to.

Tim grew up Buddhist, and when asked whether he believed as his parents do or has any different beliefs, he says, "I don't really mind religion, kinda." When asked whether he thought religion was a source of sharing or perhaps of conflict in his home, Tim says, "I think it's sharing the same sort of thing, 'cause I think if I told them I wanted to be Christian, they would really go against that," but he couldn't really identify any ways that religion affected the life of his family:

I: Do you think there is anything else about religion that affects the quality of relationships within your family?

R: I don't.

I: Do you think your family relationships are affected by faith or spiritual factors in any way?

R: Maybe, I don't know.

I: Maybe?

R: Like moral wise, like certain things we talk about and, ah, it might like influence certain ways to act around people, I guess.

Tim doesn't think of himself as a religious or spiritual person. He doesn't believe in God and thinks that Buddhism is about "how to live your life in the morally pretty well-off way. So I think it's about morals and how to live life for something." He does go to temple services, "probably maybe once or twice a month," although that's because his parents "probably make me go." He says that religion isn't that central in his life:

I: How important do you think your religion is in your life?

R: I don't think it's that important because I think if it was probably my choice, I wouldn't go to services.

I: What are some ways, if any, that you would say your religion influences you?

R: Just how to live.

Tim also occasionally attends a youth group sponsored by his temple, and when asked whether his life would be any different if he weren't involved, he said, "I think it would be same."

In general, Tim's approach to religion is that although he does see some benefit in it, at least in teaching him basic morals, he can't believe everything Buddhism—or any religion, for that matter—teaches: "All religions have something that you can believe in, and then there's something that just makes you say, 'What are you talking about?'" He says that he's taking what he can from his religion that "maybe answers some question I have or how to deal with certain things," but that some of what it teaches "just couldn't happen."

Tim seems to be a well-adjusted young man who is doing well in school, has lots of friends, and is involved in the life of his school. His religious beliefs have provided a way for him to develop a basic moral outlook on life that likely will stand him in good stead in the future. His primary goal in the religious aspects of his life, however, is more about pleasing his parents, or at least avoiding conflict with them over religious issues, than in delving into any substantive issues in Buddhism.

MARIA GONZALEZ

Maria Gonzalez is a sixteen-year-old Latina who lives in a small town in the West with her parents and her younger sister. She has thick, dark hair and dark brown eyes and says that she "gets to do a lot of stuff, but not without my parents knowing." She is involved in her school chorus, dance, and track—"good things," she says—and her favorite activities are to sing and dance. She has a very close relationship with her parents, saying that they never fight and that she can talk to them about anything. Although she says that she and her sister "get along pretty well," she does admit that they have fights over small things which siblings tend to fight over. As she says, "Well, you know, we are sisters!"

Maria was raised Catholic and says her family "used to go to church every day," but since they changed parishes they go to mass once every two or three weeks. She and her sister are involved in a youth group that she enjoys and attends every week. Maria says that although her parents are a big influence in her going to church, if it were totally up to her she would attend both the youth group and mass "about the same" as she currently does. She enjoys attending her church and says that it's "kind of like one big family," a place that is warm and welcoming, "you know, family, where they know you and you know them; you know you can go to them if you need anything."

Maria's religious beliefs are "pretty similar" to her parents' beliefs, and she thinks that religion is a source of sharing and togetherness in her family. Her ideas about God and religion come from her grandmother and from church. She thinks of herself as a religious person and says that religion is a "very important" part of her life. For her the most important parts of religion are "just believing and prayer," and she says that the core of her beliefs as a Catholic is that "God is everywhere, you know, helping. He's there when you need him; things happen for a reason." Being the kind of religious person she wants to be is "pretty easy and natural. It's not really a struggle for me 'cause I'm not looking at going to deep, deep, deep religion, you know. I think I'm fine where I'm at."

Besides attending mass and the youth group, Maria maintains her spiritual practice through prayer and reading the Bible. She says that prayer "gives me a relief of things, you know. I can take all my problems and stresses and just let them out, so it's kind of a release of things." When asked what sorts of things she prays for, she says, "the sick, the hungry, you know, anybody who's in need, for my family, my friends, really anybody who needs help."

Although Maria believes that people can be religious or spiritual without being involved in a church—that "you could do things on your own"—she says that "it's nice to be with others at a church and praise together." Going to services for her is about being with everybody else, not just on her own: "It's like praying with everybody, you know; it's more of where you're all connected, where it's not just individually, you know; it's nice to be with a lot of people."

She says she doesn't "think only one religion is just right," because "there's no say so and there's nothing written down that just one religion is truth. It could be many religions—not many, but a few religions." For Maria, in the end, it's really up to individuals and what they decide: "I just think it's however they feel."

LISA PETERSON

Lisa Peterson is a sixteen-year-old white student who has lived in a small town in the South all her life. She has fair skin, blue eyes, long brown hair, and a medium build. She is rather shy, and throughout the interview she mentions how much things "scare" her, such as what might—or might not—happen the next day, whether she'll be accepted at school, or whether she'll get a big assignment that she may have trouble completing. She lives with her mother and stepfather for one week and then with her father the next, alternating weekly throughout the year. Lisa also has two stepsisters who live in a neighboring state, whom she gets along with well, although she sees them only every other weekend. Everyone, she says, gets along in her family, even her divorced mother and father, but she's closest to her mother, whom she "tells everything" and whom she considers her best friend.

Lisa was raised Pentecostal and says that she's religious and believes in God, but that she isn't "a big religious person where I go around preaching all the time." She thinks that to be a religious person means to be faithful to your beliefs and to "not be hypocritical, to not say one thing and then do another." When she thinks of God, she "pictures it as happiness; you have nothing to fear because he'll be there . . . I don't know, it's comfortable . . . a person to talk to if you just want to sit there and talk and pray." Lisa says she is struggling somewhat with her religious views. She thinks that maybe she's being a bit of a hypocrite because she has quit going to church, despite the fact that her family has always attended together and that she had recently gone on a missions trip. When asked whether her mother is bothered that she has not attended church in a while and, as she terms it, has "gone astray" lately, she says, "I haven't talked to her about it, but I guess she sees that I have. She hasn't said anything yet, I guess." Lisa does want to, as she says, "get back on the path," and she sees the value of religion if one believes that "God, Jesus, he died on the cross for us so that we could live, and I think that we should believe and love him for that." For Lisa, believing this will serve to "help us to stay on the right path, I think; and at some points you will probably stray away like I have, and you gotta be faithful and believe and have faith that he'll help you through everything. Just stay on the path."

Lisa frames her religious experiences and practices in terms of how they serve to make her "happy" or "comfortable"—when she does them. She says that feeling close to God is having "a personal relationship with him, tell him everything and just talk, like person to person." She went on a mission trip to Central America and had a "great feeling . . . was extremely happy, very comfortable" when she saw that her drama group "got through to them about God." Spiritual practices such as praying, reading the Bible, and going to the youth group or church largely depend on her fitting them into a schedule of school and sports, "if she's not too tired from doing homework." But when she does read the Bible and pray, she says that:

It helps me out throughout the day, because I think I didn't fear the rest of the day, 'cause usually in the morning I don't want tomorrow to come, because like maybe you have a big report you have to read out for the class, and I think if reading and knowing he's going to be with you, every step of the way, you know that you don't have to be scared."

Lisa is an engaging adolescent who repeatedly made reference to being shy and to her fear of engaging in interactions or situations that may cause her to be a little uncomfortable, such as in meeting new people. Her religious beliefs operate a bit like a lifestyle accessory that serves to alleviate her shyness and fear: she knows what she should believe and be doing, but her beliefs and practices are largely in the service of making her feel good and comfortable in her life. She says that when she does pray or read the Bible, she feels like it gives her a sense "that you don't have to be scared."

The teens described here are not necessarily "representative" of their respective race or ethnicity. They do point up similarities in how teens of different groups think and talk about religion and also distinct racial and ethnic patterns in religious belief, participation, practice, and experience, which we found in our data. These differences center not only on how teens of different races and ethnicities understand and articulate their religious (or nonreligious) beliefs but on how they conceive of the role of religion in their lives and what it means to "be of" a particular religious faith. In particular, our findings show significant differences among teens across racial and ethnic groups in three distinct and key areas of religious life: religious beliefs, religious experiences and practices, and experiences in, and relationships to, religious institutions.

ONE, MANY, OR ANY: TEENS' RELIGIOUS BELIEFS

Understanding the religious beliefs of teens provides us with a good idea of how central religion is in teens' view of themselves. Christian Smith has placed teens' religious beliefs in the context of what he calls "moralistic therapeutic deism," which he argues is the dominant expression of beliefs among teens regardless of their religious tradition.[2] In short, moralistic therapeutic deism is the general belief that although God created and watches over the world and wants people to be good and go to heaven, he is somewhat removed from human affairs and functions instead as a type of cosmic butler that people can call on when they have a problem. While we do not disagree with Smith, we argue that despite this general context identifiable patterns of teens' religious beliefs vary by race and ethnicity and provide a more complex story of religion among teens. As noted above, we find generally that African-American teens are at one pole, expressing the highest levels of commitment to their religious beliefs, while Asian-American teens are at the other pole, expressing the lowest levels of commitment to particular beliefs. White and Latino teens are consistently between the two poles. For example, African-American teens are more likely than teens of any other racial or ethnic group to report a belief in God (95%), to say that only one religion is true (31%), to say that their religious faith is very or extremely important in shaping their daily life (63%) and in shaping life decisions (68%), and to believe in a judgment day (86%). Conversely, Asian-American teens are more likely to report some or many doubts about their religious beliefs (33%), that it is "okay" to practice one's own religion and another religion (52%), and that it is acceptable to pick and choose one's religious beliefs (60%). As just noted, white and Latino teens fall consistently between the responses of African-American and Asian-American teens. This remains true for third-plus-generation Latinos, although there is a slight tendency for them to show that religion is becoming less central in their lives, to think that picking and choosing religious beliefs is acceptable, and to express doubts about their beliefs. However, their responses remain within a few percentage points of other Latinos and white teens (see Table 5.1[3]).

In interviews, African-American teens exhibit an understanding of their religious beliefs that is in stark contrast to that of teens of other races and ethnicities. African-American teens tend to have the most hierarchical view of religion, in that they regularly express their respect for the authority of religion and its place in their lives, whether they are referencing God or their faith in general. When asked their views of God, African-American teens referenced a God who is above everything else and who is constantly watching over everything. Take for example these responses from a sixteen-year-old male:

I: Do you believe in God?

R: Yeah.

I: When you think about God, what do you think about?

R: I think about like this Almighty person that made heaven and earth and stuff. I think like he's the, the highest of the highest; it doesn't go no higher than him.

Or this thirteen-year-old female:

I: When you think about God, what do you think of?

R: I think of like a man who's up there, watching over everybody, but he particularly watches me, and he's waiting on me to apologize for something that I did that day.

I: Why do you think God is particularly watching you?

R: Because I think everybody feels that way, when they, when they look at they-self

TABLE 5.1

Teen Religious Beliefs by Race/Ethnicity

Percentage of teens who . . .	White	African-American	Asian-American	Latino (generation)				Total
				All	First	Second	Third+	
Believe in God	81	95	65	87	91	85	87	84
Believe in a personal God who is involved in people's lives	64	70	50	61	56	68	58	64
Maybe or definitely believe in miracles from God	90	94	86	91	91	92	90	91
Say religious faith is very or extremely important in shaping life decisions	46	63	38	47	55	43	47	49
Say it's okay to practice your religion plus another	41	31	52	39	40	34	42	39
Say it's okay to pick and choose religious beliefs	48	39	60	49	44	49	50	47
Believe only one religion is true	28	31	24	23	33	28	17	28
Believe many religions may be true	62	59	60	67	53	55	67	61
Have some or many doubts about religious beliefs	16	17	33	18	16	14	21	16

Source: NSYR survey.

Note: All differences between racial/ethnic groups are significant at $p < .01$ (Pearson's chi-square test). $N = 3,224$.

and think of God; they like, 'Oh God, he see me doing that today' and stuff like that. Like he's looking at you like, time's ticking; I'm waiting on my apology—stuff like that.

I: Do you feel like you have stuff that you need to apologize to God about?

R: Like days when I sin, when I might curse or something like that, when people get on your nerves, so I feel that I should apologize for doing that. Or doing something that my mother doesn't want me to do, and I did it already, so, I apologize, please forgive me for disobeying my mother today.

This view of God as the "highest of the high" does not, however, seem to create a distance between African-American teens and God. Rather, the responses from teens expressing their belief that God was in charge and perhaps waiting to judge them also included references to love and, in some cases, comparisons to family. For example, one seventeen-year-old, when asked what it meant for him to think of himself as a religious or spiritual person, said, "I believe in God ... that I'm promised eternal love." Similarly, a seventeen-year-old teen framed her responses this way:

I: Do you believe in God?

R: Yes. Very much.

I: When you think about God, what do you think of?

R: Peace.

I: Do you tend to see God as personal or impersonal?

R: I see God as my daddy.

I: As your daddy?

R: Oh, yeah. A father figure that I don't really have. So, um, yeah. Personal.

African-American teens also emphasized how they believed that God was active in their lives and how central their religious beliefs were in their day-to-day lives. When asked if he thought of God as personal or impersonal, close or distant, this seventeen-year-old replied, "He's close; he's here with us right now." When asked how important his faith was in his life, he said, "It's key ... it keeps me going. Like if your faith is strong, ain't too much else to worry about. Like if you got faith, a lot of good will come to you, and you have faith that bad won't. That's how I look at it." A seventeen-year-old, when asked what she thought was valuable in religion, said, "Love for others, respect. I think that religion is basically an everyday thing. The things you come in contact with every day, people, knowing how to be respectful, just being like Christ. Trying to imitate what he has done. Yeah, I think that's very valuable, love. Just overall treating others like you would want to be treated."

Although most American teens, regardless of race or ethnicity, believe that many religions may be true, African-American teens are the least likely to say that it's fine to practice one's own religion and another, or that it's "okay" to pick and choose beliefs from one's own religion (see Table 5.1). When asked this question in interviews, African-American teens often responded as this sixteen-year-old male did:

I: Some people think that it's okay for people to pick and choose religious beliefs however they want to without having to accept their religious teachings as a whole, or the religion they're a part of. Do you agree or disagree?

R: I disagree.

I: Why?

R: 'Cause you shouldn't be like, picking and choosing different religions; that's kinda like playing with God and making him mad and stuff 'cause, you know, there's a God, but some people they believe in different gods and different stuff, but I think you should believe in the one and only God, because he's the one who made the earth and stuff.

A sixteen-year-old female answered similarly:

If you're gonna dedicate your life to something, if you're gonna believe in something, if you're gonna worship something, it's not about you. It's about whatever it is that you're worshiping, so if you're gonna do it, you should do it right. Don't pick the beliefs of this one because that can fit around my schedule, or the ceremonies of this religion really work for me. That's not real worshiping, because you're not sacrificing anything; you're just picking what you want to do and creating your own universe, and it's like, it doesn't work that way; you can't dedicate your life to yourself. You can't design the way you want to worship.

In contrast to African-American teens, white teens exhibit a belief system that is highly personalized and that appears easily customizable, depending on their own judgments about what they want to believe. Further, they rarely acknowledge any external authority in religion, instead relying on their own judgment. Certainly, many teens say they believe in God and recognize parents and religious leaders as important, but these views tend to be framed in terms of "friendship," not unlike the people they usually hang out with, or as someone or something that is always there to help when they need it.

Most striking in this regard is the ability of white teens to customize their beliefs primarily on what *they* judge to be true or acceptable. One fourteen-year-old Baptist teen from the southeast, in explaining what he meant when he said he was a spiritual person, said, "Go to church; believe what you want to believe; believe what you think is real and not real, and stuff like that." This is not all that different from what a sixteen-year-old from the Midwest, who is a practicing Wiccan, explained in her answer to the same question: "I don't really follow anything too much, but I do basic principles and morals and stuff; like, with paganism, it's karma. That's the thing that's gonna get you. Do whatever you want, but whatever you do is gonna come back to you. And like if you do something bad, something bad's gonna happen to you, so that's something that I like to try to think about before I do things, you know." Or this seventeen-year-old Baptist female from Florida: "Very many people know that I believe that there is a God; they know that I pray and whatnot, but I don't believe that you should go to church every week; I don't believe that there's a certain way or a certain place to express your religion or your spirituality, I mean, no matter where you are."

Even when trying to articulate how important religion is in their lives, particularly whether it regularly influences them, they emphasize their personal authority and selecting what they think are the important influences:

I: How important or central do you think your religion or spirituality is in your life?

R [fourteen-year-old white Baptist male]: Very important. It shapes how I live; it guides me.

I: What are some examples of ways you would say your faith influences you?

R: The Ten Commandments, I try to follow them.

I: What's an example in your daily life when the Ten Commandments have influenced you?

R: Um, keep the Sabbath day holy.

I: So, what does that mean? What have you done?

R: Like, I don't want to work much on Sunday. Or overexert myself much. That's one of them.

I: All right, any other?

R: No, not really.

In contrast to African-American teens who have a hierarchical and authoritarian view of religion, white teens evidence a conception of religious authority as one of a friendly presence who is attentive to their needs:

I: Do you believe in God?

R [fourteen-year-old white Baptist male]: Yes.

I: Okay, when you think about God, what do you think of? What kind of image do you have?

R: I don't really have an image. I think of a guy and a beard in a robe.

I: Anything else, like who or what God is to you?

R: He's a role model, what I should be doing in life and, creator, and that's all.

I: Would you say that you feel close to God or not?

R: Yeah, I feel close.

I: In what ways?

R: I pray every night, and I feel safe with myself. I trust in him when I'm afraid.

I. Do you have any particular religious beliefs?

R: Well, I believe there is a God, so sometimes I, sometimes when I'm in trouble or something or in danger, then I'll start thinking about that.

A fourteen-year-old Presbyterian explains his relationship to God,

> I: Would you say that you feel close to God?
>
> R: Well, not as much close as able to get along with. Um, not close one-on-one but being protected overall; everybody is, really.

This seventeen-year-old Baptist talks about her understanding of God:

> I: What is God like to you?
>
> R: I believe that, you know, that he forgives us when we do wrong. I believe that he believes in forgiving people and, um, just that he's there to guide us, I guess, and he's there for somebody to talk to and help us through our problems.

And this seventeen-year-old Latter-Day Saint frames how he feels close to God:

> I: Um, would you say that you feel close or not close to God?
>
> R: I feel very close.
>
> I: In what ways?
>
> R: It's hard to describe. Just, um, I just feel close to him because, well, I can kind of feel him.
>
> I: What are some examples from your life of feeling this way?
>
> R: Ah, examples from my life? Well, I just, um, get a sudden feeling all day long that feels, well, like he feels, and I'm pretty sure it's him.

In their religious beliefs white teens exhibit a particularly individualistic perspective that in many ways suggests that God is there to serve their needs, whether through forgiving them or making them feel better. God is like a friend who is available whenever the teen feels a need to call but who doesn't require much commitment in return.

Latino teens are similar to white teens in that their beliefs can be framed by individual choice as to what they believe and what they find important in religion. For example, this fourteen-year-old, who had recently begun attending mass and confirmation classes at his parish, said, "Religion is whatever you want it to be. If you want it to be good, I mean, to be nice or to be real strict, you could do that, 'cause no one's going to tell you you can't, 'cause it is a free country, you know. And I think that's all right." He continued that he thought it would be all right for people to practice more than one religion "because some people have their own beliefs, and you could be going into a religion that doesn't even match with what you want to believe in. You know, there could be another religion out there for you."

Yet despite this emphasis on a personal and customizable set of beliefs, Latino teens are also highly influenced by their families in what they believe, and their beliefs often have a familial quality to them. That is, family tends to be the dominant authority through which religious beliefs and involvement are viewed:

I: Do you believe in God?

R [seventeen-year-old Catholic Latina]: Yeah, I do.

I: When you think about God, what do you think of?

R: God is like another dad for me.

I: Another dad?

R: Yeah. Well, it's like my first dad, you know, you could say that.

Or this eighteen-year-old Catholic Latino:

I: Do you believe in God?

R: Yeah.

I: When you think about God, who or what is God to you?

R: I don't know, sort of like a father figure, but like the perfect father figure, like the person that will love me no matter what the personal situation I'm in, the person that's gonna stand by you no matter what, and that's what I think; that's what I see in him.

I: Where do your ideas about God come from?

R: Come from my parents. Um, that's where they all originate. And, before my grandma passed away, she was a big influence. And she was the one that really pushed, you know, the whole religion, and, you know, I, being Catholic, is something my parents taught me through church; I always prayed; there wasn't a time when I didn't.

Similarly, this seventeen-year-old Latino, who says that his family no longer "regularly attends church" since his first communion, at age 10, maintained that religion was a source of sharing with his family. When asked what had been important influences on his religious beliefs, he said simply, "Family."

Similar to Latino teens, the religious beliefs of Asian-American teens are also related to expectations from their families, specifically from their parents, for them to participate in religious life in the same way they do. In this, Asian-American teens appear to be the most "adaptable" in their beliefs, seeking to please their parents on the one hand, generally by attending religious services and being involved in their congregations, while on the other, approaching their beliefs fairly pragmatically, which allows them to decide what they want to include in their own set of beliefs. That is, their beliefs are tied to the authority of their parents' expectations, but they seem willing and able to select what "works for them" out of the available beliefs and to leave out what they're not particularly interested in.

This sort of detached, pragmatic approach to religion came out in the interviews of Asian-American teens we interviewed and echoes what we heard from other teens, but with the additional suggestion that they select what they choose to believe with an eye toward meeting their parents' religious expectations. For example, this fourteen-year-old Asian-American Christian, who has been attending church "pretty much my whole life," says that his beliefs are "not very different" from his parents' religious beliefs. He says that his dad has "views on all these different theological topics" but he would rather not "really go into theology and all that stuff." He says that he doesn't "like going into all the details; I just like to keep it simple." But he says, "I believe with my whole heart about the stuff I do believe in, though." Similarly, this fourteen-year-old Asian-American female attends services along with her parents whenever they go and says she believes in God. When she thinks of God,

I guess it's just kind of an idea for me; I don't know if there's an actual person or being or something like that; I guess I just have an idea of something greater than us. I don't think it can really like control us or anything; I think it's just something we kind of need, like for comfort or support, just to know that there's something out there that's greater than us that can protect us or hurt us or whatever.

When asked whether people could pick and choose their religious beliefs, she said, "I agree with that. I mean, 'cause there's stuff in my religion that I don't agree with. So if I had to believe in everything, I wouldn't be very happy, and I think religion is something that you have to choose on your own; like you can't be forced to do it; you have to choose it, and be happy with it."

Perhaps the most interesting framing we heard for this approach was from a sixteen-year-old Hindu male, whose religion was primarily an identity marker rather than something he practiced on his own. He did perform rituals with his parents but said that if not for them, he would not participate in religion at all:

I: What religion, if any, do you consider yourself to be now?

R: Miscellaneous.

I: Miscellaneous. Okay. What would you say are some of the main beliefs in your family?

R: Nothing, really, just hard work. My parents really believe in hard work, so it's one of the things that really affects me.

In summary, Asian-American teens evidence a more pragmatic approach to their religious beliefs. On the one hand, they seem committed to their parents' religious expectations for them, while on the other, they manage to select the beliefs that make the most sense for them, despite their parents' expectations.

PRAYERS AND MIRACLES: RELIGIOUS EXPERIENCE
AND PRACTICE

The religious experiences and practices of American teens mirror the patterns of their religious beliefs. Although white and African-American teens are about equally likely to have had a "powerful worship experience," African-American teens are much more likely to have had a variety of religious experiences and to engage in numerous spiritual practices than are white, Latino, or Asian-American teens. For example, African-American teens are more likely to have received a "definite answer to prayer" (61%), to have experienced a miracle (64%), to feel very or extremely close to God (50%), or to have ever committed to live their life for God (70%) than white, Latino, or Asian-American teens (see Table 5.2).

Teens' responses to questions about their religious and spiritual *practices* show a similar pattern. African-American teens are more likely to pray alone at least once each day (50%), read Scripture alone at least once each week (36%), have prayer with their families at mealtime (77%), talk about religion with their families (66%), or have prayed together with their families other than at mealtime, than are white, Latino, or Asian-American teens. In fact, as one additional measure of just how integral religion is to these teenagers' lives, African-American teens are far more likely to have listened to religious music in the last year (70%) than are teens from other racial and ethnic groups (Table 5.2).

In interviews African-American teens variously express the importance of religion in their everyday lives, both through diverse experiences they may have had and through a range of practices such as prayer and Bible reading. Prayer is part of the daily life of these teens, and they often pray several times each day. This seventeen-year-old African-American male provides a typical description of the centrality of prayer in the lives of African-American teens:

I: Do you pray?

R: Yeah, I pray.

I: What do you think prayer is?

R: Calling on God, asking him for help. Expressing your feelings, expressing your needs.

I: How often do you pray?

R: I pray every day at some point.

I: What kinds of things do you pray for?

R: Uh, guidance. Strength, like the motivation to keep me going, to keep me focused, at least try to keep me focused at all times.

I: Are your prayers answered?

TABLE 5.2

Teen Religious Practice and Experience by Race/Ethnicity

Percentage of teens who . . .	White	African-American	Asian-American	Latino (generation)				Total
				All	First	Second	Third+	
Practice								
Pray alone at least once per day	34	50	19	39	45	40	36	37
Read scripture alone at least once per week	24	36	15	26	24	28	23	40
Pray with family at mealtime	48	77	29	47	49	51	42	47
Talk with family about religion at least once per week	37	66	33	48	53	53	43	45
Pray together with parents other than at mealtime	37	54	31	45	47	49	42	62
Listened to religious music in the past year	49	70	38	38	37	36	39	51
Experience								
Ever had a powerful spiritual worship experience	54	53	27	37	40	33	39	51
Ever had a definite answer to a prayer	48	61	38	47	53	45	47	50
Ever experienced a miracle	43	64	33	42	47	40	42	47
Feel very or extremely close to God	34	50	23	34	44	34	29	37
Ever committed to live life for God	54	70	29	43	39	46	43	55

Source: NSYR survey.
Note: All differences between racial/ethnic groups are significant at $p < .01$ (Pearson's chi-square test).
$N = 3,224$.

R: Most of the time, yeah, eventually.

I: And how do you feel about praying?

R: It's helpful; it's just, I mean, it's one of the healthy part of my, of my religion; it's like the healthiest parts, you know.

A seventeen-year-old African-American female presents a similar perspective:

I: Do you pray?

R: Yes, I do.

I: What is prayer to you?

R: Having a conversation and listening with the Lord.

I: How often do you pray?

R: Every night, every day, anytime. You know, I got a free second, I'll be like, "Lord, help me." You know, anything, anything is prayer with us.

Bible reading is also an important part of the lives of African-American teens. They read the Bible several times each week and, when asked why, give answers that demonstrate the importance of this practice in their lives. One sixteen-year-old said that he reads the Bible every day because "it gives me wisdom, and certain books show you how to deal with certain situations; like with anger, it shows you how to deal with that, shows you how to deal with lusts and lying and adultery and stuff like that." A seventeen-year-old said that he reads the Bible "two to three times a week" and that for him, "the Bible is like a motivational speaker. It really keeps you going; it's like it's a rush, like a big drive, and it will keep you with it at all times." When asked how important his practices of praying and Bible reading were in his life, he said, "They define me. They sort of mold me to the person I am."

African-American teens evidence a dimension that suggests that their religious beliefs and practices are not only about themselves but about other people, whether family, friends, or even the broader world. For example, when asked what types of things they prayed for, African-American teens would often list first their family, their friends, church, or their community. One teen said he prays for "family issues, for the family to be in unity. I pray for the United States and stuff during the war times, that we'll all be protected and stuff." Similarly, religious experiences, while on one level being about the individual, were often framed beyond the individual:

I: Have you personally had any significant religious experiences?

R: Oh, yeah. Like that really affected me was like, my dad, once I moved in with my grandparents, he told me he didn't want to have nothing else to do with me. And then, I knew it was God that made him change his mind, 'cause now we're really, really, really, really close together now. And he comes almost every other weekend; he comes and picks me up.

I: How did you feel about it?

R: I felt hurt about it, but, um, like my grandmother said, just pray about it and God will figure it out for you, he'll help you; and I said okay, and I prayed about it, and now we're like, me and my Dad are like the bestest friends.

I: Did that change your way of thinking about religion?

R: Oh, yes. It really changed; I was like if God can do that, then he can do other things for me, too.

In contrast to African-American teens, white, Latino, and Asian-American teens are less likely to have personal religious practices such as prayer and Scripture reading or to engage in similar religious practices with their families. In this as with religious beliefs, Asian-American teens are the least likely to pray alone (19%), to read Scripture alone (15%), to pray together with their families other than at mealtime (31%), or to talk about religion with their families once a week (33%). Latino teens are slightly more likely than white teens to engage in these personal and family practices; when we look at successive immigrant generations, we find some differences in practices between generations, but Latino teens are still more likely than white teens to engage in these practices regardless of immigrant generation (Table 5.2).

In the interviews white, Latino, and Asian-American teens express a more personalized religious experience and approach to practice, which is based largely on their personal preferences and desires. As with religious beliefs, white teens report the most individualized experience and practice, and are the least concerned with religious authority and tradition. What seems to be most important to them is that their experiences make them feel good and that their practices are customizable, requiring neither change nor sacrifice on their part for any sort of religious expectations or requirements. This fifteen-year-old Jewish female says that she prays "sometimes, if I want something," although she allows that she doesn't think she's "ever gotten an answer that I felt was from God." Similarly, this sixteen-year-old white respondent said that she prays only "when I need something or when I need guidance or something, you know. Like it doesn't play a big part in my life, but it's still there." When asked what kinds of things she prays for, she said, "I don't know, like whatever I need in my life right now. Like if I need help with which guy I like, which should I go out with, you know, then I'll do that; or if I need help on a test, I'll hopefully ask him to help me to remember everything better."

Similar to white teens, and mirroring their religious beliefs, Latino and Asian-American teens have very personalized practices and experiences, although few report having the latter. For Latino teens the family is again the filter through which their experiences and practices are understood and oriented. Although many Asian-American teens report that they don't have any religious experiences or practices, when they do, their practices tend to be what they believe their parents expect of them. For Latino and Asian-American teens, as

with white teens, there is little if any talk of conforming to a religious authority in their practices or experiences. Rather, for Latino teens experiences and
practices tend to revolve around the family as the locus of authority, while for
Asian-American teens, authority tends to reside with parental expectations.

Among teens of each racial and ethnic group, the importance of family
in their religious understandings is often expressed. This is particularly true
among African-American teens, as we have already heard. But it is striking how
often Latino teens express their religious experiences and their religious practices—in particular, whom and what they pray for—in terms of their families.
As noted above, the family is the locus of authority; religion operates in support of the family. For example, when asked if they have ever had a significant
religious experience, those that have relate a story (usually without hesitation)
about how things worked out well in their family or for a family member. For
example, this fourteen-year-old Latino sees an improvement in his family's financial situation as a result of their faith:

I: Have you personally had any significant religious experiences?

R: Well, recently we've been going through a little bit of a money problem, and I
think some checks have been coming in that don't usually come in. And I think that's
kind of odd. And then we're like getting—my mom's boyfriend owns a company where
he designs, you know, and uh, he's been getting a lot of deals. He went from zero to five
recently, and it looks like, you know, we're in debt, but we're getting pulled up quick. So
it seems like we've got an open road right now. And I think that's because of our faith.

I: How does that make you feel?

R: It makes me feel happy. It makes me feel that there is a God. That's why I have
more of a belief in him. More than ever.

A sixteen-year-old Latina expressed a similar experience with her great-grand-
mother: "There was this time my great-grandma, she was really sick, and I
prayed for her, and it's like a couple of days; I didn't expect for her to get better
the way she did, so I felt that he helped out a lot." These religious experiences
are not particularly spectacular; what is notable is that in response to a question about their *personal* religious experiences these teens relate stories in the
context of their *families*.

This extends as well to how Latino teens tend to pray. When asked whether
they prayed and what they prayed for, often the first item on their prayer list
was family. The same fourteen-year-old just quoted said that he prays "once a
week," some weeks more and some weeks less, and that he prays, "Please, God,
help my mom; help my little brother." Does he think his prayers will be an-

swered? "I think they will be answered not too far along yet. I think that what he does is that he just does a little bit here and there, and the rest is up to us." A seventeen-year-old Latina prays similarly: "Dear God, I just want to thank you that I have a beautiful family. Help my grandparents; help my grandpa in Mexico." Yet when asked how important these practices are in their lives, although some say they are important, most say they are not. One teen said she didn't really know. "I guess I'm just used to it." Once again, others frame the importance of these religious practices in the context of their family:

> I: How important are your religious practices to you?
> R [fourteen-year-old Latino]: They're not really important; well, they're kind of important to me, but they're important to my family because, you know, if I'm doing religious things and my family is too, that means a religious family, so that's kind of what I'm hoping for.
> I: Do you think that these religious practices affect your life?
> R: Um, not really. It, it—it just really brings faith. And I've seen that happen.

Among Asian-American teens many simply reported that they had never had any religious experiences and that they had no religious practices. Those who did report having religious experiences and practices often described them in terms that suggested they were not central in their lives. One fourteen-year-old said that in general she prays only in religious services and religious school so that "It's not really, like a voluntary thing." When asked what she thought prayer was, she replied, "I guess it's like what you hope and what you want, what you dream, what you're thankful for, and what you'd like." She said that when she prayed on her own, she would usually "pray for good fortune, or health for my family, and happiness for my family." She said that in general she didn't think prayer was particularly important but that "if it's important to somebody else or if it makes them feel better, then it's good." When asked if she thought her prayers were answered, she replied, "No."

Other Asian-American teens allowed that their practices had a more central part in their lives. For example, this fourteen-year-old from the northeast prays every day and reads his Bible several times each week. His prayers, he says, consist of him just talking to God, "telling him something I would like to happen or telling him what's bad and I shouldn't do something." He admits that it has been difficult to maintain his Bible reading. "Well, I used to have the chronological Bible that you could read over a year, but I gave up on that after like a month 'cause I didn't have the motivation—maybe not motivation—I didn't have the patience . . . I got to like Leviticus, and then I was just like, this crap!"

ATTENDING OR PRETENDING: RELIGIOUS INSTITUTIONS

The involvement of teens in religious institutions is an important part of how they are influenced by different institutions in their socialization. In many ways, their involvement in and relationship to religious institutions reinforces socialization experiences in other areas of their lives. In how teens experience religious institutions there are many similarities, with only slight differences, across racial and ethnic groups, including second- and third-generation Latinos. For example, about half of all teens attend services at least two or three times a month, with about 20–30 percent of teens across all racial and ethnic groups attending Sunday school every or almost every week. About a third have been in a religious youth group at some time in their life, and about a third are currently involved in a youth group (see Table 5.3).

Yet even with these similarities, when we listen to what these survey responses actually mean to teens, we begin to see differences across different racial and ethnic groups. For example, although a majority of teens attend religious services regularly, as we hear them talk about why they attend or what importance it has in their lives, we hear different responses, which follow along racial and ethnic lines. Asian-American teens, regardless of their religious tradition, report that their involvement in religious institutions seems to be primarily motivated by their parents' expectations for them. Take, for example, this seventeen-year-old Asian-American Buddhist male who regularly attends religious services:

I: How do you feel about going to religious services?

R: I don't know; I don't want to wake up in the morning.

I: Besides getting up too early, are there things that you like or don't like about it?

R: I don't hate it, but I don't like it, either; it's kind of like, there.

I: Why do you go?

R: I don't really know; maybe because mostly my parents want me to go.

I: So your parents are probably the biggest influence in that?

R: Yeah.

I: What kind of influence do they have in whether or not you attend?

R: They probably make me go. Like if I haven't been in a long time, they probably like force me to go.

Another Asian-American teen gives a similar response in regard to performing religious rituals with his parents, explaining, "I wouldn't do them myself, 'cause I don't know how, but I would do them with my parents."

When asked how important activities like attending services or youth group

TABLE 5.3

*Teen Involvement in and Attitudes Toward Religious
Institutions by Race/Ethnicity*

Percentage of teens who ...	White	African- American	Asian- American	Latino (generation)				Total
				All	First	Second	Third+	
Attend services two to three times month	51	51	50	49	48	52	47	51
Attend Sunday school every or almost every week	30	29	19	24	24	31.2	20	28.7
Would attend same congregation as currently attending if up to them*	67	71	63	68	75	68	66	68
Are currently in a religious youth group	41	33	27	25	21	24	27	37
Have ever been in a religious youth group	31	33	35	33	31	33	34	32
Think adults at church are very or somewhat easy to talk to	52	59	44	46	51	41	48	53
Think church is a very or fairly good place to talk about serious issues	46	51	33	42	41	44	42	46

Source: NSYR survey.
Note: All differences between racial/ethnic groups are significant at $p < .01$ (Pearson's chi-square test), except for *, where $p < .10$. $N = 3,224$.

are in their lives, Asian-American teens, while affirming that they enjoyed, for example, belonging to a youth group, also said that being in the group wasn't a very significant part of their lives:

I: Do you enjoy the youth group?
R [seventeen-year-old Asian-American Buddhist male]: Yes.
I: What is it that you get out of it?
R: Meeting people and then meet more friends.

I: How important is the youth group in your life?
R: Not really important; I wouldn't mind if I didn't go or not.
I: Other than meeting friends, is there anything else that is important about the youth group for you?
R: Not really.

I: How, if at all, do you think your life would be different if you were not in the youth group?

R: I think it'd be the same.

Similarly, one fourteen-year-old, who maintained that if attendance were totally up to her, she would "never" go, said, "I don't really feel a need to go. I mean, it doesn't fulfill anything for me." Even for a fourteen-year-old Christian teen whose father is a pastor, participation in his youth group doesn't sound all that important in his life:

I: If you didn't go to youth group, would you feel like something was missing in your life?

R: I mean, I don't do it like every day, but I guess I would have an open Sunday night; I mean, it's not a huge factor.

I: What affect does being part of the youth group have on you?

R: I guess it's just, it's just good to be around like all these Christians like after school and all these crazy people.

In contrast to Asian-American teens, African-American teens exhibit a much stronger affinity for being involved in the life of their church, and a sense of commitment to their church as the best place to gain religious knowledge and direction. In this, African-American teens evidence a commitment to the authority of the church and to their pastors, and an understanding of their participation in the church as a chance to serve both the church and others. This seventeen-year-old African-American from a large city in the southeast describes her church this way:

First off, my denomination is a people denomination. So what I mean by that is, we have only one God. We read the Bible, we believe the Bible, we practice the teachings in the Bible, and when I say people church, a people denomination, it's based on others and helping other people. Volunteering, food drives. A couple of years back, we had over a thousand pairs of tennis shoes sent to Africa, 'cause, you know, they didn't like that whole barefoot idea kind of thing. So, clothing drives, things like that—so we try to help the community here in this city, as well as across countries.

This same teen is very involved in different activities in her church and is quite enthusiastic, not only about her activities but about the church as a whole. She sees it in many ways as family:

R: Yeah, youth choir and stuff like that, we have youth bells, bell choir, those kind of things. We're like a church of activities. Vacation Bible school, which was this week, a lot of things for the kids . . . we try to keep them in the church so they'll help build the church in the future.

I: How much do you like or dislike your church?

R: I like my church a lot. When I walk into the doors of my church, I know that I'm myself. It's your family in there. There's no tension at my church; it's very open. So I love my church, I love it.

When asked whether a person needed to be involved in a church or not in order to be religious, African-American teens responded, as did most teens regardless of their race or ethnicity, that churches and religious institutions weren't necessary for a person to be religious, that they might practice the religion of their choice, on their own, if they wanted to. But these teens followed up with the idea that while that was all right, it wasn't really optimal. Listen to this thirteen-year-old African-American female:

I: In order to be religious do you need to be involved in a church or do you think you can do it on your own, be by yourself?

R: You know, you don't need to be involved in a church; you can learn and be religious without being in a church. You can know about God without being in church. Just read the Bible, and you will understand it. But to feel the power, you need to be in church.

I: What do you mean, feel the power?

R: Like, to get understanding from the preacher. You know how sermons give you more understanding.

Similarly, one sixteen-year-old African-American male said, "Christianity, I think it's not something you just live; I feel like you have to practice. And it's something that you . . . you can't live it all by yourself; you need to go to church because like church, it helps you . . . get closer to God and it helps you to solve certain problems."

As we have seen, for Latino teens the relationship between religion and family seems particularly close. Many of the Latino teens talked about their church as a large family where everybody cares about everybody else, whether the minister, priest, or the parishioners. Recall Evelyn Cabrera from Chapter Two, who receives support from women at her church and who said about these ladies, "They help me out the same way as my parents. They're like another part of my family." Other Latino teens gave similar responses to questions about their church:

I: How much do you like or dislike your church?

R [fifteen-year-old Latina]: I like it a lot.

I: How good or not good a place is your church to go if you wanted to talk about serious issues like family problems, alcohol, sex and stuff like that?

R: It's good. Like youth group, you can go, and if you don't want to say it out loud, you can talk to a youth leader by themselves, and they're like people who are, you know, really godly centered; they'll give you good advice, they'll support you, they'll cry with you, they'll laugh with you.

When we asked in interviews whether religion was a source of conflict or togetherness in their families, most teens, regardless of race or ethnicity, replied that it was in some way a source of sharing or togetherness. Although most teens said that their common beliefs were a source of sharing in their families, few offered any specific experiences of this sense of sharing beyond just knowing that they held the same beliefs. But many Latino teens, when talking about religion—whether attending church together or "becoming more religious"—offered experiences in which they believed religion had contributed to family solidarity with demonstrated effects. For example, this eighteen-year-old describes how his involvement in church encouraged his parents to start attending with him, thus in his view making the whole family feel more together:

Yeah. When I started going to church, it's like they sent me, but they didn't really participate. But when I started going to church, I know they hadn't gone to confession, and when I was going to confession, they decided to go too, so it was kind of like they decided to go with me.

Similarly, this seventeen-year-old provides an example of how her family benefited from going to church together:

I: Do you think religion is something that brings you guys together? Is it something that you share?

R: I think so, yeah. Well, I mean, my brother used to be so negative, you know, but we said, oh, let's all just go to church; let's, you know, let's do this; let's hang out with some friends at church, you know. And then one day, he showed up to church; I mean, I guess God really changes some personalities, you know, from inside somehow. Like my brother, everybody's fine; we get along. I guess God brought us together, to be there for each other.

I: When your brother started going to church, did everybody's relationship with him get better or not?

R: Oh, yeah, way better.

A fourteen-year-old describes how his mother's relationship with her boyfriend and her pregnancy motivated the whole family to become more involved in religious activities:

I: Why do you think you guys started getting more active a year ago?

R: Uh, because a year ago was when she told me she was pregnant . . . she figured out she was pregnant, and we started getting more religious. . . . When she had me she wasn't really into religion, so she kind of tried to do something different this time. So I am baptized and everything.

Since they all have been attending church and "doing religious things," the best result, he believes, is that they are all becoming a "religious family."

White teens, once again in contrast to other teens, tend to talk about their experiences in religious institutions in very individualistic ways, in general detailing how the institution benefits their personal lives, whether by helping them to develop their spiritual lives, hang out with their friends, or just feel better about themselves. This fourteen-year-old male from the South belongs to a youth group that meets each week:

I: What do you get out of the youth group? What does it do for you?

R: Lessons on how to be a better Christian, and stuff like that.

I: Any other things you enjoy or you get out of it or it does for you, the youth group?

R: Makes me feel better about myself.

I: Can you tell me more about that?

R: If I've like had a bad day at school, it makes me feel better when I go down there.

I: How does it make you feel better?

R: If I had a bad grade, it makes me realize that grades really don't matter; they're not that important in your life.

Similarly, this white fourteen-year-old from the West describes that what he really enjoys about his youth group is just hanging out with his friends:

I: What's been your experience with adults in your church? Have you found them to be helpful to you, or interested in you at all?

R: All the adults are supportive of the youth, pretty much, because it's trying to get the youth to believe. . . . They're actually active about trying to get youth involved and get them understanding and excited about coming.

I: How do the youth usually respond to that?

R: It's fun, because our youth group, instead of sitting in church every week or whatever and just listening to the person talk, we actually go out on activities; we go to the park and just hang out there sometimes. It's not as much a church group as it is a group of friends that all met at the church, and are getting into the church.

And this fifteen-year-old white respondent from the southeast describes why she likes her church and what she gets out of it:

R: I think it does open me up. It's kind of what's helped me make a lot of different kinds of friends and being nice to everyone.

I: Do you think your life would be different if you weren't involved at all?

R: I probably wouldn't be nice to everyone. I'd probably feel like, well, I already have enough friends, so you don't really matter. It's probably how it would be.

I: Okay, and if it were totally up to you, how often would you attend?

R: Hopefully, I'd attend almost every Sunday. I'd probably only attend like two times a month, though. 'Cause like I said, I'm not a morning person, and it's early in the morning, so.

I: And what do you like about your church?

R: Everyone there is very friendly, and they're not that judgmental, and they all believe in you, and they all care about you, and they all pray about you when you want them to.

I: Is there anything you don't like about it?

R: No. I think I like everything.

For white teens, participation in religious institutions tends to be more oriented around what they might be able to "get out of it" personally, whether hanging out with friends or learning how to get along with different types of people. As this seventeen-year-old Latter-Day Saint told us about attending his youth group, "I just feel good from it."

It is not overly surprising that we found, for example, that African-American teens are on most measures the most religious among American teens. Studies over several decades have shown African-Americans to be more likely to attend church, participate in church-related activities, and belong to more church-related organizations than are whites. Further, the African-American church, particularly in the rural South, has been described as a "semi-involuntary institution" in which participation has been largely shaped by generally accepted norms and expectations within the African-American community.[4] But we want to move beyond such observations toward an understanding of how the relative centrality of religion in teens' lives—and how teens of different races and ethnicities understand religion in their lives—may have an effect on their development and their futures.

CONCLUSION

We believe that our analysis of the religious lives of American teens tells a more complex, though related, story than the "moralistic therapeutic deism" described by Christian Smith.[5] As this chapter has shown, teens from different racial and ethnic groups differ in their religious beliefs and understandings, practices, and involvements in religious institutions. We will now describe in ideal-typical form the diverse roles, understandings, and involvements religion has in the lives of teens from different racial and ethnic groups.

African-American teens exhibit a *personalistic absolutism* in regard to their religious beliefs and commitments. As repeatedly shown throughout this chapter, most African-American teens reported a strong belief in the absolute truth of the Christian religion and Scriptures. They were the most likely to see God as someone demanding something from them and having authority that must be obeyed, but also as someone with whom they have a strong personal relationship that affects every aspect of their lives. Thus we heard African-American teens talk about God as the "highest of the high," or as watching them specifically and "waiting on an apology" for some wrongdoing. Yet they also framed their religious beliefs, their views of God, and even their involvement in church in love and acceptance toward themselves and others. As well, most African-American teens expressed the central role of religion in their lives not only through what they believed but through their religious practices; these teens often pray several times a day and read the Bible several times a week. This emphasis expressed among African-American teens is quite different from how other teens talked about the importance of religion in their lives. White, Latino, and Asian-American teens tended to report that religion functioned primarily as a support or backdrop for other parts of their lives; in contrast, for African-American teens religion seemed to function more as a realm that has its own rewards. Finally, for African-American teens religion not only played an authoritative role in what they believed and in what was expected of them, but was necessarily about caring for and serving family, community, and others.

White teens displayed the most diversity in terms of religious belief and practice, yet despite this diversity most shared a therapeutic and individualistic orientation toward religion. Thus, in contrast to African-American teens, white teens show a *therapeutic individualism* in their religious beliefs and commitments. More than any other group white teens tended to see God as someone who exists primarily to help them through problems and make them happy. Religious organizations were embraced by white teens to the extent that they met a personal need but not necessarily as an authority that demanded allegiance or required their service. In this, white teens often spoke of their belief that God is there to "forgive us" and to "help us through our problems." Further, they didn't think there is only one way to believe but rather that people should "believe what they want to believe." Similarly, the religious practices of white teens appear to be less central in their lives, again being oriented toward what they might need at a particular point in time, whether having a prayer answered or feeling good because of their particular religious practice. Finally, white teens' involvement in religious organizations also centers on their personal needs and desires. White teens told us, for example, that they enjoyed church or youth group because they could "hang out" with friends or because they "felt better" about themselves when they attended services or were otherwise involved.

The emphasis among Latino teens that religion functions to serve the needs of their families can be described as *religious familism*. Latino teens often reported strong religious beliefs, yet more than any of the other racial or ethnic groups this was tied to family relationships rather than a commitment to a religious institution per se. Religion for many of these teens serves as a support for their family and is variously cited as a catalyst for family unity. Latino teens often sound like white teens in how they understand religion to be about personal fulfillment. Yet unlike white teens, they most often spoke of the importance of family as the frame through which they understood the role of religion in their lives, and in how they viewed religious institutions. We heard Latino teens speak of God as "like another dad" or as "a father figure," and they repeatedly told us that their beliefs came from their families. Similarly, Latino teens often understood their religious experiences in the context of their families, in which one's individual experience was often filtered through a positive outcome for one's family and, further, was interpreted to have supernatural origins. Their involvement in religious institutions tended also to be framed in familial terms. The church was most often viewed "like another family" and a place a person could go to with personal problems or, again, where families might be served together.

Asian-American teens' approach to religion is best described as *relativistic instrumentalism*. Asian-American teens most often reported their religious involvement and beliefs in the context of expectations their parents had for them in this area of their lives. Asian-American teens are somewhat similar to white teens in how they believe and participate in religion, and also to Latino teens in their primary emphasis on family. But with Asian-American teens it is much more about acquiescing to parents' desires and expectations while adapting their own beliefs, feelings, and participation patterns within that context. Thus Asian-American teens told us about the general value of religion in providing meaning to life or a moral outlook but that religion wasn't necessarily all that central in their daily lives. These teens rarely reported any religious experiences or practices, but when they did, they suggested again that these were not central in their lives and, in some cases, were "not really a voluntary thing." Even when these teens provided evidence of a greater commitment to personal religious practice, they would often say that they wouldn't really miss it if it were not part of their lives. This was true as well with their participation in religious institutions—they would often say that they enjoyed meeting friends at services or in the youth group but that their parents generally required them to go, and that they would be just as happy if they could stay in bed. Asian-American teens then, more than any other racial or ethnic group, exhibit a pragmatic, even relativistic approach to religion. Religion is much less central in their lives, and they exhibit a lack of commitment to a fixed set of beliefs, tending instead toward a "pick and choose" approach to religion. Beliefs, practices, and institutional involvements may be chosen out of a larger pool of possibilities, with the goal being to please their parents—and perhaps other authorities—while maintaining their own pragmatic approach.

Christian Smith has theorized that the constructive influence of religion in the lives of American youth can be understood by observing several factors in their lives, two of which are particularly important for this discussion: *cultural capital* and *social capital*.[6] Teens are able to develop different forms of cultural and social capital as a result of their participation in various forms of religion. Regarding cultural capital, Smith argues that religion provides opportunities to "acquire elements of cultural capital that may directly enhance the well-being of youth and may be transposable to other social settings for constructive purposes in youth's lives."[7] He suggests types of cultural capital that are distinct to religion and available to young people, which range from gaining a better understanding of the Western historical context and major religious traditions to receiving musical education through participation in choirs or by just singing along during religious services. Similarly, for social capital, he argues that as one of the few major American social institutions that is "not rigidly age stratified and emphasizes personal interactions over time," religion provides opportunities for youth to interact with older adults in their communities. These interactions may result in "cross-generational network ties with the potential to provide extra-familial, trusting relationships of care and accountability, and linking youth to wider sources of helpful information, resources and opportunities."[8] As a result of developing important forms of cultural and social capital through their religious involvements, Smith suggests, teens may gain a relative edge over peers who do not develop such capital. Owing to intergenerational relationships they may have developed in their religious communities, these teens are perhaps able to take advantage of a greater range of networks and, in exercising their cultural capital, perform better in various interactions ranging from basic conversations to job interviews.

We agree with Smith's assessment that religious involvements provide many opportunities for teens to develop important forms of social and cultural capital. Such capital may lead to significant payoffs, whether in the concrete form of jobs and career paths or in a greater likelihood of positive outcomes in youths' lives. Yet our research suggests an additional point: the forms of cultural and social capital that teens may develop through their religious involvements are bounded in many ways by distinctively racial and ethnic patterns. Thus, for example, religion can be seen to reinforce the sense among white teens that institutions and authority figures are there to serve them rather than the other way around, giving them a sense of entitlement and confidence. For African-American teens, religion demands service and obedience, perhaps inhibiting a sense of entitlement but providing relational and emotional benefits in return. Similarly for Latino teens, religion, reinforcing the authority and importance of family in their lives, serves as both an extension and a support of the family. Again, religion demands obedience and service but results in similar types of relational and emotional benefits as suggested for African-American teens. This pattern may disadvantage African-American and Latino teens hoping to advance in white-dominated institutions, but it does give them relational resources to lead healthy lives as adults. For Asian-American teens, religion reinforces the role of parental authority in their lives yet also allows them an arena in which they can pragmatically adapt their religious participation, beliefs, and practices while submitting to their parents' expectations. As a result, Asian-American teens may gain pragmatic decision-making skills and spiritual and ideological resources to pursue upward mobility as they move out of adolescence.

In sum, religion acts as a socializing agent in the lives of teens that tends to reinforce their experiences in their families, among their peers, and in their schools but that also provides them a place to develop different forms of social and cultural capital, as well as distinct forms of religious capital. White teens exhibit a decision-making process in which religious authority is effectively leveled and in which they decide what they will believe and practice as well as how religious institutions can meet their needs. In contrast, African-American, Latino, and Asian-American teens variously demonstrate that their religious beliefs, practices, and institutional involvements are oriented around an authoritative presence in their lives, whether that is religion per se, or family, or parents. In this they reveal an understanding that even while they may gain certain things from religion, they are expected to serve the needs of religious institutions and their families through their religious involvements. Finally, for teens overall, religion reinforces autonomy, authority, and community as it is experienced in the other areas of their lives.

6 CONCLUSION

Race matters. Contrary to the view of many people that American society is, or should be, color-blind and that we should all get along despite our differences, or that anyone with just a little hard work can overcome any obstacle and become rich or famous or attain some other measure of success, race still matters—not only in how one experiences the world but more specifically in how individuals are prepared from their earliest ages for participation in the American social system. Of course, class matters too and so does gender, yet one of the primary findings in this book is that when we hold variables like social class constant, race still matters in teens' socialization, in their preparation for the roles they will take on as they grow up, and in how the American socioeconomic system rewards some groups over others, thereby reproducing structures of inequality across generations.

In this concluding chapter we will summarize the different patterns of socialization we have observed throughout the book, showing how race makes a difference in how young people are socialized in their preparation to participate in American society. We will then discuss what we see as the primary implications of our findings and argue that teens, through their experiences in each of the institutional spheres of society, are building stores of capital—social, cultural, human, religious—and, further, that the types of stored capital and how they are combined are in large part a result of the race or ethnicity of the teen. We argue that teens of different racial and ethnic groups have a different mix of what we are calling their *capital portfolio*, which they will draw on as they move out of adolescence and into young adulthood, and which will lay the foundation of success and well-being in their future life.

RACIAL AND ETHNIC DIFFERENCES IN
SOCIALIZATION PATTERNS

White teens are in general socialized to be more autonomous and in many ways separated from their families, and to view relationships with their parents and other authority figures as more peerlike than do minority teens. Further, they tend to find their friends through their involvement in school and activities in other organizational contexts and to spend a large amount of time with their peers in unsupervised settings and activities. As a result, peers tend to exert a larger influence in the lives of white teens than is the case for teens of other races and ethnicities. Finally, white teens' involvement in formal organizations like schools and religious institutions is characterized by an assumption that these institutions exist to enhance their educational and personal lives, whether that includes extra tutoring or personal counseling and mentoring, however formal or informal that may be.

For African-American teens, who are embedded in more authoritarian families, a pattern of socialization emerges in which they learn to respect their subordinate role in relation to parental authority. Finding emotional support from their families, they are expected to have respect for authority and to develop personal responsibility for their behaviors. Authority figures and symbols of authority, whether in family, school, or religious organizations, remain important in the lives of African-American teens. They are more intimately tied to a smaller group of extended family than are other teens, with "best friends" often being cousins, aunts, or uncles. In a related manner, African-American teens experience formal institutions as loci of authority, not—as with white teens—as resources for enhancing their personal or educational lives. Rather, for African-American teens institutions serve certain formal functions, such as teaching or imparting religious knowledge. Institutions then are a locus of authority in that they not only wield power in teens' lives but reinforce existing social hierarchies and boundaries. African-American teens receive less attention in formal institutions such as schools and generally receive more individual attention in institutions like churches. However, churches are relatively closed networks, not unlike relationships with family and peers, and thus do not introduce teens to a wider range of people and networks. This serves to reinforce the forms of authority they experience in their family and peer relationships.

Latino teens are embedded within their families, extended kin ties, and family friendship networks, in which they are nurtured and their behavior monitored.

In this, they find that they are part of a larger whole and learn to respect their role in relation to parental and other authorities in their networks. Authority figures and symbols of authority remain important in the lives of Latino teens; this includes the extended family and also school and religious authorities. Peers tend to be drawn mostly from these extended-family and family friendship networks. These teens thus have a fairly supervised adolescence; much of their lives is oriented around activities in which community authority figures are often integral, serving to socialize Latino teens into the wider extended family and community. Similar to African-American teens, Latino teens experience formal institutions such as schools and religious institutions as simply serving authoritative functions, such as education or religious training, rather than as attending to their personal needs. As well, they receive less personal attention in school, and while they may receive more attention in religious institutions, their experiences there reinforce existing hierarchies and the forms of authority they encounter in their families and peer relationships.

These patterns hold less in the socialization experiences of third-or-more-generation Latino teens. The experiences of these teens look more like how white teens are socialized, particularly in their separation from family and in the influence of peers, who are drawn from a broader pool than that of first- and second-generation Latino teens. In this, however, third-plus-generation Latino teens don't seem to have developed the resources that would help them resist or successfully move beyond negative outcomes and behaviors, and they don't get personal care and attention from the authority figures in their lives. Further, third-plus-generation Latino teens neither expect nor receive the same sort of attention to their needs from formal institutions as white teens do.

The socialization experiences of Asian-American teens are similar to the experiences of white teens, particularly in their interaction with and separation from family. However, they also feel an almost constant sense of parental authority in their lives, which serves both as a governor for negative behavior and outcomes and as an impetus to achievement in a variety of areas. Their peers are most often from different racial and ethnic backgrounds, and as with white teens friends are found mostly through school and various organizations and activities outside the family. Asian-American teens spend a great deal of time with their peers in unsupervised settings and activities, again like white teens, yet the importance of their parents in their lives seems to result in their being less affected by peer pressure than are white teens. Finally, Asian-American teens have internalized a form of instrumental rationality whereby their conception of their efforts in school and even their religious beliefs tends toward what will help them achieve their goals rather than any intrinsic value education or religion may have.

AMERICAN TEENS AND THEIR CAPITAL PORTFOLIOS

As we noted in the Introduction, the fact that teens of different races and ethnicities have different socialization experiences, and that these are related to relative advantages or disadvantages as they prepare for their future roles in society, may seem obvious. Yet what we are suggesting is not simply that teens are different in their experiences and outcomes but that as they are growing up they are also developing their capital portfolio—their mix of social, cultural, human, and religious capital—that will lay the groundwork for their future success and well-being in life. We argue that the patterns uncovered in the previous chapters show that teens' capital portfolios, while certainly varying from individual to individual, are bounded by the types of capital that tend to develop within different racial and ethnic groups. In what follows, we trace the formation of teens' capital portfolios and suggest that by thinking about the positive and negative effects stemming from their particular forms and mixes of capital, we might be able to adopt a broader emphasis on well-being rather than focusing on more narrowly defined measures of economic success.

DEFINING FOUR FORMS OF CAPITAL

In discussing social, cultural, human, and religious capital, we are less interested in, for example, the many streams of research on social capital that emphasize its relation to civil society,[1] economic development,[2] or more macrolevel issues—although these are of course related to our concerns. Our interests focus instead on the various forms of capital teens are developing through socialization and how these may influence and improve their overall well-being and preparation for a successful life. Our emphasis on well-being is intentional in that we want to move away from a narrower emphasis on socioeconomic success (while not minimizing this) and point toward a broader preparation for adult life. We note here as well that this discussion, while based on our findings, is conjectural; that is, we don't know how these teens will utilize their capital portfolios in the future, or how they may be able to develop them further. As Amanda Lewis and others have suggested, if left unused, capital yields no specific benefits for the owner.[3] These are important questions that future investigations will be able to answer.

We now briefly define the different types of capital that will inform our discussion. *Social capital* is the value of social networks and the "norms of reciprocity," or inclinations to do things for others within those networks. This includes norms of cooperation, trust, and information-sharing as people and groups interact within and across different networks. As norms of reciprocity are enacted in these different ways—and, for our purposes, passed down across generations—social capital is developed.[4] *Cultural capital* refers to the different forms of cultural knowledge and experience that teens gain throughout their life, which enables them to succeed relative to others. Some forms of cultural capital are more highly valued and thus rewarded in the larger society. Cultural capital is passed on to teens and learned in their participation in the various institutional spheres of their lives.[5] *Human capital* is simply the stock of knowledge, education, skills, and so on that allows or prepares teens for future participation in the labor force. Teens build this part of their capital portfolio in their formal education but also informally through the skills and knowledge they may gain outside the formal educational sphere which may prepare them for the world of work.[6] *Religious capital* refers to the "products" of religion and spirituality that are performed at the individual and aggregate levels and that influence people in particular ways.[7] That is, religious capital is religious or spiritual knowledge, beliefs, behaviors, and social structures that can be leveraged for an individual or collective good. In our conception, religious capital provides teens with "goods" related to a sense of meaning and belonging, as well as a broad ethical framework that frames their approach to life.[8]

Our concept of the capital portfolio is metaphorically similar to Ann Swidler's "cultural toolkit" in that it implies a storehouse or, better, a bank from which teens can draw as they engage the world.[9] Yet the capital portfolio is more than a repertoire of culturally acceptable strategies of action; rather, it is a baseline of different forms of capital available to teens as they begin to engage the wider worlds of education, employment, and involvement in large social institutions. Thus, for Swidler one can reach into one's cultural toolkit in any given situation and put together an appropriate course of action based on what is culturally available, while the capital portfolio essentially *defines* the social world and its possibilities for teens. To put this in the extreme, networks either exist for teens or they don't; teens have been taught culturally valued information or they haven't; young adults either have a certain level of education and skills or they don't; and religious beliefs and institutions either provide knowledge and resources that are valuable to teens or they don't.

We are not arguing that there is only one form each of social, cultural, human, or religious capital; rather, there are several forms of each, some more valued by the larger socioeconomic system than others, and they combine into capital portfolios in different ways. Further, as noted above, we argue that the capital portfolio can and does change with time and with experience, particularly as teens enter young adulthood. Thus, what teens have in their capital portfolio when they reach the end of adolescence will be invested, diversified, and built on as they gain education, knowledge, and experience. All that said, what do the capital portfolios of the teens we have been describing look like, and how might these portfolios affect their life trajectories?

Thinking back to the patterns we found in how teens are differentially socialized by race and ethnicity, we can begin to sketch out the different types of social, cultural, human, and religious capital that teens of different races and ethnicities possess in their capital portfolios.

Social Capital

The way that white teens tend to be socialized, for example, into independence, autonomy, and peer networks and organizations outside the family's sphere of influence, helps build greater amounts of what Robert Putnam has called "bridging" forms of social capital, in which connections form with a broader range of people and organizations than family or even a family- or community-oriented religious congregation can offer.[10] White teens tend to be oriented *outward* toward relationships with organizations, peers, and groups that expand their experience and thus help them develop social capital which may be better used in the larger socioeconomic system. For example, recall the teen whose time was consumed with so many outside activities that she defined her parents' support as simply being in attendance at her school functions and sporting events since she didn't otherwise spend much time with them. Or recall other teens who variously expressed that they preferred not to spend too much time with their parents and that they rather preferred to be with friends or involved in different activities. Through these experiences in organizations and with others outside the realm of their families, white teens are broadening their network relationships, thus building forms of social capital that potentially put them at an advantage over teens who do not have those experiences.

In comparison to white teens, African-American and Latino teens appear to be developing greater amounts of what Putnam has called "bonding" social capital, that is, social capital formed through relationships with similar types of people, embedding teens into networks of relational ties with people who provide oversight and otherwise pay attention to teens' lives.[11] These teens' socialization experiences are mostly based on relationships with family, peers, and even religious institutions that emphasize commitment and deference to established authority and traditions. African-American and Latino teens tend to be oriented *inward* toward relationships with organizations, peers, and groups that promote cohesion and form a sort of support system but which also limit their external relationships, creating a form of social capital that may have less payoff for them in the larger social system.

For example, recall Derek Williams, a fifteen-year-old African-American youth whom we met in Chapter Two. He has close relationships with his mother and other members of his extended family, and he likes being around them and admires them. His mother has set down strict "house rules" that include daily and weekly chores, a curfew, and attending church together each week. Overall Derek felt supported, not only by his mother and his extended family but by his church "family" as well, which provided him with an extended network of support and discipline. This is similar to what we heard from first- and second-generation Latino teens like Evelyn Cabrera, who not only likes spending time with her mother and father but also has many of her activities supervised, whether formally or informally, by her parents, friends' parents, or other relatives. Like Derek she has felt the interest and support of members of her church and considers them "like another part of my family." Evelyn's life is embedded in a dense network of family and friends who always seem to know where she is and what she is doing, and who provide her with love and support. This pattern changes when looking at third-or-more-generation Latinos, whose family structures and relationships with parents are much more similar to those we found among white teens.

Teens like Derek and Evelyn are developing strong sources of "bonding" social capital, which may not have the same potential to help them socioeconomically as the "bridging" capital being developed by white teens, even if it does help them gain other social and psychological goods, such as living in a close community, family unity, and relational thriving.

Asian-American teens seem to have significant autonomy and the freedom to develop their own peer networks and involvement in organizations outside their family's sphere of influence. This might lead to the expectation that they would develop the sort of social capital that white teens tend to develop; in reality, it seems that their development of social capital is limited by an emphasis on authority and by a distance in communicating with their parents, all of which limits their ability to engage authority figures as equals and get what they need from them. The almost constant psychological presence of parents, as positive as this might be, may limit these teens' ability to develop a broader set of networks, organizational affiliations and involvement, and independence, which would be more highly valued by the larger socioeconomic system. Recall Erik Li, who talked about his parents' high expectations for his doing well in school and ultimately in a career, while at the same time saying he was much less interested in their measures of success. He also reported regular conflict with his parents over his schooling and future plans and that he rarely talks to his parents about personal things. Thus while Asian-American teens perceive their parents' support and high expectations, they also experience more distant relationships with them—relationships characterized by a parental authority that seems to restrain the development of broader forms of social capital.

Cultural Capital

Developing cultural capital among teens is seen most clearly in how they interact within formal organizations like schools and religious institutions. White teens' autonomy, sense of equality with authority figures, and desire to be without parental or other supervision suggest a sense of entitlement, particularly as they act within these organizations. These teens just seem to know, or expect, that the institutions are there to serve their needs. For example, the expectations of white teens that teachers and schools are there not only to teach them subject matter but also to serve their personal needs, including mentoring, counseling, or even assisting them in the college admissions process, is a form of cultural capital which follows from their sense of entitlement and equality with authority. White teens have learned that institutions are "supposed" to serve them in these ways, which when extrapolated beyond their middle school and high school years, suggest a form of cultural capital in which white teens have a significant knowledge base to operate within formal organizations to their own advantage. We repeatedly heard white teens report that teachers care not only about their academic performance but about their personal lives; teachers spend time providing individualized counseling on coursework and college admissions tips, and are generally interested in their lives. Recall what Valerie, who told us that her volleyball teacher was advising her how and when to take the SAT exam, said about this teacher: "I really like her; I enjoy being with her. . . . She's real supportive." Similarly, Jonathan, who reported that his teacher (who was also his football coach) would take the time to individually tutor him "when I'm not too sure about a test or something." White teens' understanding of themselves in relation to authority figures and formal institutions, and their expectation that their needs will—or should—be met by these entities, is a form of cultural capital that sets them apart from the other teens in this study.

For African-American and Latino teens, formal organizations are experienced as loci of authority, where they must operate within given rules. Both the organization and its personnel are seen as authorities with power over them rather than as equals—as white teens tend to see them. Thus African-American and Latino teens don't expect these formal organizations to serve their personal needs, which puts them at a disadvantage in comparison to white teens. African-American and Latino teens are building a type of cultural capital in which their expectations and abilities to use institutions to their personal advantage are bounded within a much narrower range of possibilities than white teens enjoy.

As an example, African-American and Latino teens' expectations that schools and teachers are there only to teach them subjects and not to be their friends or mentors put them at a disadvantage relative to white teens, who expect schools to provide a much broader range of service. Minority youth are more focused on whether teachers impart information knowledgeably and respectfully rather than on personal attention to their academic needs or receiving encouragement and direction. As such, they must rely on other institutions, particularly the family, without much input from teachers or schools to aid in their academic success. Over and over minority teens reported that they wanted to do well in school so that they could go to college or get a good job, yet rare was the minority teen who described a teacher who might be tutoring one-on-one, or providing individual advice on taking the SAT, or for that matter taking any sort of personal interest in the student. In contrast to white teens, who engage these institutions as resources for their personal, academic, and career advancement, the experience of minority teens in school teaches them that public institutions are primarily places which disseminate information and establish boundaries and hierarchies.

Asian-American teens, who emphasize more pragmatic concerns, particularly in the context of the ever present parental authority, appear to be developing forms of cultural capital in which they are able both to accede to authority and to use the resources available to them, whether from their families or the organizations in which they are active, as they pursue their goals. In this, however, they face the same limits as African-American and Latino teens, in that their learned respect for authority is likely to restrain them from demanding the resources they need from organizations and to keep them from seeing authority figures as equals, which in turn will likely hinder them socioeconomically. Recall Lana, a fourteen-year-old Asian-American student who reported doing well in school but said about her teachers, "I mean, they teach me stuff, for the most part. Not all of them do, but most of them try to." But as with African-American and Latino teens, these teens function in community, putting the needs of others first, participating in reciprocal relationships, taking responsibility, and in general being successful within the contexts in which they are located. Thus even here, although there may be socioeconomic deficits, there are gains in other aspects of well-being.

Human Capital

Human capital refers generally to formal and informal education, training, knowledge, and experience that translate into jobs, careers, and income. We assume that teens don't at this point possess much in the way of human capital but that their experiences and achievements, particularly in school, are vital as they develop their own forms of human capital. Indeed, in our interviews most teens reported that they were doing well in school. Yet our earlier discussions of differences between white teens and racial minority teens, particularly in schooling experiences, suggest that white teens—through the more personalized attention they receive from schools and teachers regarding their educational futures—are building forms of human capital that have a greater potential for future payoff in the kinds of knowledge and skills they are likely to receive. For example, white teens' parents, teachers, and schools essentially partner together to help them do well in school and even gain admittance to college. In the end, this not only results in better performance in school but also may lead to better college placement, thereby enhancing these teens' stock of human capital.

African-American and Latino teens, while expressing their desires to do well in school and ultimately attend college, to have a good job, and to "be a success," are much more reliant on their parents because they lack the support of schools and teachers to provide academic direction and personal advice. Thus, although they may attain educational achievements similar to white teens, pursuing their academic goals and developing human capital will be much more difficult for them.

Similarly, Asian-American teens tend not to enjoy the same sort of relationships with their schools and teachers as white teens. However, owing to their parents' higher levels of human capital and their influence in their teens' lives, including specific expectations for their children's future careers, these teens receive more direct benefit from parents in the development of their human capital. The direct influence of parents may thus mitigate the absence of partnering with schools and teachers, which white teens enjoy and which African-American and Latino teens also lack.

A related, equally important issue is the differential development of human capital among some African-American and Latino teens as a result of their being less prepared academically than white and Asian-American teens. Studies show a variety of causes of this disparity, such as inferior or overcrowded schools, inappropriate tracking of minority youth, and continued segregation in schools.[12] We would add to this list our finding that African-American and Latino teens have more difficulty than white teens in getting personal attention to their educational development from their teachers and schools, even in the best of situations. This leaves them more reliant on themselves and their families for the development of basic educational skills—an essential part of their human capital—and it puts them at a disadvantage relative to other teens.

Religious Capital

The concept of religious and spiritual capital is an emerging area of research; there is some discussion over exactly how to conceptualize these ideas and whether they are even a separate form of capital and not simply a subset of social capital. Although that larger discussion is beyond the scope of our purposes here, we believe religious capital can be thought of as a separate type of capital, which has its own benefits but which also reinforces other forms of capital. Thus for the teens in our study, socialization within religious institutions—and teens' understanding of and approach to religion—results in the development of forms of religious capital that are similar to and reinforce the other forms of capital in their portfolio. But we also believe that religious capital benefits teens in its own right, providing a sense of meaning and belonging and a sort of "life ethic" which frames their approach to life.

White teens, more than teens from other racial and ethnic groups, tend to approach religious institutions—even God—as something that is there to serve them, depending on their needs. Similar to their experiences with educational institutions, white teens expect their religious involvements to net them particular benefits, often without their acknowledging any sort of authority of tradition or set of beliefs. Instead, their beliefs are often malleable and are completely up to them to choose. Recall the teen who said that to be a spiritual person means "go to church, [and] believe what you want to believe"; or similarly, the teens who reported that what they enjoyed about church or youth group was that they were able to "hang out" with friends there or that they "just feel good from it." The forms of religious capital being developed by white teens, similar to their social capital, seem to let them reap particular benefits, such as belonging, meaning, and belief, from their involvement in religious institutions with less commitment to the authority of the institution, religious tradition, or congregation. That is, white teens tend to develop a form of religious capital in which personal fulfillment is paramount and in which their general approach to life suggests, in a phrase, that "it's all about me."

The expression of religious beliefs and the experiences of African-American teens within religious institutions are much different from those of white teens, leading to different forms of religious capital. Similar to their socialization experiences in school and family, African-American teens are embedded in belief systems and institutions where religious authority is assumed and where they are expected to serve. In other words, their experience causes them to understand that they are part of a larger institution, which has authority in their lives and in their families and to which they are expected to be personally committed. Recall the African-American teen who said that he thought about God as "this almighty person . . . he's the highest of the high"; or similarly, the teen who said, "If you're gonna dedicate your life to something, if you're gonna believe in something, if you're gonna worship something, it's not about you." Religious capital provides these teens with support and guidance and with a life ethic that values authority and respect for others. This conception of religion certainly benefits teens individually, but it also requires them to serve the institution instead of the institution primarily serving their needs. For African-American teens religious meaning and fulfillment are derived from participating in the religious institution and from being a part of its structure or tradition, not (as with white teens) from interactions with the structure that seek to customize their religious experience.

Latino teens' expressions of their religious beliefs and experiences within religious institutions sound similar to African-American teens', particularly in that they understand religion to be an authority in their lives. Yet the emphasis for Latino teens was centered primarily on the family rather than religion per se; that is, religious beliefs and involvement were understood as supporting the family and were often seen as a means to family unity. Latino teens also sounded somewhat like white teens in that they often framed their understanding of religion in terms of personal fulfillment. Yet while white teens were seeking their own fulfillment, Latino teens most often spoke of the importance of family as the frame through which they understood the role of religion in their lives and viewed religious institutions. Recall the Latino teens who spoke of God as "like another dad" or as "a father figure" and who said that their religious beliefs came from their families. Latino teens also understood their involvement in religious institutions in familial terms. They spoke of their church as being "like another family," which in turn functions as a support and extension of the family. Latino teens are developing a form of religious capital that promotes family unity and their role in the family, as well as a sense of personal well-being which is itself contextualized through their understanding of their families and how they contribute to them.

Asian-American teens seem to be developing a fairly pragmatic or flexible form of religious capital. Their openness to multiple perspectives in the service of "what works," particularly in meeting their parents' expectations, suggests that their religious attachments, activities, and satisfaction are often more a function of pragmatism than of intrinsic belief. For example, recall Tim Hirano, who said that religion wasn't all that important in his life but who nonetheless attended services, because his parents "probably make me go"; he even allowed that he enjoyed youth group at times and thought that religion provided him with at least some basic morals to guide his life. Asian-American teens seem to be building stores of religious capital that, as with teens of other racial and ethnic groups, provides them with a sense of meaning and belonging and that enhances their sense of well-being. Whether drawn from one or more religious traditions, this capital gives them a set of beliefs that can improve their ability to achieve their goals.

One final note on religious capital: With the different forms of religious capital that teens from each racial and ethnic group are developing, they are able to "purchase" different forms of thriving. White teens learn to value their individual journey and their emotional well-being and to experience God as loving and supportive of their desires. African-American and Latino teens learn to live in a community that is bound by a set of nonnegotiable beliefs and practices; they thus experience a level of "social integration" that white teens are less able to enjoy with their particular brand of religious capital. Asian-American teens, in contrast, are able to meet their parents' expectations, perhaps with an eye toward upward socioeconomic mobility, while pragmatically selecting those parts of religion that will give them versions of community, belonging, and moral direction which are in accord with their desires and goals.

Looking at these four forms of capital, which combined together compose the capital portfolios of American teens, we can see that teens are developing mixes of capital which show relatively distinct differences along racial and ethnic lines.

White teens show a mix of capital that encourages individual, autonomous action in which authorities, whether parents, teachers, or institutions, are leveled; that is, these teens believe themselves to be equals in their relationships to authority figures. They understand and act in institutions so that they are able to make demands, receive benefits, and have their needs served rather than serving the needs of the institution themselves. Further, their separation from the family into involvement with public institutions and outside relationships makes available to them a broad range of networks, which they can then put into action to increase their cultural and human capital. Religious capital functions as a support to their autonomy and serves their needs and desires for personal meaning and an ethic customized to their preferences.

African-American teens reveal a mix of capital that encourages commitment to family, church, and community; they understand themselves to be part of a larger entity, which they experience as authoritative and which they are expected to serve, while being served in return. As such, African-American teens have a narrower set of interaction networks and thus more "network closure" with significant ties and commitments to family and church. In turn, the family and the church look out for the teen, which reinforces these networks, limiting the teen's range of social capital but providing more relational and emotional well-being and further developing a commitment to community. Religion reinforces other forms of capital, particularly in the small community and family contexts. African-American teens, more than any other teens, seem to be developing significant stores of religious capital through their investment in religious institutions, their personal religious practice, and their religious beliefs. For African-American teens religion is an institution to believe in and serve, and it is authoritative in their life. This promotes a life ethic that will include a commitment to family, community, church, and so on.

Latino teens demonstrate a similar mix of capital that encourages commitment to family, community, and church. They understand themselves to be part of this larger reality, which they experience as an authoritative presence. As such, Latino teens have narrower or more insular networks. They thus experience more network closure, with generally larger numbers of people close to them, primarily in their extended family and community but also through church involvement. Again, this serves to reinforce these networks, thereby limiting these teens' range of social capital but providing for more community and relational well-being. Religion is in service to other social institutions, such as the family, and it reinforces other forms of capital, sometimes within the context of the extended family or community, and other times when it supports family solidarity. For Latino teens, religion is an authoritative institution that they believe in, although they see it too as serving the well-being of the family. As with African-American teens, this view reinforces their understanding of authority in general, yet religious authority doesn't seem to be as integral to their daily lives as with African-American teens.

Third-and-more-generation Latino teens are developing a mix of capital in which they have separated from family, but they have not developed the autonomy and sense of equality with authority that white teens have. They have developed broader networks, particularly through peer relationships, than have first- or second-generation teens, but they do not seem to have the resources to obtain what they need from formal institutions such as schools. Further, they show more distance from religious belief and institutional involvement than first- or second-generation Latinos, thus leaving them with less religious capital, less sense of community and belonging, and less of a moral compass than other teens.

Asian-American teens have a mix of capital that combines a commitment to highly authoritarian parents and their expectations with the freedom to pursue friends and interests outside the family. This may provide Asian-American teens with broader network interactions beyond their families and religious institutions, but because of the power of their parents' authority they are limited in how these networks may be developed. This in turn limits the amount of cultural capital these teens may be able to gather. Further, their authoritarian perspective limits their ability to act as white teens do in relation to institutions; that is, they understand formal institutions as they understand their families, namely, as authorities in their lives, and thus they are less able to exercise the same sort of cultural capital in getting what they want from institutions. Asian-American teens benefit, however, from their parents' human capital inputs—

more so than African-American and Latino teens—which may compensate somewhat for their lack of social and cultural capital. Owing to their need to meet parental expectations and still pursue their own interests, they develop pragmatic forms of cultural and religious capital that allow them to figure out roles within organizational hierarchies while gaining the benefits of relational and community belonging from their families, communities, and religious institutions.

It is clear that one capital portfolio mix may favor one form of success over other forms of success or well-being. For example, it might seem obvious (and in fact is supported by much research) that the American socioeconomic system favors the type of capital portfolio diversification that white teens tend to develop, since the behaviors and roles they have invested in are more closely aligned with that dominant system. Yet we would point out that what on the surface appears to be strengths—individualism, independence, separation from family, and the like—also holds the potential for less than optimal outcomes. Excessive individualism and independence can lead to a lack of commitment in relationships, to selfishness, and to an unhealthy emphasis on what others think, which as we have seen can result in such negative outcomes as unhealthy self-image or alcohol or drug abuse. By contrast, while other capital portfolios, such as those developed by minority teens, may not seem to favor the same sort of success in the economic system, they do offer many rewards that most people admit to seek out in their lives, such as strong families, community support and accountability, strong moral boundaries, and a commitment to others. At the same time, these forms of capital are not without their potentially negative outcomes. For example, a more insular emphasis on family, kin, and neighborhood may increase commitment to unhealthy alliances, simultaneously reducing commitment to the larger social order, which is essential in modern social life.

Most discussions of any form of capital tend to focus on the positive aspects: the mere possession of the "right kinds" of capital, whether social, cultural, human, or religious, will enhance one's life and benefit society. We argue that there are two sides of the capital coin, as it were—positive forms and negative (or "bad investment") forms of capital, *either* of which can lead to less than optimal outcomes for teens. We have alluded to this, generally in the context that the larger socioeconomic system favors certain forms of capital over others, thereby enhancing the likelihood of economic success for teens of certain races and ethnicities over other teens. Yet as we have heard from these teenagers, there are negative payoffs related to the forms of capital that are rewarded by the dominant system, just as there are negative payoffs associated with capital that is not as valued by that system. The point, it seems, is to keep in mind the larger goal: to develop teens who will thrive economically, emotionally, educationally, and spiritually. If we really believe that children are our future, perhaps a better socialization strategy within families, schools, and religious institutions would be to focus less on preparing teens for career success (although that is an important goal) and more on developing a balanced emphasis on well-being—economic, social, emotional, spiritual, and so on. Such an emphasis would give teens a diverse capital portfolio, one that leads to greater life success rather than primarily career or economic success. If this is so, then we would be wise to diversify the capital portfolios of all teens, adopting and borrowing from each of the forms found within each racial and ethnic group.

APPENDIXES

APPENDIX A

Methodology

The National Survey of Youth and Religion (NSYR) is a nationally representative telephone survey of 3,290 U.S. English- and Spanish-speaking youth between the ages of thirteen and seventeen, and their parents. The survey also includes eighty oversampled Jewish households, bringing the total number of completed cases to 3,370. The NSYR was conducted from July 2002 to April 2003 by researchers at the University of North Carolina at Chapel Hill using a random-digit-dial (RDD) telephone survey method and employing a sample of randomly generated telephone numbers representative of all household telephones in the fifty states. The national survey sample was arranged in replicates based on the proportion of working household telephone exchanges nationwide. This RDD method ensures equal representation of listed, unlisted, and not-yet-listed household telephone numbers. Eligible households included at least one teenager between the ages of thirteen and seventeen living in the household for at least six months of the year. In order to randomize responses within households to help attain representativeness of age and gender, interviewers were asked to conduct the survey with the teenager in the household who had the most recent birthday. The NSYR was conducted with members of English- and Spanish-speaking households. Participants were offered a financial incentive to participate. Each randomly generated telephone number was dialed a minimum of twenty times over a minimum of five months, over varying hours during weekdays, weeknights, and weekends. The calling design included at least two telephone-based attempts to convert refusals. Households refusing to cooperate with the survey but established by initial screening to include children ages 13–17 in residence and to have telephone numbers that could be matched to mailing addresses were mailed information about the survey, contact information for researchers, and a request to cooperate and complete the survey. Those records were then called back for possible refusal conversion. Ninety-six percent of households achieving parent completes also achieved teen completes. Diagnostic analyses comparing NSYR data with 2002 U.S. Census data on comparable households and with comparable adolescent surveys—such as Monitoring the Future, the National Household Education Survey, and the National Longitudinal Study of Adolescent Health—confirm that the NSYR provides a nationally representative sample without identifiable sampling and nonresponse biases of U.S. youth ages 13–17 and their parents living in households. For descriptive purposes, a weight was created to adjust for the number of teenagers in the household, the number of household telephone numbers, census region of residence, and household income. A separate weight is used in multivariate analyses that control for census region and household income, which adjusts only for the number of teenagers in the household and the number of household telephone numbers. The eighty Jewish oversample cases are omitted from our analysis in this book (see Smith 2005, Appendix B "Survey Methodology" and Appendix C "Interviews Methodology" for further details on NSYR methodology).

APPENDIX B

Frequencies of Racial/Ethnic Groups

Racial/Ethnic Group	Frequency	Valid Percent
White	2,136	65
African-American	578	18
Asian-American	47	1.4
Latino (generation)		
All	385	12
1st	75	2
2nd	125	4
3rd	185	6
All Other	144	4
TOTAL	3,290	100

Source: NSYR survey.

APPENDIX C

Regression Analyses of NSYR Survey Data

TABLE C.1

Logistic Regression Model Predicting Likelihood of Teen Living in Female-Headed Single-Parent Household

Variable	β
Independent Variables	
White	Reference
African-American	.64**
Latino (generation)	
1st	−.63**
2nd	−.03
3rd	.23***
Asian-American	.04
Control Variables	
Household Income > $80K	Reference
$60–79K	.53**
$40–59K	1.32***
$20–39K	2.31***
< $20K	3.13***
Age 17	Reference
Age 16	−.17
Age 15	−.18
Age 14	−.02**
Age 13	.11
Female	.06
Nagelkerke R^2	.26

Note: 1 = female-headed single-parent household; 0 = other household.
*** $p < .01$, ** $p < .05$, * $p < .10$

TABLE C.2

Logistic Regression Model Estimating Likelihood of Teen Spending at Least One Evening per Week with No Adult Supervision

Variable	β
Independent Variables	
White	Reference
African-American	−.44***
Latino (generation)	
1st	−1.66***
2nd	−.33***
3rd	−.08
Asian-American	−.42
Control Variables	
Household Income > $80K	Reference
$60–79K	.01
$40–59K	−.20*
$20–39K	−.17
< $20K	−.12
Age 17	Reference
Age 16	−.31**
Age 15	−.51***
Age 14	−.73***
Age 13	−1.14***
Female	−.24***
Nagelkerke R^2	.08

Note: 1 = one or more nights without supervision; 0 = no nights without supervision.

*** $p < .01$, ** $p < .05$, * $p < .10$

TABLE C.3

Logistic Regression Model Estimating Likelihood of
Teen Spending Eight Hours per Week or More in One
or More Weeknight Extracurricular Activity

Variable	β
Independent Variables	
White	Reference
African-American	−.27**
Latino (generation)	
1st	−.87**
2nd	−.31**
3rd	−.02
Asian-American	−.36
Control Variables	
Household Income > $80K	Reference
$60–79K	−.21*
$40–59K	−.52***
$20–39K	−.77***
< $20K	−1.17***
Age 17	Reference
Age 16	−.12
Age 15	−.05
Age 14	−.24*
Age 13	−.75***
Female	−.09
Nagelkerke R^2	.07

Note: 1 = eight hours or more of outside activities; 0 = less than eight hours.
*** $p < .01$, ** $p < .05$, * $p < .10$

TABLE C.4

Logistic Regression Model Estimating Likelihood of Teen Having Been Drunk at Least Once in the Past Year

Variable	β
Independent Variables	
White	Reference
African-American	−1.22***
Latino (generation)	
1st	−1.01***
2nd	−.34***
3rd	.11*
Asian-American	−1.00**
Control Variables	
Household Income > $80K	Reference
$60–79K	−.05
$40–59K	−.11
$20–39K	−.04
< $20K	.07
Age 17	Reference
Age 16	−.29***
Age 15	−.77***
Age 14	−1.46***
Age 13	−2.59***
Female	−.19**
Nagelkerke R^2	.19

Note: 1 = drunk once or more in the past year; 0 = not drunk in the past year ($N = 3,089$).

*** $p < .01$, ** $p < .05$, * $p < .10$

TABLE C.5

Logistic Regression Model Estimating Likelihood of
Teen Having Had Sex at Least Once

Variable	β
Independent Variables	
White	Reference
African-American	.35***
Latino (generation)	
1st	−1.14***
2nd	−.19
3rd	.14**
Asian-American	−1.15**
Control Variables	
Household Income > $80K	Reference
$60–79K	.01
$40–59K	.25*
$20–39K	.52***
< $20K	.72***
Age 17	Reference
Age 16	−.63***
Age 15	−1.45***
Age 14	−2.41***
Age 13	−3.51***
Female	−.19**
Nagelkerke R^2	.26

Note: 1 = had sex once or more; 0 = never had sex (N = 3,063).
*** $p < .01$, ** $p < .05$, * $p < .10$

TABLE C.6

Ordered Logistic Regression Model Estimating
Likelihood that Female Teen "Feels Happy About
Her Physical Appearance"

Variable	β
Independent Variables	
White	Reference
African-American	.75***
Latino (generation)	
1st	−.08
2nd	.14
3rd	.35*
Asian-American	.78**
Control Variables	
Household Income > $80K	Reference
$60–79K	−.09
$40–59K	−.07
$20–39K	−.15
< $20K	.01
Age 17	Reference
Age 16	−.07
Age 15	.22
Age 14	.03
Age 13	.44***
Nagelkerke R^2	.03

Note: 1 = very unhappy; 2 = somewhat unhappy; 3 = neither; 4 = somewhat happy; 5 = very happy (N = 1,670) (females only).
*** $p < .01$, ** $p < .05$, * $p < .10$

TABLE C.7

*Odds Ratios of Academic Views and Future Aspirations
Predicted by Race/Ethnicity*

Variable	Extremely important to do well in school		Would like to go to college		Thinks will actually go to college	
	Odds Ratio	S.E.	Odds Ratio	S.E.	Odds Ratio	S.E.
Independent Variables						
African-American[a]	2.95***	0.36	1.43**	0.25	1.23	0.18
Latino (generation)[a]						
1st	2.52***	0.83	0.83	0.32	0.48**	0.15
2nd	1.05	0.12	0.97	0.16	0.99	0.14
3rd	1.00	0.06	1.07	0.10	0.96	0.07
Asian-American[a]	0.76	0.25	2.38	1.77	2.66	1.67
Control Variables						
Grades[b]	0.71***	0.02	0.79***	0.03	0.71***	0.02
School Activities[c]	1.06**	0.03	1.52***	0.10	1.46***	0.07
$60–79K[d]	1.04	0.14	0.90	0.24	0.79	0.17
$40–59K[d]	1.57***	0.18	0.54***	0.12	0.48***	0.08
$20–39K[d]	1.61***	0.20	0.43***	0.09	0.40***	0.07
< $20K[d]	1.69***	0.28	0.27***	0.07	0.24***	0.05
Age 17[e]	0.60***	0.08	0.59**	0.13	0.80	0.14
Age 16[e]	0.71***	0.09	0.52***	0.11	0.86	0.15
Age 15[e]	0.62***	0.08	0.87	0.19	0.91	0.15
Age 14[e]	0.72**	0.10	0.82	0.18	0.87	0.15
Female	1.35***	0.11	1.51***	0.20	1.33***	0.14
R^2	0.09		0.12		0.15	

Note: Net other factors.

[a] Reference: white.

[b] 1 = all A's; 2 = mostly A's; 3 = A's and B's; 4 = mostly B's; 5 = B's and C's; 6 = mostly C's; 7 = C's and D's; 8 = mostly D's; 9 = D's and F's; 10 = mostly F's.

[c] Number of school activities in which teen participates (range: 0–11).

[d] Reference: Household Income > $80K.

[e] Reference: Age 13

*** $p < .01$, ** $p < .05$, * $p < .10$

TABLE C.8

*Logistic Regression Model Predicting Likelihood of
Teen Saying Religious Faith Is Very or Extremely
Important in Shaping Daily Life*

Variable	β
Independent Variables	
African-American	Reference
White	−.81***
Latino (generation)	
1st	−.47*
2nd	−.44***
3rd	−.30***
Asian-American	−1.05***
Control Variables	
Household Income > $80K	Reference
$60–79K	.19
$40–59K	.28***
$20–39K	.25**
< $20K	.20
Age 17	Reference
Age 16	−.14
Age 15	−.23*
Age 14	−.22*
Age 13	.12
Female	.37***
Nagelkerke R^2	.05

Note: 1 = religious faith very or extremely important; 0 = other response.
*** $p < .01$, ** $p < .05$, * $p < .10$

TABLE C.9

Logistic Regression Model Predicting Likelihood of
Teen Praying Alone at Least Once a Day

Variable	β
Independent Variables	
African-American	Reference
White	−.68***
Latino (generation)	
1st	−.23
2nd	−.25**
3rd	−.20***
Asian-American	−1.38***
Control Variables	
Household Income > $80K	Reference
$60–79K	.24*
$40–59K	.22**
$20–39K	.18
< $20K	.18
Age 17	Reference
Age 16	.21*
Age 15	.03
Age 14	.18
Age 13	.15
Female	.57***
Nagelkerke R^2	.05

Note: 1 = pray alone at least once a day; 0 = other response.
*** $p < .01$, ** $p < .05$, * $p < .10$

TABLE C.10

Logistic Regression Model Predicting Likelihood of
Teen Saying Their Church Is a Very or Fairly Good
Place to Talk to Adults

Variable	β
Independent Variables	
African-American	Reference
White	−.23**
Latino (generation)	
1st	−.45
2nd	−.14
3rd	−.13**
Asian-American	−.90***
Control Variables	
Household Income > $80K	Reference
$60–79K	.25**
$40–59K	.09
$20–39K	−.01
< $20K	−.08
Age 17	Reference
Age 16	.22*
Age 15	.42***
Age 14	.40***
Age 13	.30**
Female	.37
Nagelkerke R^2	.02

Note: 1 = church very or fairly good place to talk to adults; 0 = other
response.
*** $p < .01$, ** $p < .05$, * $p < .10$

REFERENCE MATTER

NOTES

Chapter 1

1. Newacheck et al. 2004.
2. DeBell and Chapman 2003.
3. Lieberson 1980.
4. Takaki 1993.
5. Lopez 1996.
6. Takaki 1993. This tax is commonly known as the "miner's tax on foreign miners." Foreign miners had to pay a tax on the precious metals they collected during the California Gold Rush. Since foreign workers in California at the time were overwhelmingly nonwhite, this law gave working-class white miners a supreme advantage over their Asian and Latino counterparts.
7. Grebler et al. 1970; Mirande 1985.
8. Bonilla-Silva 2001, 2003.
9. Bobo et al. 1997; Bonilla-Silva 2001, 2003.
10. Murray 1984; Mead 1986.
11. Lin 1999.
12. Bonilla-Silva 2001, 2003; Bobo et al. 1997.
13. Wilson 1997.
14. We also acknowledge considerable ethnic and cultural diversity within these broad racial and ethnic categories (African-American, Asian-American, Latino, and white). However, in this study we chose to analyze differences in these broad racial and ethnic categories instead of fine-grained ethnic categories because (a) in American society these are the social categories into which most immigrants are socialized by the second generation; (b) the number and combination of groups within each racial and ethnic category limits the practicality of comparing each of them with every other one;

and (c) America's racial formations suggest the presence of significant inequalities between these large racial and ethnic categories, which is the focus of this study.

15. Lewis 2003, p. 156.

16. Ibid., p. 155.

17. Lee and Zhou 2005.

18. Tatum 2003.

19. Giordano 2003; Peterson and Hann 1999.

20. Lareau 2003.

21. Pattillo-McCoy 1999.

22. Portes and Rumbaut 2001.

23. Ogbu 2003.

24. Ainsworth-Darnell and Downey 1998; Cook and Ludwig 1997; Fergus 2004.

Chapter 2

1. Peterson and Hann 1999.

2. Arnett 1995.

3. We realize that many scholars do not consider teen sex, in and of itself, risky. For our purposes we do not distinguish between risky and safe sex because (a) our data do not allow us to distinguish between protected and unprotected sex, and (b) we view protected sex among teens as carrying other physical and emotional risks.

4. Each table incorporates multiple survey questions. The counts (N's) of each racial/ethnic group were slightly different for each survey question included because of missing values, for example. For the frequency distributions of the racial/ethnic groups in the overall sample, see Appendix B.

5. "Statistically significant" means that the differences between the racial/ethnic groups in our sample are so large that they cannot be attributed to chance.

6. Unfortunately, we did not have enough Asian-American teens in our sample to explore differences between first-, second-, and third-generation Asian-American teens or to explore differences between different Asian cultural groups.

7. Peterson and Hann 1999; Arnett 1995; Baumrind 1991; Peterson and Leigh 1990.

8. Baumrind 1978, 1980, 1991.

9. Peterson and Hann 1999.

10. Dornbusch et al. 1987; Steinberg et al. 1992; Baumrind 1991; Smetana and Asquith 1994.

11. Peterson and Hann 1999.

12. Bellah et al. 1985.

13. Human Rights Watch 2003.

14. Eisenberg 1989; Hoffman 1980.

15. Eckenrode et al. 1993; Straus 1994.

16. Chao 1994.

17. See, for example, Romero and Ruiz 2007; Sabogal et al. 1987.

18. See, for example, McClanahan and Sandefour 1994.

19. Peterson and Hann 1999.

20. Dillworth-Anderson et al. 1993; Giordano et al. 1993.

21. Harrison et al. 1990; Delgado-Gaitan 1987.

22. Aponte 1999; Goldscheider and Goldscheider 1989.

23. See, for example, Kohn 1977; Lareau 2003.

Chapter 3

1. Giordano 2003.

2. See, for example, Brittain 1963; Floyd and South 1972.

3. Giordano 2003.

4. Ibid.

5. Ibid.

6. Youniss and Smollar 1985.

7. Giordano 2003.

8. For a definition of "statistically significant," see Chapter 2, note 5.

9. Each table incorporates multiple survey questions. The counts (N's) of each racial/ethnic group were slightly different for each survey question included because of missing values, for example. For the frequency distributions of the racial/ethnic groups in the overall sample, see Appendix B.

10. See Appendix C for results of regression analyses.

11. Orenstein 1997; Field et al. 2007; Neff et al. 1997; Riolo et al. 2005.

12. CDC 2006b.

13. CDC 2007.

14. See Bradshaw et al. 2006.

15. Regnerus 2007.

16. Youniss and Smollar 1985.

17. Giordano 2003.

18. Anderson 1989; Coates 1999; Savin-Williams and Berndt 1990.

19. Giordano 2003.

20. Giordano et al. 1993; Larson et al. 2001.

21. See, for example, Eckert 1989.

22. McLanahan and Booth 1989.

23. Carr 2002; and Sanchez-Jankowski 1991.

24. CDC 2006a; CDC 2006b.

25. Getz and Bray 2005; Wallace and Bachman 1991.

26. Field et al. 2007; Neff et al. 1997.

27. Portes and Rumbaut 2001.

Chapter 4

1. Schaefer 2008;Charter and Sherman 1996; Woodard 1998.
2. Touraine 1974.
3. Lucas 1999; Oakes and Lipton 1996; Maldonado and Willie 1996.
4. Crosnoe et al. 2003.
5. Kao and Thompson 2003.
6. Ogbu 2003; Steel 1997; Portes and Zhou 1993.
7. Ainsworth-Darnell and Downey 1998; Cook and Ludwig 1997; Tyson et al. 2005.
8. Each table incorporates multiple survey questions. The counts (N's) of each racial/ethnic group were slightly different for each survey question included because of missing values, for example. For the frequency distributions of the racial/ethnic groups in the overall sample, see Appendix B.
9. Swanson 2004.
10. Ibid.
11. Fisher and Hout 2006.
12. Kao and Thompson 2003.
13. Wirt et al. 2004; Kao and Thompson 2003.
14. Oian and Blair 1999; Farmer 1985; Solorzano 1991; Wilson and Wilson 1992; Chang et al. 2006; Ainsworth-Darnell and Downey 1998; Cook and Ludwig 1997; Tyson et al. 2005.
15. Ainsworth-Darnell and Downey 1998.
16. Cheng and Starks 2002.
17. Kao and Thompson 2003.
18. Rosen 1959.
19. Ogbu 2003; Steele 1997; Portes and Zhou 1993.
20. Mickelson 1990.
21. Downey et al. 2009.
22. Ibid.
23. Davis 1982; Davis et al. 2005, pp. 2050–51.
24. Comparing white and Asian-American students, even though the standard for academic excellence is set lower for white youth, their privileged status as members of the dominant racial group, in combination with the smaller population of Asian-American youth in the United States, minimizes the effect the lower standard may have on the life chances of white youth.
25. Kao 2000.
26. Farkas et al. 1990.
27. Welsh 2000.
28. Gay 1975; Jeter 1975; Oakes 1989, 1985; Epps 1995.
29. Downey and Pribesh 2004.

30. Beady and Hansell 1981.

31. Ainsworth-Darnell and Downey 1998.

32. Ainsworth-Darnell and Downey 1998; Crosnoe et al. 2003.

33. Crosnoe et al. 2003.

34. Grant and Sleeter 1988.

35. Epps 1995; Dunham and Wilson 2007.

36. Kao 2002.

37. Cook and Ludwig 1997; Gutman and Eccles 1999.

38. Duncan and Magnuson 2005; Gutman and Eccles 1999; Jeyenes 2005.

39. Qian and Blair 1999.

40. Sherrod 2003.

Chapter 5

1. See, for example, Harker 2001; Regnerus 2003; Smith 2003a; Wallace and Forman 1998.

2. Smith 2005.

3. Each table incorporates multiple survey questions. The counts (N's) of each racial/ethnic group were slightly different for each survey question included because of missing values, for example. For the frequency distributions of the racial/ethnic groups in the overall sample, see Appendix B.

4. Ellison and Sherkat 1995; Glenn 1964; Jackson et al. 1990; Roof and McKinney 1987.

5. Smith 2005.

6. Smith 2003b.

7. Ibid., p. 24.

8. Ibid., p. 25.

Chapter 6

1. For example, Putnam 2000; Putnam and Feldstein 2003.

2. For example, Woolcock 1998.

3. Lewis 2003; see also Lareau 2003, p. 277.

4. For example, Bourdieu 1983; Coleman 1988; see also Portes 2000.

5. Bourdieu 1983; Bourdieu 1984; Lamont and Lareau 1988.

6. Becker 1994.

7. In this discussion we conflate the ideas of religious capital and spiritual capital, simply using the term *religious capital*, because the degree to which these concepts are separable is not always clear in the literature.

8. For a range of definitions of spiritual and religious capital, see Finke 2003; Iannaccone and Klick 2003; Iannaccone 1990; Woodberry 2003.

9. Swidler 1986.

10. Putnam 2000.

11. Ibid.

12. See, for example, Eitle 2002; Frankenberg et al. 2003; Hallinan 2003; Renzulli and Evans 2005.

REFERENCES

Ainsworth-Darnell, James W., and Douglas B. Downey. 1998. "Assessing the Oppositional Culture Explanation for Racial/Ethnic Differences in School Performance." *American Sociological Review* 63: 536–53.

Anderson, E. 1989. "Sex Codes and Family Life Among Poor Inner-City Youths." *Annals of the American Academy of Political and Social Sciences* 501: 59–79.

Aponte, R. 1999. "Ethnic Variation in the Family: The Elusive Trend Toward Convergence." In M. Sussman, S. K. Steinmetz, and G. W. Peterson (eds.), *Handbook of Marriage and the Family*, 2nd ed. (111–41). New York: Plenum.

Arnett, J. J. 1995. "Broad and Narrow Socialization: The Family in the Context of a Cultural Theory." *Journal of Marriage and Family* 57(3): 617–28.

Baumrind, D. 1978. "Parental Disciplinary Patterns and Social Competence in Children." *Youth and Society* 9(3): 239–76.

———. 1980. "New Directions in Socialization Research." *American Psychologist* 35: 639–52.

———. 1991. "Effective Parenting During the Early Adolescent Transition." In P. A. Cowan and M. Hetherington (eds.), *Family Transitions* (111–63). Hillsdale, NJ: Erlbaum.

Beady, Charles H., and Stephen Hansell. 1981. "Teacher Race and Expectations for Student Achievement." *American Educational Research Journal* 18: 191–206.

Becker, Gary S. 1994. *Human Capital: A Theoretical and Empirical Analysis, with Special Reference to Education*, 3rd ed. Chicago: University of Chicago Press.

Bellah, R., R. Madsen, W. M. Sullivan, and A. Swidler. 1985. *Habits of the Heart: Individualism and Commitment in American Life.* Berkeley: University of California Press.

Bobo, Lawrence, James Kluegel, and Ryan Smith. 1997. "Laissez-Faire Racism: The Crystallization of a Kinder, Gentler, Anti-Black Ideology." In S. Tuch and J. Martin (eds.), *Racial Attitudes in the 1990s: Continuity and Change* (15–42). Westport, CT: Praeger.

Bonilla-Silva, Eduardo. 2001. *White Supremacy and Racism in the Post-Civil Rights Era.* Boulder, CO: Lynne Rienner.

———. 2003. *Racism Without Racists: Color-Blind Racism and the Persistence of Racial Inequality in the United States.* Lanham, MD: Rowman and Littlefield.

Borman, Geoffrey D., and Laura T. Oyerman. 2004. "Academic Resilience in Mathematics Among Poor and Minority Students." *Elementary School Journal* 104: 177–95.

Bourdieu, Pierre. 1983. "Forms of Capital." In John G. Richardson (ed.), *Handbook of Theory and Research for the Sociology of Education* (241–58). New York: Greenwood Press.

———. 1984. *Distinction: A Social Critique of the Judgment of Taste.* Cambridge, MA: Harvard University Press.

Bradshaw, C. S., S. N. Tabrizi, R. H. Read, S. M. Garland, C. A. Hopkins, L. M. Moss, and C. K. Fairley. 2006. "Etiologies of Nongonococcal Urethritis: Bacteria, Viruses, and the Association with Orogenital Exposure." *Journal of Infectious Diseases* 193: 336–45. http://www.journals.uchicago.edu/doi/full/10.1086/499434-fn1#fn1http://www.journals.uchicago.edu/doi/full/10.1086/499434-fn2#fn2.

Brittain, C. V. 1963. "Adolescent Choices and Peer-Parent Cross Pressures." *American Sociological Review.* 28(3): 385–91.

Carr, Patrick. 2002. "Bullets Don't Have No Name on Them: Young People, Exposure to Violence, and Informal Social Control in Three Philadelphia Neighborhoods." Presented at American Sociological Association Meetings, Chicago, August.

Centers for Disease Control (CDC) 2007. *National Youth Risk Behavior Survey.* Washington DC: Department of Health and Human Services.

Centers for Disease Control (CDC) 2006a. *Health, United States, 2006.* Washington DC: Department of Health and Human Services.

Centers for Disease Control (CDC 2006b). Web-Based Injury Statistics Query and Reporting System (WBISQRS). Available at http://www.cdc.gov/ncipc/wisqars/.

Chang, Esther, Chuansheng Chen, Ellen Greenberger, David Dooley, and Jutta Heckhausen. 2006. "What Do They Want in Life? The Life Goals of a Multiethnic, Multigenerational Sample of High School Seniors." *Journal of Youth and Adolescence* 35: 321–32.

Chao, R. 1994. "Beyond Parental Control & Authoritarian Parenting Style: Understanding Chinese Parenting Through the Cultural Notion of Training." *Child Development* 65: 1111–19.

Charter, David, and Jill Sherman. 1996. "Schools Must Teach New Code of Values." *London Times*, January 15, 1.

Cheng, Simon, and Brian Starks. 2002. "Racial Differences in the Effects of Significant Others on Students' Educational Expectations." *Sociology of Education* 75: 306–27.

Coates, D. L. 1999. "The Cultured and Culturing Aspects of Romantic Experience in Adolescence." In Wyndol Furman, B. Bradford Brown, and Candice Feiring (eds.),

The Development of Romantic Relationships in Adolescence (ch. 13). Cambridge, UK: Cambridge University Press.

Coleman, James S. 1988. "Social Capital in the Creation of Human Capital." *American Journal of Sociology* 94: S95–S120.

Cook, Philip J., and Jens Ludwig. 1997. "Weighing the 'Burden of "Acting White"': Are There Race Differences in Attitudes Toward Education?" *Journal of Policy Analysis and Management* 16: 256–78.

Crosnoe, Robert, Shannon Cavanaugh, and Glen H. Elder. 2003. "Adolescent Friendships as Academic Resources: The Intersection of Friendship, Race, and School Disadvantage." *Sociological Perspectives* 46: 331–52.

Davis, James A. 1982. "Up and Down Opportunity's Ladder." *Public Opinion* 5: 11–15, 48–51.

Davis, James A., Tom W. Smith, and Perter V. Marsden. 2005. *General Social Surveys 1972–2004: Cumulative Codebook.* Chicago: National Opinion Research Center.

DeBell, M., and C. Chapman. 2003. *Computer and Internet Use by Children and Adolescents in the United States, 2001* (NCES 2004-014). Washington, DC: National Center for Education Statistics, U.S. Department of Education.

Delgado-Gaitan, C. 1987. "Tradition and Transitions in the Learning Process of Mexican Children: An Ethnographic View." In G. Spindler and L. Spindler (eds.), *Interpretive Ethnography of Education: At Home and Abroad* (333–59). Hillsdale, NJ: Erlbaum.

Dillworth-Anderson, P., L. M. Burton, and W. L. Turner. 1993. "The Importance of Values in the Study of Culturally Diverse Families." *Family Relations* 42: 238–42.

Dornbusch, S. M., P. L. Ritter, P. H. Leiderman, D. F. Roberts, and M. J. Fraleigh. 1987. "The Relation of Parenting Style to Adolescent School Performance." *Child Development* 59: 1244–57.

Downey, Douglas B., James W. Ainsworth, and Zhenchao Qian. 2009. "Rethinking the Attitude-Achievement Paradox Among Blacks." *Sociology of Education* 82: 1–19.

Downey, Douglas B., and Shana Pribesh. 2004. "When Race Matters: Teachers' Evaluations of Students' Classroom Behavior." *Sociology of Education* 77: 267–82.

Duncan, G. J., and Magnuson, K. A. 2005. "Can Family Socioeconomic Resources Account for Racial and Ethnic Test Score Gaps?" *Future of Children* 15: 35–54.

Dunham, R. G., and G. Wilson. 2007. "Race, Within-Family Social Capital, and School Dropout: An Analysis of Whites, Blacks, Hispanics, and Asians." *Sociological Spectrum* 27: 207–21.

Eckenrode, J., M. Laird, and J. Doris. 1993. "School Performance and Disciplinary Problems Among Abused and Neglected Children." *Developmental Psychology* 29: 53–62.

Eckert, P. 1989. *Jocks and Burnouts: Social Categories and Identity in the High School.* New York: Teachers College Press.

Eisenberg, N. 1989. "Prosocial Development in Early and Mid-Adolescence." In R. Montemayor, G. R. Adams, and T. P. Gullottta (eds.), *Advances in Adolescent Development, from Childhood to Adolescence: A Transitional Period?* (240–68). Newbury Park, CA: Sage.

Eitle, Tamela McNulty. 2002. "Special Education on Racial Segregation: Understanding Variation in the Representations of Black Students in Educable Mentally Handicapped Programs." *Sociological Quarterly* 43(4): 575–605.

Ellison, Christopher G., and Darren E. Sherkat. 1995. "The 'Semi-Involuntary Institution' Revisited: Regional Variations in Church Participation Among Black Americans." *Social Forces* 73(4): 1415–37.

Epps, Edgar. 1995. "Race, Class, and Educational Opportunity: Trends in the Sociology of Education." *Sociological Forum* 10: 593–608.

Farkas, George, Daniel Sheehan, Robert P. Grobe, and Yuan Shuan. 1990. "Cultural Resources and School Success: Gender, Ethnicity, and Poverty Groups Within an Urban School District." *American Sociological Review* 55: 127–42.

Farmer, Helen S. 1985. "Model of Career and Achievement Motivation for Women and Men." *Journal of Counseling Psychology* 32: 363–90.

Fergus, Edward. 2004. *Skin Color and Identity Formation: Perceptions of Opportunity and Academic Orientation Among Mexican and Puerto Rican Youth.* New York: Routledge.

Finke, Roger. 2003. "Spiritual Capital: Definitions, Applications, and New Frontiers." Spiritual Capital Planning Meeting, Cambridge, MA, October 10–11.

Fischer, Claude S., and Michael Hout. 2006. *Century of Difference: How America Changed in the Last One Hundred Years.* New York: Russell Sage Foundation.

Floyd, H. H., and D. R. South 1972. "Dilemma of Youth: The Choice of Parents or Peers as a Frame of Reference for Behavior." *Journal of Marriage and Family* 52: 941–58.

Frankenberg, Erica, Chungmei Lee, and Gary Orfield. 2003. *A Multiracial Society with Segregated Schools: Are We Losing the Dream?* Cambridge, MA: Civil Rights Project, Harvard University.

Gay, G. 1975. "Teachers' Achievement Expectations of and Classroom Interactions with Ethnically Different Students." *Contemporary Education* 46: 166–71.

Getz J. G. and J. H. Bray 2005. "Predicting Heavy Alcohol Use Among Adolescents." *American Journal of Orthopsychiatry* 75(1):102–16.

Giordano, P. C. 2003. "Relationships in Adolescence." *Annual Review of Sociology* 29: 257–81.

Giordano, P. C., S. A. Cernkovich, and A. DeMaris. 1993. "The Family and Peer Relations of Black Adolescents." *Journal of Marriage and Family* 55: 277–87.

Glenn, Norval D. 1964. "Negro Religion and Negro Status in the United States." In Louis Schneider (ed.), *Religion, Culture and Society* (623–39). New York: Wiley.

Goldscheider, F. K., and C. Goldscheider. 1989. "Ethnicity and the New Family Economy: Synthesis and Research Findings." In F. K. Goldscheider and C. Goldscheider (eds.), *Ethnicity and the Family Economy: Living Arrangements and Intergenerational Financial Flows* (185–97). Boulder, CO: Westview Press.

Grebler, Leo, Joan Moore, and Ralph Guzman. 1970. *The Mexican American People.* New York: Free Press.

Gutman, Leslie M., and Jacquelynne Eccles. 1999. "Financial Strain, Parenting Behaviors, and Adolescents' Achievement: Testing Model Equivalence Between African American and European American Single- and Two-Parent Families." *Child Development* 70: 1464–76.

Hallinan, Maureen. 2003. "Ability Grouping and Student Learning." In Diane Ravich (ed.), *Brookings Papers on Education Policy* (95–140). Washington, DC: Brookings Institution Press.

Harker, Kathryn. 2001. "Immigrant Generation, Assimilation, and Adolescent Psychological Well-Being." *Social Forces* 79: 969–1004.

Harrison, A. O., M. N. Wilson, C. J. Pine, S. Q. Chan, and R. Buriel. 1990. "Family Ecologies of Ethnic Minority Children." *Child Development* 61: 347–62.

Hoffman, M. L. 1980. "Moral Development in Adolescence." In J. Adelson (ed.), *Handbook of Adolescent Psychology* (295–343). New York: Wiley.

Human Rights Watch. 2003. "Incarcerated in America." Available at www.hrw.org/backgrounder/usa/incarceration; accessed 10/30/08. (Calculated from data from the National Corrections Reporting Program 1996 and Bureau of the Census 2000.)

Iannaccone, Laurence R. 1990. "Religious Practice: A Human Capital Approach." *Journal for the Scientific Study of Religion* 29: 297–314.

Iannaccone, Laurence R., and Jonathan Klick. 2003. "Spiritual Capital: An Introduction and Literature Review." Spiritual Capital Planning Meeting, Cambridge, MA, October 10–11.

Jackson, Cardell K., Tim B. Heaton, and Rutledge M. Dennis. 1990. "Black-White Differences in Religiosity: Item Analyses and a Formal Structural Test." *Sociological Analysis* 51: 257–70.

Jeter, J. T. 1975. "Can Teacher Expectations Function as Self-Fulfilling Prophecies?" *Contemporary Education* 46: 161–64.

Jeyenes, W. H. 2005. "The Effects of Parental Involvement on the Academic Achievement of African American Youth." *Journal of Negro Education* 74: 260–75.

Kao, Grace. 2000. "Group Images and Possible Selves Among Adolescents: Linking Stereotypes to Expectations by Race and Ethnicity." *Sociological Forum* 15: 407–30.

———. 2002. "Ethnic Differences in Parental Aspirations." *Sociology of Education* 13: 85–94.

Kao, Grace, and Jennifer Thompson. 2003. "Racial and Ethnic Stratification in Educational Achievement and Attainment." *Annual Review of Sociology* 29: 417–42.

Kohn, M. L. 1977. *Class and Conformity: A Study in Values*, 2nd ed. Chicago: University of Chicago Press.

Lamont, Michele, and Annette Lareau. 1988. "Cultural Capital: Allusions, Gaps, and Glissandos in Recent Theoretical Developments." *Sociological Theory* 6: 153–68.

Lareau, Annette. 2003. *Unequal Childhoods: Class, Race, and Family Life*. Berkeley: University of California Press.

Larson, R. W., M. H. Richards, B. Sims, and J. Dworkin. 2001. "How Urban African American Young Adolescents Spend Their Time: Time Budgets for Locations, Activities and Companionship." *American Journal of Community Psychology* 29: 565–95.

Lee, Jennifer, and Min Zhou. 2005. *Asian American Youth: Culture, Identity, and Ethnicity*. New York: Routledge.

Lewis, Amanda E. 2003. *Race in the Schoolyard: Negotiating the Color Line in Classroom and Community*. New Brunswick, NJ: Rutgers University Press.

Lieberson, Stanley. 1980. *A Piece of the Pie: Blacks and White Immigrants Since 1880*. Berkeley: University of California Press.

Lin, Nan. 1999. "Social Networks and Status Attainment." *Annual Review of Sociology* 25: 467–87.

Lopez, Ian F. Haney. 1996. *White by Law: The Legal Construction of Race*. New York: New York University Press.

Lucas, Samuel R. 1999. *Tracking Inequality: Stratification and Mobility in American High Schools*. New York: Teachers College Press.

Maldonado, Lionel A., and Charles V. Willie. 1996. "Developing a 'Pipeline' Recruitment Program for Minority Faculty." In Laura I. Rendon and Richard O. Hope (eds.), *Educating a New Majority: Transforming America's Education System for Diversity* (330–71). Jossey-Bass: San Francisco.

Mead, Lawrence. 1986. *Beyond Entitlement: The Social Obligations of Citizenship*. New York: Free Press.

McLanahan, S., and K. Booth. 1989. "Mother-Only Families: Problems, Prospects, and Politics." *Journal of Marriage and Family* 51: 557–80.

McLanahan, S., and G. Sandefur, 1994. *Growing Up with a Single Parent: What Hurts, What Helps*. Cambridge: Harvard University Press.

Mickelson, Roslyn Arlin. 1990. "The Attitude Achievement Paradox Among Black Adolescents." *Sociology of Education* 63: 44–61.

Mirande, Alfredo. 1985. *The Chicano Experience: An Alternative Perspective*. Notre Dame, IN: University of Notre Dame Press.

Murray, Charles. 1984. *Losing Ground: American Social Policy 1950–1980*. New York: Basic Books.

Neff, L. J., R. G. Sargent, R. E. McKeown, K. L. Jackson, and R. F. Valois, 1997. "Black-White Differences In Body Size Perceptions and Weight Management Practices Among Adolescent Females." *Journal of Adolescent Health* 20(6): 459–65.

Newacheck, P. W., M. J. Park, C. D. Brindis, M. Biehl, and C. E. Irwin Jr. 2004. "Trends in Private and Public Health Insurance for Adolescents." *Journal of the American Medical Association* 291: 1231–37.

Oakes, Jeannie. 1985. *Keeping Track: How Schools Structure Inequality*. New Haven, CT: Yale University Press.

————. 1989. "What Educational Indicators? The Case for Assessing the School Context." *Educational Evaluation and Policy Analysis* 11: 181–99.

Oakes, Jeannie, and Martin Lipton. 1996. "Developing Alternatives to Tracking and Grading." In Laura I. Rendon and Richard O. Hope (eds.), *Educating a New Majority: Transforming America's Educational System for Diversity* (168–200). San Francisco: Jossey-Bass.

Ogbu, John U. 2003. *Black American Students in an Affluent Suburb: A Study of Academic Disengagement.* Mahwah, NJ: Erlbaum.

Orenstein, P. 1995. *Schoolgirls: Young Women, Self Esteem, and the Confidence Gap.* New York: Anchor.

Pattillo-McCoy, Mary. 1999. *Black Picket Fences: Privilege and Peril Among the Black Middle Class.* Chicago: University of Chicago Press.

Peterson, G. W., and D. Hann. 1999. "Socializing Children and Parents in Families." In M. Sussman., S. K. Steinmetz, and G. W. Peterson (eds.), *Handbook of Marriage and the Family*, 2nd ed. (327–70). New York: Plenum.

Peterson, G. W., and G. K. Leigh. 1990. "The Family and Social Competence in Adolescence." In T. P. Gullotta, G. R. Adams, and R. Montemayor (eds.), *Developing Social Competency in Adolescence: Advances in Adolescent Development* (vol. 3, 97–138). Newbury Park, CA: Sage.

Portes, Alejandro. 2000. "The Two Meanings of Social Capital." *Sociological Forum* 15: 1–12.

Portes, Alejandro, and Ruben Rumbaut. 2001. *Legacies: The Story of the Immigrant Second Generation.* Berkeley: University of California Press.

Portes, Alejandro, and Min Zhou. 1993. "The New Second Generation: Segmented Assimilation and Its Variants." *Annals of the American Academy of Political and Social Science* 530: 74–96.

Putnam, Robert. 2000. *Bowling Alone: The Collapse and Revival of American Community.* New York: Simon and Schuster.

Putnam, Robert D., and Lewis M. Feldstein. 2003. *Better Together: Restoring the American Community.* New York: Simon and Schuster.

Qian, Zhenchao, and Sampson Lee Blair. 1999. "Racial/Ethnic Differences in Educational Aspirations of High School Achievement." *Sociological Perspectives* 42: 605–25.

Regnerus, Mark. 2003. "Religion and Positive Adolescent Outcomes: A Review of Research and Theory." *Review of Religious Research* 44(4): 394–413.

————. 2007. *Forbidden Fruit: Sex and Religion in the Lives of American Teenagers.* New York: Oxford University Press.

Renzulli, Linda, and Lorraine Evans. 2005. "School Choice, Charter Schools, and White Flight." *Social Problems* 52(2): 398–418.

Riolo, Stephanie, Tuan Anh Nguyen, John F. Greden, and Cheryl A. King, 2005. "Prevalence of Depression by Race/Ethnicity: Findings from the National Health and Nutrition Examination Survey III ." *American Journal of Public Health* 95(6): 998–1000.

Romero, A. J., and M. Ruiz. 2007. "Does Familism Lead to Increased Parental Monitoring? Protective Factors for Coping With Risky Behaviors." *Journal of Child and Family Studies* 16(2): 143–54.

Roof, Wade Clark, and William C. McKinney. 1987. *American Mainline Religion.* New Brunswick, NJ: Rutgers University Press.

Rosen, Bernard C. 1959. "Race, Ethnicity, and the Achievement Syndrome." *American Sociological Review* 24: 47–60.

Sabogal, F., G. Marin, P. O. Sabogal, B. V. Marin, and E. J. Perez-Stable. 1987. "Hispanic Familism and Acculturation: What Changes and What Doesn't?" *Hispanic Journal of Behavioral Sciences* 9(4): 397–412.

Sanchez-Jankowski, M. 1991. *Islands in the Street: Gangs and American Urban Society.* Berkeley: University of California Press.

Savin-Williams, R. C., and T. J. Berndt. 1990. "Friendship and Peer Relations." In S. S. Feldman and G. R. Elliot (eds.), *At the Threshold: The Developing Adolescent* (277–307). Cambridge, MA: Harvard University Press.

Schaefer, Richard T. 2008. *Sociology: A Brief Introduction.* New York: McGraw-Hill.

Sherrod, Lonnie R. 2003. "Promoting the Development of Citizenship in Diverse Youth." *Political Science and Politics* 36: 287–92.

Smetana, J. G., and P. Asquith. 1994. "Adolescents' and Parents' Conceptions of Parental Authority and Personal Autonomy." *Child Development* 65: 1147–62.

Smith, Christian. 2003a. "Religious Participation and Parental Moral Expectations and Supervision of American Youth." *Review of Religious Research* 44(4): 414–24.

———. 2003b. "Theorizing Religious Effects Among American Adolescents." *Journal for the Scientific Study of Religion* 42: 1, 17–30.

Smith, Christian (with Melinda Lundquist Denton). 2005. *Soul Searching: The Religious and Spiritual Lives of American Teenagers.* New York: Oxford University Press.

Solorzano, Daniel. 1991. "Mobility Aspirations Among Racial Minorities, Controlling for SES." *Sociology and Social Research* 75: 182–88.

Steele, Claude M. 1997. "A Threat in the Air: How Stereotypes Shape Intellectual Identity and Performance." *American Psychology* 52: 613–29.

Steinberg, L., S. Lamborn, S. Dornbusch, and N. Darling. 1992. "Impact of Parenting Practices on Adolescent Achievement: Authoritative Parenting, School Involvement, and Encouragement to Succeed." *Developmental Psychology* 63: 1266–81.

Straus, M. A. 1994. *Beating the Devil Out of Them: Corporal Punishment in American Families.* New York: Lexington Books.

Swanson, Christopher B. 2004. "Sketching a Portrait of Public High School Graduation: Who Graduates? Who Doesn't?" In Gary Orfield (ed.), *Dropouts in America: Confronting the Graduation Rate Crisis* (ch. 1). Cambridge, MA: Harvard Education Press.

Swidler, Ann. 1986. "Culture in Action: Symbols and Strategies." *American Sociological Review* 51(2): 273–86.

Takaki, Ronald T. 1993. *A Different Mirror: A History of Multicultural America*. Boston: Little, Brown.

Tatum, Beverly. 2003. *Why Are All the Black Kids Sitting Together in the Cafeteria? And Other Conversations About Race*. New York: Basic Books.

Touraine, Alain. 1974. *The Academic System in American Society*. New York: McGraw-Hill.

Tyson, Karolyn, William Darity, and Domini R. Castellino. 2005. "'It's Not a Black Thing': Understanding the Burden of Acting White and Other Dilemmas of High Achievement." *American Sociological Review* 70: 582–605.

Wallace, J. M., and J. G. Bachman. 1991. "Explaining Racial/Ethnic Differences in Adolescent Drug Use: The Impact of Background and Lifestyle." *Social Problems* 38(3): 333–57.

Wallace, John, and Tyrone Forman. 1998. "Religion's Role in Promoting Health and Reducing Risk Among American Youth." *Health Education and Behavior* 25: 721–41.

Welsh, Wayne N. 2000. "The Effects of School Climate on School Disorder." *Annals of the American Academy of Political and Social Science* 56: 88–107.

Wilson, William Julius. 1987. *The Truly Disadvantaged: The Inner City, the Underclass, and Public Policy*. Chicago: University of Chicago Press.

———. 1997. *When Work Disappears: The World of the New Urban Poor*. New York: Random House.

Wilson, Patricia M., and Jeffrey R. Wilson. 1992. "Environmental Influences of Adolescent Educational Aspirations: A Logistic Transform Model." *Youth and Society* 24: 52–70.

Wirt, John, Susan Choy, Patrick Rooney, Stephen Provasnik, Anindita Sen, and Richard Tobin. 2004. *The Condition of Education 2004*. National Center for Education Statistics (NCES 2004-077). Washington, DC: Institute of Education Sciences, U.S. Department of Education.

Woodard, Colin. 1998. "When Rote Learning Fails Against the Test of Global Economy." *Christian Science Monitor*, April 15, 7.

Woodberry, Robert D. 2003. "Researching Spiritual Capital: Promises and Pitfalls." Spiritual Capital Planning Meeting, Cambridge, MA, October 10–11.

Woolcock, M. 1998. "Social Capital and Economic Development: Toward a Theoretical Synthesis and Policy Framework." *Theory and Society* 27(2): 151–208.

Youniss, J., and J. Smollar. 1985. *Adolescent Relations with Mothers, Fathers and Friends*. Chicago: University of Chicago Press.

INDEX

Note: Tables are indicated by "*t*" following the page number.

Academic achievement, 79–86, 81*t*, 100–105

Acting white, 9, 101

Adaptation, family socialization and, 34–37, 39–40

African-American teens: and academic achievement, 9, 79–80, 82, 84–85, 101–5; academic investment in, 107–9; capital portfolios of, 158; cultural capital of, 153; educational/career aspirations of, 86–89, 107; family relationships/communication of, 31; household structure of, 21–24; human capital of, 154–55; male family mentors for, 23–24; parenting styles involving, 35–36; peer pressure among, 60–61, 64; peer relationships among, 43, 53–54, 69; religious beliefs of, 111, 118–22, 140; religious capital of, 156–57; religious experiences/practices of, 111, 127–30, 135–36, 139–40; risky behavior of, 43, 59 (*see also* sexual activity among; substance use among); sexual activity among, 62–65, 69–70; social capital of, 150–51; socialization of, 146; substance use among, 59–60; supervision of, 24–26; teacher perceptions of, 106; and teacher-student relations, 96–98, 109; violence involving, 60–61

Asian-American teens: and academic achievement, 79–80, 83, 102–4; academic investment in, 107–9; capital portfolios of, 159–60; cultural capital of, 153–54; educational/career aspirations of, 86, 89–90; family relationships/communication of, 31–32, 56–57; household structure of, 21; human capital of, 155; identity formation of, 5; life chances of, 184*n*24; parenting styles involving, 36; peer pressure among, 57; peer relationships among, 43, 52, 70; religious beliefs of, 111, 119, 125–26, 141–42; religious capital of, 157–58; religious experiences/practices of, 111, 130–35, 141–42; responsibilities of, 30; risky behavior of, 30, 36, 43, 56, 70 (*see also* sexual activity among; substance use among); sample size of, 182*n*6; sexual activity among, 66; social capital of, 151–52; socialization of, 147–48; substance use among, 55–57; supervision of, 29–30; and teacher-student relations, 96, 98, 109

Asians, immigration laws on, 2
Assimilation, 69. *See also* Latino teens:
  third-or-more-generation
Attitude-achievement paradox, 100
Authoritarian parenting style, 34–36
Authoritative parenting style, 34–35
Autonomy. *See* Independence

Baumrind, D., 34–35
Bible reading, 129–30, 132
Bionuclear families, 21–22
Body image, 54, 55t, 60

California, 2
Capital: Asian-American access to, 107;
  cultural, 142–43, 149, 152–54; forms of,
  148–61; human, 149, 154–55; religious,
  149, 155–58; social, 142–43, 149–52
Capital portfolios: benefits and
  detriments of different, 160; defined,
  4–5, 149; development of, 148;
  diversification of, 161; race/ethnicity
  and, 145, 158–60; societal values and, 11;
  types of well-being favored by, 160–61
Career aspirations, 86–93. *See also*
  Human capital
Centers for Disease Control and
  Prevention, 60, 64
Chao, R., 36
Class: academic encouragement
  influenced by, 108; family socialization
  influenced by, 7, 38–39; peer
  relationships and, 67–68; race/ethnicity
  and, 8. *See also* Lower class; Middle
  class
College aspirations. *See* Educational
  aspirations
Communal nurturant parenting style,
  37
Compensation hypothesis, 67
Concerted cultivation, 7, 68, 70
Counseling, 107
Cultural capital: defined, 149; by
  race/ethnicity, 152–54; religion's
  contribution to, 142–43

Dating, 63t
Discipline, 24–26
Discrimination, 1–2

Educational aspirations, 72, 81t, 84–93,
  100, 107. *See also* Human capital
Ethnicity. *See* Race/ethnicity

Family, 12–40; academic encouragement
  provided by, 108; adaptation through
  socialization styles of, 34–37, 39–40;
  case examples, 13–21; class as factor
  in, 38–39; Eurocentric bias of research
  on, 38; household structure, 21–24;
  influence of, 41; peer relationships
  influenced by, 67; pros and cons
  of socialization styles, 39–40;
  relationships and communication
  in, 31–34, 32t; religion and, 131–32,
  136–38, 141, 157; similarities among
  racial/ethnic groups concerning, 12–13;
  socialization by, 7, 12; supervision in,
  24–30, 25t, 68; typologies of, 34, 35t
Fathers, absent/distant, 22–24, 38
Freedom. *See* Independence
Friendships. *See* Peers

Generation status, 9
Giordano, P. C., 67
Girls, fights involving, 61
God, perceptions of, 113, 119–21, 123–26
Graduation, attitudes toward, 85–86

Homeschooling, 27–28, 60–61
Household structure, 21–24, 22t
Human capital: defined, 149; by race/
  ethnicity, 154–55. *See also* Educational
  aspirations

Identity formation, 5–6
Immigrants' experiences, 8–9
Independence: of Asian-American
  teens, 70; dangers of, 40, 42–43, 68,
  69; parenting style promoting, 34; of
  third-or-more-generation Latinos, 69;

of white teens, 13, 26, 28, 32–33, 37, 40, 42–43, 68

Inequalities: capital portfolios and, 4, 11; discriminatory practices leading to, 2; in human capital, 155; school experience and, 72, 109; teen socialization and, 3

Institutions: African Americans' relations with, 36, 146, 153; Asian-Americans' relations with, 52; class as factor in relations with, 7; Latinos' relations with, 37, 69, 147, 153; minority groups' relations with, 40, 109; religious groups as, 110, 133–39; schools as, 71, 108–9; whites' relations with, 39, 52, 108–9, 143, 146, 152, 155–56; youth relations with, 71

Instrumental authoritarian parenting style, 36

Intergenerational relationships, formed through religion, 142–43

Jews, sexual activity among, 65

Kao, Grace, 104

Lareau, Annette, *Unequal Childhoods*, 6–7

Latent functions of school, 107–9

Latino teens: and academic achievement, 79–80, 82–85, 101–5; academic investment in, 107–9; capital portfolios of, 158–59; cultural capital of, 153; educational/career aspirations of, 86–87, 89–92, 107; family relationships/communication of, 33–34; first- and second-generation, 28, 33, 36–37, 43, 52–53, 58–59, 69, 80; household structure of, 21–24; human capital of, 154–55; parenting styles involving, 36–38; peer relationships among, 43; religious beliefs of, 111, 119, 124–25, 141; religious capital of, 156–57; religious experiences/practices of, 111, 130–32, 136–38, 141; responsibilities of, 28; risky behavior of, 37 (*see also* substance use among); social capital of, 150–51;

socialization of, 146–47; substance use among, 58–59; supervision of, 28–29; and teacher-student relations, 96–98, 109; third-or-more-generation, 22–24, 29, 37–38, 43, 52–53, 58–59, 69, 80, 101, 119, 147, 159

Lee, Jennifer, *Asian American Youth*, 5

Lewis, Amanda, 4, 148

Life chances, 3, 184n24

Lower class: family socialization practices of, 7, 39; peer relationships among, 68

Mainline Protestants, sexual activity among, 65

Manifest functions of school, 107–9

Middle class: family socialization practices of, 7, 39; racial/ethnic influences on, 8

Miner's tax on foreign miners, 181n6

Moralistic therapeutic deism, 118, 139

National Origins Act (1924), 2

National Study of Youth and Religion (NSYR), 9–10

Network closure, 48, 158–59

Nurturant authoritarian parenting style, 36

Ogbu, John, *Black American Students in an Affluent Suburb*, 9

Oral sex, 65

Parenting styles, 34–39

Pattillo-McCoy, Mary, *Black Picket Fences*, 8

Peers, 41–70; attributes of, 53t; case examples, 43–51; characteristics of relationships with, 41–42, 52–54, 66–67; class and, 67–68; family influence on, 67; importance of, 52, 67; influence of, 41–42, 54–62; minority youth and, 67; pros and cons of, 68; sexual activity among, 62–66; similarities among racial/ethnic groups concerning, 42

Permissive parenting style, 34–35

Physical appearance, 54, 55*t*, 60
Portes, Alejandro, *Legacies*, 8–9
Prayer, 127–32
Protestants. *See* Mainline Protestants;
   Religious conservatives
Putnam, Robert, 150

Race/ethnicity: capital portfolios
   influenced by, 145, 158–60; class and, 8;
   family socialization and, 13; research
   on, 5–9; social investment influenced
   by, 1; socialization and, 3, 6, 146–48;
   social significance of, 1–3, 145
Regnerus, Mark, 65
Religion, 110–44; beliefs concerning,
   118–26, 120*t*; case examples, 111–18;
   cultural and social capital available
   from, 142–43; experiences/practices
   involving, 127–32, 128*t*; family and,
   131–32, 136–38, 141, 157; ideal-typical
   descriptions of, 140–42; institutional
   aspect of, 133–39, 134*t*; minority group
   control of, 9, 110; perceptions of
   God, 113, 119–21, 123–26; racial/ethnic
   patterns in, 143–44; and sexual activity,
   62–66; similarities among racial/ethnic
   groups concerning, 110–11. *See also*
   Religious capital
Religious capital: defined, 149; by
   race/ethnicity, 155–58; well-being
   "purchased" by, 157–58
Religious conservatives, sexual activity
   among, 65–66
Research, 5–9
Respect, in teacher-student relations,
   98–99
Responsibilities, 26, 28
Risky behavior: of African-American
   teens, 43, 59; of Asian-American teens,
   30, 36, 43, 56, 70; of Latino teens,
   37; permissive parenting and, 35;
   prevalence of, 42; sex as, 182*n*3; of white
   teens, 40, 43. *See also* Sexual activity;
   Substance use
Rumbaut, Ruben, *Legacies*, 8–9

School, 71–109; academic achievement
   in, 79–86, 81*t*, 100–105; academic
   encouragement in, 107–9; case
   examples, 72–79; functions of,
   71, 107–9; future aspirations, 81*t*,
   86–93; importance of, 71; institutional
   experiences provided by, 108–9;
   similarities among racial/ethnic
   groups concerning, 72; teacher-student
   relations in, 72, 93–100, 105–6, 108–9,
   152–53
Self-segregation, 6
Sexual activity, 62–66; of African-American teens, 43, 62–65, 69–70; of Asian-
   American teens, 66; by race/ethnicity,
   63*t*; religion and, 62–66; risk associated
   with, 182*n*3; of white teens, 65
Sexually transmitted diseases (STDs),
   64–65
Single-parent families, 22–23, 38
Smith, Christian, 118, 139, 142–43
Smollar, J., 41, 66
Social capital: "bonding," 150–51;
   "bridging," 150; defined, 149; by
   race/ethnicity, 150–52; religion's
   contribution to, 142–43
Social investment, 1, 3
Socialization: concept of, 4; family as
   means of, 12; race/ethnicity and, 3, 6,
   146–48; of teens, 3, 7
Student-teacher relations, 72, 93–100,
   105–6, 108–9, 152–53
Substance use, 54–59, 56*t*
Swidler, Ann, 149

Tatum, Beverly, *Why Are All the Black
   Kids Sitting Together in the Cafeteria?*,
   5–6
Teacher-student relations, 72, 93–100,
   105–6, 108–9, 152–53
Teens: research on, 5–9; socialization of,
   3, 7
Tracking, academic, 107

Violence, 60–62

Well-being, 148, 157–58, 160–61

White teens: and academic achievement, 79–81, 102–4; academic investment in, 107–9; capital portfolios of, 158; cultural capital of, 152; educational/career aspirations of, 86–87; family relationships/communication of, 32–33; family socialization of, 13; household structure of, 21–22; human capital of, 154–55; life chances of, 184n24; parenting styles involving, 34–35, 39–40; peer pressure among, 54–55; peer relationships among, 42–43, 52, 68; religious beliefs of, 111, 119, 122–24, 140–41; religious capital of, 155–57; religious experiences/practices of, 111, 130–31, 138–41; research emphasis on, 34, 38, 41, 67; responsibilities of, 26; risky behavior of, 40, 43 (*see also* sexual activity among; substance use among); sexual activity among, 65; social capital of, 150; socialization of, 146; substance use among, 54–55; supervision of, 26–28, 68; and teacher-student relations, 93–96, 106, 108–9

Youniss, J., 41, 66

Zhou, Min, *Asian American Youth*, 5